60–Second CPD

239 ideas for busy teachers

Hanna Beech
with Ross Morrison McGill

First published 2020

by John Catt Educational Ltd,
15 Riduna Park, Station Road
Melton, Woodbridge IP12 1QT

Tel: +44 (0) 1394 389850
Fax: +44 (0) 1394 386893
Email: enquiries@johncatt.com
Website: www.johncatt.com

ISBN: 978 1 913622 10 7

Set and designed by John Catt Educational Limited

Reviews

It is said that the best CPD can be measured by what you do the next time you are in the classroom. *60-Second CPD* exceeds this measure, packed full of clear, concise and incredibly practical strategies and tips 'oven-ready' for the classroom. I cannot recommend this highly enough – it has been a pleasure to read and I know this will be a game-changer in schools across the country.

Richard Cahill, principal, Hinckley Academy, Leicestershire

In a notoriously time-poor profession, *60-Second CPD* provides a collection of quick wins and sections to promote deeper staff discussion and thinking. Easy to navigate, covering many aspects of school life, this guide collates experience and wisdom for teachers and leaders to provide a wealth of tried-and-tested approaches alongside some fresh, new ideas.

Emma Turner, research and CPD lead at Discovery Schools Academy Trust and author of *Be More Toddler*

Hanna Beech and Ross Morrison McGill have created a real gem of a book that is a must for every teacher's bookshelf. Whether you are primary or secondary-focused, this book provides an abundance of ideas.

Claire Vickery, head of D&T, Buckler's Mead Academy, Somerset

If you want an easy-to-read text packed full of useful ideas and tips for practice in the school setting, this is a must-read. What a wonderful book to have and use to reflect on your own practice, take new steps and grow as an educator.

Kiki Amin, Ramsgate Arts Primary School, Kent

Beech and McGill have come together to produce a compendium of ideas and top tips on a range of topics. It is a book that you will return to time and time again on your leadership journey.

Dr Kulvarn Atwal, headteacher and author of *The Thinking School*

Having devoured this book in a matter of days, I was left brimming with ideas that I needed to go straight out and try in my classroom. Beech and McGill offer easily digestible, bite-sized chunks that are perfect as staff meeting starters.

Lynn How, educator and SENCO

A teacher's time is precious and the little they get for CPD often isn't targeted or meaningful. *60-Second CPD* allows a teacher to own their professional learning and hone in on a topic. It allows teachers to focus their time and effort on what will make a meaningful impact on their learners. The book is full of well-researched ideas and there really is something for everyone.

Darren Leslie, principal teacher of learning and teaching (acting), Scotland

This is a great dip-in, dip-out book for busy teachers, which covers a wide variety of practical ideas across a wide range of topic areas. It's great to see so many of the ideas backed up by research evidence that will give teachers the confidence to try them in their classrooms.

Dr Rachel Dodge, wellbeing consultant

Whether you are a trainee teacher or school leader, an educational research enthusiast or a fan of the quick tools, *60-Second CPD* will be a companion to your development for years. If I had to recommend one book for any educator training library, it would be this one.

Hanaé Berton, MFL teacher

60-Second CPD is a fantastic resource for teachers and leaders regardless of their point on their professional journey. The accessibility of the tips and suggestions enables you to consider challenging questions that open and support thinking while not having to wade through weighty academic tomes. The combination of personal anecdotes supported by research and excellent tips makes this a stand-out book for those working in schools. A thoroughly enjoyable and informative read.

Matt Dechaine, leadership and wellbeing coach

Contents

Foreword

I was busy and another request came in asking for my input. Two weeks went by and I didn't get round to it. A polite email landed asking, 'Please, Diana, what do you think of this?'

Twenty minutes later I am hooked on the content, making notes in the margins, jousting with the ideas that spring up in my mind because I am challenged by what I am reading. *60-Second CPD* stepped into my life in June 2020 and I will keep a copy of this by my side for a very long time.

Hanna and Ross have managed to find the elusive balance between educational research and what is useful for educators at the chalkface. Their 239 ideas will do the following:

- Prevent you from making ridiculous but very common mistakes.
- Give you templates to start conversations (at those times when your tongue is stuck to the roof of your mouth).
- Give you frameworks that will help your daily interactions within school and deal with those times when you are unsure, unconfident and feel like you don't know what you are doing.

Where was this book when I was an NQT and trying to understand why my Year 10 science class were acting up every Thursday, period 5? Where was this book when I had my first leadership position and I didn't know how to handle the situations that made my heart thump with fear? Where was this book when I was first appointed headteacher and sat staring at the school development plan waiting for it to miraculously turn into a useful tool to help shape my community?

The answers are here, now, and you lucky lot have them in one book, by your side every day. Thousands of books are written every year – some make it to the public domain and a small percentage of these are worth bothering with. Bother with this book. You will be glad you did. (Then buy another copy and give it to the teacher or leader in the next room.)

Diana Osagie, director of Courageous Leadership and
The Academy of Women's Leadership

Introduction

Time is a commodity – and that is especially true in education. Limited time can leave many teachers feeling unable to fulfil all aspects of the role as well as they would like. Teaching is the job that can never be 'finished'.

In its purest form, the role of the educator is to teach, but anyone who has spent more than five minutes in a school knows that things are not that simple. Moving through the curriculum objectives while addressing the pupils' social issues and helping them to become autonomous, confident individuals is no easy feat. There is a huge amount of knowledge to share with our young people and so many skills to foster, and naturally we want to do this really, really well.

Teaching requires not only effective preparation and delivery, but also deep thought and reflection, which demand more time. Unfortunately, tight budgets can leave schools with little capacity to provide staff with quality CPD, meaning that professional development is often left for teachers to manage themselves. We know that CPD is invaluable, but when we're pushed for time as it is, how can we realistically continue to advance our practice?

There are a million and one ideas out there. Sifting through hundreds of research articles, blogs and books is not a practical option for all educators. We need easy-to-digest ideas and theories for incremental professional development. That's what this book is for: to provide a summary of a range of ideas, from the conventional to the controversial, each digestible in roughly 60 seconds.

The chapters focus on areas such as: behaviour; equality, equity and inclusion; leadership; learning environments; and mental health and wellbeing. In each one you'll find ideas and research that could make all the difference to your pupils, your school, your team or your teaching. And at the end of each chapter you'll find suggestions for further reading.

I can't create more time for you to spend on CPD. But I hope you'll find that the ideas in this book are a great way to make the most of the time you do have. You can, of course, read the book in one hit. Alternatively, you can dip in and out as you wish. This is a book that you can refer back to time and time again as the year moves on and your career progresses. Remember to share the ideas with your colleagues. We are all in this together, so sharing practice, ideas and research is a fantastic way for us to grow as teachers and as teams.

A note on the authors

The majority of this book is written by Hanna Beech, with additional insights, contributions and ideas from Ross Morrison McGill, who has supported Hanna with the publication. Some of the CPD ideas come from our own personal experiences, some are gathered from research, and some come from other educators or specialists from the education world and beyond!

Chapter 1: Behaviour

Behaviour. Now there is a word to spark debate among educators (and parents, for that matter). The reason that behaviour in schools is such a trigger for debate is pretty straightforward: challenging behaviour obstructs teaching and hinders learning, as well as affecting the wellbeing of staff and pupils.

It's likely that you have heard – or even made – comments such as 'It wasn't like this last year' or 'In my day, we didn't have all these behaviour problems'. But the data indicates that, on the whole, behaviour isn't getting much worse – or any better. According to the 2018 Teacher Voice Omnibus Survey,[1] 73% of teachers in England think behaviour in their school is good or very good. And the Education Endowment Foundation's *Improving Behaviour in Schools* document (see idea #1) says the proportion of teachers reporting behaviour that is good or better has been fairly stable over the past 10 years. Yet it's also worth considering the results of the NASUWT's 2019 Big Question survey,[2] which found that 82% of teachers believed there was a widespread behaviour problem in schools today. Whatever your views or experiences, I'm sure we can all agree on one thing: challenging behaviour can place teachers under considerable pressure.

When talking about behaviour, there tends to be an assumption that we are referring to problematic behaviour. I find it more useful to consider behaviour in terms of the dictionary definition: 'The way in which one acts or conducts

1   Robert Smith, Caroline Sharp, David Sims, Sarah Millar, Jo Nossiter, Rebecca Menys and Chloe Rush (National Foundation for Educational Research), *Teacher Voice Omnibus Survey: research report*, Department for Education, 2018, tinyurl.com/ugo9vgx
2   *The Big Question 2019: an opinion survey of teachers and headteachers*, NASUWT, 2019, tinyurl.com/vfd9tuv

oneself, especially towards others.'[3] If we think about how children are acting, rather than about how badly they are behaving, we move from a closed stance to an open and reflective one. More often than not, the behaviour in schools is positive, or at least comprehensible. Call me naive, but I like to believe that there is always more good than bad, more joy than dismay, and more hope than despair. I've met pupils who do bad things, say bad things and behave badly – but I've never met a 'bad' child.

Schools are very likely to have a behaviour policy. If you are a leader, your role will be to ensure that this is clearly defined. If you are a teacher or teaching assistant, your role is to apply it in your classroom. Sticking to the school's approach will undoubtedly help to deliver whole-school consistency and have a positive impact on behaviour. Having said that, it's worth noting that expectations vary from teacher to teacher. As long as the school policy is adhered to, there will be behaviours that you as an individual expect and other teachers don't – and that is OK.

Taking the time to reflect upon the behaviour of the pupils in your care can reap rewards. Before delving into the ideas and research presented in this chapter, consider what the desirable and undesirable behaviours are *for you*. It may be useful to think about these five categories of disruptive behaviour, as defined by RJ Cameron (1998):[4]

1. Aggressive behaviour (e.g. hitting, pulling hair, kicking, pushing, using abusive language).
2. Physically disruptive behaviour (e.g. smashing, damaging or defacing objects, throwing objects, physically annoying other pupils).
3. Socially disruptive behaviour (e.g. screaming, running away, exhibiting temper tantrums).
4. Authority-challenging behaviour (e.g. refusing to carry out requests, exhibiting defiant verbal and non-verbal behaviour, using pejorative language).
5. Self-disruptive behaviour (e.g. daydreaming, reading under the desk).

The problematic behaviours we encounter will vary according to the cohort of pupils, their age, the school's catchment area and so on. In order to establish

---

3   en.oxforddictionaries.com/definition/behaviour

4   RJ Cameron, 'School discipline in the United Kingdom: promoting classroom behaviour which encourages effective teaching and learning', *School Psychology Review*, 27.1, 1998, tinyurl.com/yx4pmtzr

where your priorities and boundaries lie, take a few moments here to jot down the behaviours that you consider desirable and undesirable in the classroom.

Desirable	Undesirable
1	1
2	2
3	3
4	4
5	5

Finding ways to communicate these expectations to your pupils will help to establish clear boundaries – you could try class discussions, displays or charts, whatever floats your boat! As long as the children understand your expectations, they have a fair chance of meeting them. After all, there is no point in you holding expectations for behaviour if these expectations are kept under wraps until someone pushes boundaries. Young people often just need direction; clear expectations give them a solid foundation to build upon.

When I first started teaching, behaviour was a huge concern for me. Will they behave? What if they don't? Behaviour management is likely to be a hotspot for most newly qualified teachers: a six-year longitudinal study of the experiences of trainee teachers and NQTs found that pupil behaviour was frequently associated with negative experiences of being a student teacher.[5] And a report published by the NASUWT suggests that behaviour issues have an impact on a newly qualified teacher's desire to remain in the profession.[6] That's no big surprise. When considering teacher retention, we need to take misbehaviour very seriously. There are three key messages about behaviour that I wish I could tell my newly qualified self:

1. They won't always behave well. (At least, not all of them and certainly not all the time.)
2. It's not about you. (Even when it is about you, it's not about you as a person, just your approach.)
3. Act cross, don't be cross. (When you're actually cross, step back, take a breath and remember messages 1 and 2.)

Expecting some form of challenging behaviour will help your wellbeing. This is absolutely not to suggest that teachers should *accept* the challenging behaviour. But when you're working with young, hormonal humans whose prefrontal cortexes are far from fully developed, there are bound to be self-regulation issues and emotional outbursts. Some young people have personal lives that are incredibly traumatic, leaving them emotionally fragile and sometimes defensive. If you expect perfect behaviour, you will be disappointed. It's more effective to arm yourself with strategies that address negative behaviours, and to learn how to look after your own wellbeing and stress levels, too.

The aim of this chapter is to empower and prepare you to manage a range of behaviours. But teaching pupils who display very challenging behaviour on a daily basis can leave educators feeling exhausted, frustrated and alone. If you feel too much of any negative emotion when attempting to handle behaviour, talk to a colleague, union or member of your SLT.

---

5   Andrew J Hobson, Angi Malderez, Louise Tracey, Matthew S Homer, Patricia Ashby, Nick Mitchell, Joanna McIntyre, David Cooper, Tom Roper, Gary N Chambers and Peter D Tomlinson, *Becoming a Teacher: teachers' experiences of initial teacher training, induction and early professional development, final report*, Department for Children, Schools and Families, 2009, tinyurl.com/v9nkrnp

6   Katy Owen, Kate Broadhurst and Gemma Keats, *Sink or Swim? Learning lessons from newly qualified and recently qualified teachers*, NASUWT, 2009, tinyurl.com/sjk8r8g

#1 The EEF approach to improving behaviour

Here are the six recommendations made in the Education Endowment Foundation's *Improving Behaviour in Schools* guidance report.[7]

1. Know and understand your pupils and their influences.
2. Teach learning behaviours alongside managing misbehaviour.
3. Use classroom management strategies to support good classroom behaviour.
4. Use simple approaches as part of your regular routine.
5. Use targeted approaches to meet the needs of individuals in your school.
6. Consistency is key.

Why it works
A clear and comprehensive approach to managing behaviour in your school will allow teachers to focus on teaching and pupils to focus on learning.

Top tip
Read the full report and keep a copy of the summary poster in the staffroom. Both can be found at educationendowment foundation.org.uk/tools/guidance-reports/improving-behaviour-in-schools

---

7   Igraine Rhodes and Michelle Long, *Improving Behaviour in Schools: guidance report*, Education Endowment Foundation, 2019, tinyurl.com/y2pqq7zt

#2 Words of warning

No one likes to give sanctions, but unfortunately they are sometimes needed in order to maintain standards of good behaviour. Here's how to make sure sanctions are given fairly and received as well as they can be.

1. **Warning.** Always give a warning before you deliver a sanction. Use simple statements such as, 'Sienna, you are ignoring my instructions. If this continues, you will lose a point. Take this as your warning. If I have to ask you again, you will lose a point.'
2. **Check for understanding.** Follow your warning with a question to make sure it has been understood – for example, 'Do you understand?' or 'Is that clear?' This gives the pupil the opportunity to fully absorb your expectations.
3. **Praise or sanction.** If the behaviour changes, praise Sienna, telling her why the change made a positive difference to the learning. If the behaviour continues, give the sanction. Do not give additional warnings. Simply explain that, despite the warning, the behaviour has continued: 'We discussed that if you continued to ignore instructions, you would lose a point. Sadly, you have continued. Now you will lose a point.'
4. **Consequences.** Now you're back at the warning stage. Warn once more that if the behaviour continues, there will be further consequences. Highlight these in line with your school's behaviour policy.

Why it works
Clear warnings allow the pupil to really own their behaviour. You've shown yourself to be clear and fair, and the pupil knows you mean what you say.

Top tip
Know your school's behaviour policy and make clear to the class that you will follow it.

#3 De-escalating challenging behaviour

Working with a challenging pupil? Every child is different, but here are some key approaches you can take to de-escalate problematic behaviour.

1. Know the pupil. Know their triggers and what helps them to calm down.
2. Keep an eye on them. Big outbursts can appear to come out of nowhere, but careful monitoring can reveal clues that the pupil's behaviour is worsening (over-excitement, agitation, lethargy, withdrawal, etc).
3. Distract them. Give them a job or offer them a way out (e.g. reading a book).
4. Humour (but not sarcasm) can work, if well timed.
5. Allow them sufficient time and space to calm down. We often assume a young person has settled, only for them to have a second outburst. In many cases, it isn't a second outburst at all – the first one wasn't actually over.
6. Avoid getting into an argument and don't ask why they are acting in a certain way, at least not initially. Generally, asking 'why' questions at the time of a meltdown is unhelpful.
7. Listen to them. If they are communicating a problem, try to listen and offer a solution if you can.
8. Show empathy. Let them know that you understand their problem and how they must be feeling.
9. Enlist the help of others. There are often key people who connect with the pupil; use them to support you and the child.
10. Create an action plan. If things are getting out of control or outbursts are becoming more frequent, it's time to gather with the relevant parties to create a behaviour plan. You shouldn't have to deal with outbursts on your own.

Why it works
Outbursts can be reduced (or even completely avoided) by knowing and applying de-escalation techniques.

Top tip
When an outburst happens, log everything: the date, the time, the place, the people involved, the triggers, the outcomes, etc. You never know when you might need to refer back to the details of an incident. Be sure to talk to someone in your team if you've been affected by a pupil's challenging behaviour.

#4 The positivity-first approach

It can be easy to focus on undesirable behaviour, but there is much to be gained from celebrating good behaviour through praise and recognition. Try this positive approach to give your pupils' behaviour (and your wellbeing) a boost.

1. Jot down three desirable behaviours shown by your class as a collective. Do this in isolation from the class.
2. When teaching, every time the pupils demonstrate one of these desirable behaviours as a collective, praise and thank them, explaining the positive impact this behaviour has on the learning.
3. Jot down three undesirable behaviours shown by your class as a collective. Again, this is for your own reflection so don't involve the pupils.
4. For each of the undesirable behaviours, make a mental note of one pupil who always maintains good behaviour during this time (e.g. when everyone else chats during transitions, Bradley sits patiently and has his equipment ready).
5. When the pupils demonstrate an undesirable behaviour as a collective, look for that one pupil and draw all attention to their positive behaviour. Be careful not to make comparisons between pupils, just praise what is going well and why.
6. If there isn't one pupil to draw positive attention to, refer to a different class or group who behave in the model way.

Isn't this a bit obvious?
This approach is nothing new. The trouble is, in the moment, we don't always do what we know to be right, so take this as a little reminder of that go-to strategy that really does work!

Phrasing tip
'When you [insert desirable behaviour] it has a positive impact on the learning. This makes me feel really proud. I'd like to see more of this so we can all benefit.'

#5 **Reliable role models**

Everyone needs a good role model. And everyone can *be* a good role model in one way or another (even the most troubled pupils). Try this strategy to build a class of behavioural heroes.

1. Begin by watching the class carefully. Identify and note admirable traits in each pupil.
2. Tell the class you've been watching them and you're really proud that they have all proven themselves a role model in one way or another.
3. Read out their admirable traits, explaining why these make them reliable role models.
4. Create a poster or display showing each pupil's main strength.
5. Throughout the day, use the reliable role model traits to praise and remind pupils about their behaviour. For example, 'Raf has clearly been inspired by Margo as he has been supporting his group really well, which is Margo's reliable role model trait.' Or 'Frankie, I think you might need to take a leaf out of Rayanesh's book by showing good manners.'

Why it works

Making every pupil feel looked up to will promote positive behaviours. They will want to live up to the traits you've noticed in them.

Top tip

Partner up role models who will compliment each other. For example, if Frank shows work ethic but needs to develop his manners, pair him with Bella, who shows great manners but lacks work ethic.

#6 The consistency quiz

Young people like to know where they stand, so consistent and predictable approaches will help you immensely when it comes to managing behaviour. Use this quick quiz to help you reflect upon how consistent you are.

1. Do you have consistent routines for each part of the day?
2. Do pupils often ask you what is coming next?
3. Are your plans always carefully considered?
4. Do you always follow the school's behaviour policy?
5. Do you treat all pupils equally?
6. Do transitions between activities or lessons feel smooth and seamless?
7. Are your expectations the same each day, despite your own mood?
8. Is behaviour in your classroom unpredictable and inconsistent?

What do my answers mean?

You can decide what your answers mean – just reflect on each question and how happy you are with your response. Which question sticks with you? That's the one you might want to spend some more time thinking about.

Top tip

The more consistent you are with your pupils, the more secure they will feel. This will have a positive impact on behaviour.

 Stability and routine

Pupils settle well when there is stability in class and sometimes even a slight change in routine can lead to chaos. Studies have shown that instability at home can have negative effects on child development,[8] so we don't want to provide instability at school. Follow these suggestions to make sure a change in routine has as little impact on behaviour as possible.

1. Display a visual timetable for a regular week.
2. To begin each day, briefly run through what will be happening and when.
3. Explain that sometimes the unexpected happens. Discuss examples.
4. Always inform pupils of planned changes to timetable or routine in the coming weeks. This can be especially important for pupils who have autistic spectrum conditions. Offer reminders on the day, too.

Why it works
Being prepared for a change in routine will help pupils to cope.

Top tip
When something unexpected occurs, remind the class that these things happen and we need to be adaptable.

---

8   Heather Sandstrom and Sandra Huerta, *The Negative Effects of Instability on Child Development*, Urban Institute, 2013, tinyurl.com/twwecsb

#8 Helping pupils to manage unexpected interruptions[9]

When a parent is hovering at the door, a colleague pops in to ask a question or the phone rings, behaviour can slip. Unexpected interruptions are the perfect opportunity for pupils to go off-task. If your class are easily distracted by interruptions, try this simple method to tackle the issue.

1. Get yourself a push lamp (Ikea have these) or a touch lamp of some kind. Alternatively, use a piece of red card that can be quickly stuck to the whiteboard.
2. Explain to the class that interruptions will occur from time to time. Ask them to share ideas about what they think they should do if an interruption occurs – call these 'ways to wait'.
3. Explain that when an interruption occurs, you will turn on the lamp or stick the red card on the whiteboard. When that happens, the pupils should remember their ways to wait.
4. Put this into practice, praise success and feel proud when an interruption happens and your classroom doesn't descend into chaos!

Why it works
Children often want to please, but if they don't realise how important it is to maintain focus, they won't stay on-task when interruptions happen.

Top tip
When you first start using this strategy, ask a colleague to spontaneously pop in. This gives the pupils a chance to practise their ways to wait.

---

9 Hanna Beech, 'Beating interruptions', *Teacher Toolkit*, 2017, teachertoolkit.co.uk/2017/10/13/one-minute-cpd-5

WAYS TO WAIT

Sometimes our lessons might be interrupted. If this happens, remember our ways to wait...

Continue with your task

If you are working on something, an interruption doesn't change that. Keep working on your task. If I was teaching, you may need to just wait patiently and quietly until I am ready again.

Work quietly and sensibly

Remember that you should be calm and sensible even when an interruption happens! I will be proud if you can remain quiet and sensible when our lesson is interrupted.

Avoid interrupting me

Unless there is an emergency, avoid interrupting me as I handle something that has popped up unexpectedly. The sooner I can deal with this, the sooner we can carry on with the lesson.

Be patient. I won't be long!

You might need my help or want to tell me something. Please be patient and wait for me to be ready to help or listen to you. I will be with you as quickly as I can!

#9 The rule is...

Do you have a pupil who often defies school rules or codes of conduct? This highly effective strategy helps you to direct them towards the expected behaviour without demanding that they meet your personal expectations.

1. Identify what the undesirable behaviour is. For example, the pupil is messing around during the lesson.
2. Tell them what they are doing: 'You are messing around during the lesson.'
3. Tell them what the rule is. For example, 'The rule is, during lessons we focus on our work and make a good effort to achieve.'
4. Ask them to abide by the school rules.

Why it works

This suggestion was shared with me by a SENCO. I've tried it multiple times and found it to be far more effective than sharing the rules as if they belong to me. There's something about the phrase 'the rule is' that makes the expectations less personal.

Top tip

This method seems to work particularly well with pupils who have special educational needs or autistic spectrum conditions.

#10 Non-verbal behaviour management

Never underestimate the power of non-verbal signals and the influence they can have on a pupil's cognitive development. Here are three silent strategies for dealing with misbehaviour.

1. **The pause.** Stop talking and stare towards the back of the classroom with a neutral expression. If the pupil stops the behaviour, wait for five seconds before carrying on. If they do not, direct your eyes towards them and wait for another count of five. If they still do not stop, you might resort to saying their name (but usually another pupil will do this for you in protest against their behaviour!).
2. **The stop signal.** Using your hand to signal 'stop' is an effective way to get a pupil to cease misbehaving.
3. **Arms and eyebrows.** Your arms and eyebrows give away a lot about what you're thinking. Try folding your arms or gesturing as if to say, 'Really?' Raising an eyebrow often has a magical effect on pupils.

Why it works
Strategies such as these enable you to take control of behaviour without unnecessary 'telling off'. They reduce interruptions and allow you to make expectations clear without repeating yourself.

Top tip
Non-verbal cues can sometimes be confusing for young people with autistic spectrum conditions or other SEN; they may require additional explanation. For strategies and considerations relating to autism, refer to chapter 4.

#11 Breaking down problematic behaviour[10]

Problematic behaviour is what NQTs often worry about and experienced teachers often grumble about. The best way to start tackling the issue is to ask yourself the following questions about challenging behaviour in your classroom.

1. What is the behaviour? Write down three behaviours, from the most to the least concerning.
2. When is the behaviour? Identify when the behaviour occurs – and when it doesn't.
3. Why is the behaviour happening? This is the single most significant question you can ask, because it helps you to understand the situation, build your empathy and increase your chance of solving the problem.
4. Who has the relationship? Someone, somewhere in the school, has a connection with this pupil. You're going to need them. If no one has the relationship, why is this the case?
5. What is of high value to the pupil? Finding out what they care about can help you to motivate them.
6. What are the school's expectations? What resources or support do you need to put in place?
7. Who has authority? In order to feel supported, you need someone with authority to regularly monitor behaviour.
8. What do parents/carers need to know?
9. In an ideal world, what will the outcome be? Forget zero-tolerance.

Why try this?
In the words of the entrepreneur Tony Robbins,[11] 'If you do what you've always done, you'll get what you've always gotten.'

Top tip
Keep the end goals in mind. Don't expect things to go perfectly; you'll likely be disappointed. Be persistent, positive and consistent. It will be worth it, for you and for the pupil involved.

---

10 Hanna Beech, 'Breaking down behaviour', *Teacher Toolkit,* 2019, teachertoolkit.co.uk/2018/06/06/one-minute-cpd-26
11 tonyrobbins.com

#12 Behaviour interventions

If you think a behaviour intervention might have a positive impact on a pupil, follow these steps to help get the ball rolling.

1. Who needs to be in the know? Before planning an intervention, you need to make sure the senior leadership team and the pupil's family are on board. Set up a meeting with senior leaders and behaviour mentors to discuss ideas for interventions.
2. What type of intervention will work? Be sure to consider the young person in question. What might work for them? Why?
3. Successful intervention relies on timing. When should you start? On what day should the intervention happen? Why?
4. How will the pupil respond? Consider how they will feel about a potential intervention and define your expected outcomes.

Why it works

According to the Education Endowment Foundation, evidence suggests that behaviour interventions, particularly one-to-one interventions, can 'produce moderate improvements in academic performance along with a decrease in problematic behaviours'.[12]

Top tip

Interventions usually run for between three and six weeks.

---

12 'Behaviour interventions', Education Endowment Foundation, tinyurl.com/yapckfx9, accessed 2019

#13 Engaging the pupil: breaking the behaviour cycle

If a child's behaviour has spiralled out of control, it might be necessary to begin proactive intervention. Such negative behaviours may indicate that the child has reached crisis point, and if they are to improve their behaviour, they must first feel that they trust those around them (read more about the importance of trust in idea #192). Break the cycle with this social-connection strategy.

1. Chat to the pupil outside of lesson time. Say that you've noticed a negative behaviour pattern and discuss the impact of this on their learning.
2. Ask them why they think this behaviour is happening. A surprising answer might allow action to be taken to resolve the issue, but often the pupil will say they don't know.
3. Challenge the pupil to change the behaviour, explaining the positive impact this would have on their learning.
4. Tell them that every time they avoid the behaviour, you will silently record one point (tick on the board, marble into a jar, five minutes of free time, phone call home, anything!). And every time they show the negative behaviour, you will remove one point.
5. Keep a log of the points gained in each lesson and discuss their progress with them at the end of the day or week. Reward as you wish, but be sure to recognise successes.

Why it works
Explaining the impact of a negative behaviour can encourage a pupil to change. Visual cues and consistent rewards keep the strategy motivating and easy to follow.

Top tip
Start with a negative behaviour that is easy to amend. Once success has been achieved, move on to the next behaviour.

#14 Engaging the peers: getting friends onside

Worried that a pupil is losing their way? Enlist their friends to get them back on the right track.

1. Decide on your main aim – for example, for the pupil to get to school on time, build their confidence in maths, learn to ask for help or express their needs calmly.
2. Find out who their closest friend is.
3. Speak to the pupil and their friend, too. Describe your aim for the pupil, explaining how this would make a big difference to their education or school life.
4. Give the friend some suggestions for how they could help, explaining that having the support of a good friend is vital for success.
5. Check in with the pupil and their friend separately to see if progress is being made.

Why it works

The pupil in question will want to make their friend proud. In turn, the friend will feel proud when their influence has a positive impact.

Top tip

Be careful not to put too much pressure on peers – they need to know that their role is to be a friend, not a life coach!

#15 Engaging the pastoral team: looking to the future

Do you wish you could show a pupil how their behaviour now will affect them later in life? Ask the pastoral team to try this idea to help them map out their future.

1. Block out 10-20 minutes to work with a pupil one-to-one. Have a strip of paper and some pens at the ready.
2. Tell the pupil that you want to help them make a timeline of their future.
3. Note where they were five years ago, talking briefly about what has changed since. Continue the timeline to where they are now, sticking to basics such as their year group, age and favourite activities.
4. Ask the pupil to suggest the skills they might like to develop in the next year, plotting these as the next milestone on their timeline.
5. Do the same for two years and five years from now. Make notes along the timeline as they discuss their aims. They might need some question prompts to help them think ahead.
6. Ask them what might get in the way of their goals. Be open about their behaviours, desirable and undesirable, explaining how these will help or hinder their progress.
7. Explain that what they do now will directly affect their options later on. Talk about desirable behaviours that will enable them to reach their goals.

Why it works
This activity holds a mirror up to the pupil, helping them to see how their current actions may be more important than they realise.

Top tip
When the pupil shows undesirable behaviours, remind them of their future intentions and how their actions now could change things for them.

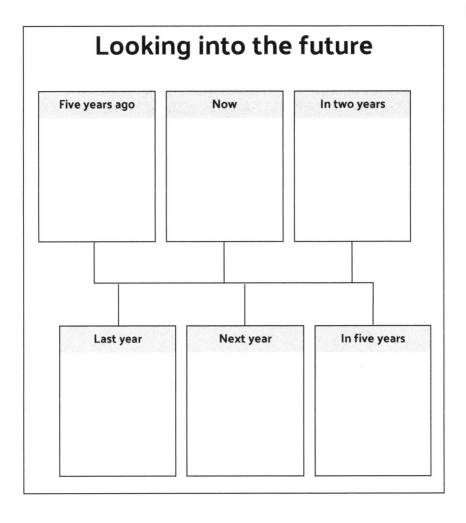

#16 Engaging the parents: identifying common aims

Engaging parents can be a powerful behaviour management strategy. Try this five-step method to connect with parents over common aims for a pupil.

1. Make contact. Invite the parent or carer into school for a meeting. Don't explain too much over the phone but do indicate the purpose of the meeting – for example, 'I'd like to discuss our thoughts, hopes and ideas about making positive changes to Gemma's behaviour.'
2. Set the scene. Start the meeting with a positive discussion about working together to improve the child's behaviour. Be very explicit about your thoughts, hopes and ideas.
3. Listen. The parent or carer will have contributions to make to the discussion. Allow them to share their hopes and ideas, and listen with the intention of including them in the processes for improvement.
4. Clarify the next steps. End the meeting with a plan; discuss the intended outcomes and some realistic timescales.
5. Involve the pupil. Invite them to join the meeting and present a united front as you share the thoughts, hopes and ideas. Give them the aims and the timescale, and discuss any consequences of the changes you expect to see.

Why it works

Getting parents onside shows the pupil that expectations at home and school are shared and consistent.

Top tip

See chapter 3 for more strategies to engage parents and carers.

#17 Reflection: what went wrong?

Metacognitive thinking can help pupils to become more reflective and better regulate their emotions. A restorative justice approach can be a valuable tool for improving behaviour. Here is a simple model.

1. When negative behaviour occurs, start by asking what went wrong. Allow the pupil to explain in their own way, while you listen, clarify and paraphrase.
2. When you've established what went wrong, ask why. Again, listen carefully. If the pupil isn't sure, prompt with questions. If they're still not sure, just tell them.
3. Once you know why, ask: 'Which way next?' Discuss alternative responses and reactions, and their consequences.

Why it works
As adults, we often spend time thinking about what went wrong, why and what should happen next. This strategy helps young people to practise the skill of self-reflection.

Top tip
Don't try to have these conversations when emotions are flying high – allow the pupil sufficient time to calm down. Remember, don't poke the bear.

#18 Promoting self-regulation to improve behaviour

Dr Stuart Shanker, a professor of psychology and philosophy, defines self-regulation as 'the ability to manage stress'. And he describes dysregulation as: 'When a child's stress levels are too high, various systems for thinking and metabolic recovery are compromised. The signs of dysregulation show up in the child's behaviour, or mood, or attention, and physical well-being.'[13]

When it comes to behaviour in school, it's useful to view self-regulation as recognising one's own responses to a perceived stressor and aiming to keep your behaviours in line with your long-term goals. Common stressors in the classroom include finding the work too challenging, being irritated by a peer, losing equipment or feeling unwell. So, how can you encourage self-regulation in your pupils?

1. Help young people to define their long-term goals and personal ethos. They can keep these in mind when a stressor occurs.
2. Teach stress-reducing techniques such as mindful breathing.
3. Give pupils time and space to recover after a behavioural or emotional outburst. Then talk through what happened and how they wish they had responded.
4. Praise pupils when they show high self-regulation (e.g. completed work despite distractions or challenges, calmed emotions after a stressful event).

Why try this?
Fostering the skill of self-regulation in your pupils will result in many benefits for them and for you.

Top tip
Explore the work of my intellectual crush, the self-regulation expert Dr Stuart Shanker. His website, self-reg.ca, offers a wide range of information and resources, including free downloadable posters and fact sheets about self-regulation.

---

13 'Self-reg definitions', Mehrit Centre, tinyurl.com/tsv475m, accessed 2020

#19 Culture over strategies

According to the behaviour specialist Paul Dix, 'In behaviour management, culture eats strategy for breakfast. Getting the culture right is pivotal. With the right culture the strategies that are used become less important. The culture is set by the way that the adults behave.'[14] Here are a few thought-provoking questions for senior leaders about setting the behavioural culture in a school.

1. What are the expectations for behaviour? Why?
2. How are these shared with the team?
3. How are these shared with the pupils?
4. How will parents know and support the expectations?
5. How are the expectations encouraged?
6. What will the outcome be if expectations are adhered to?
7. What will the outcome be if expectations are not adhered to?

Why it works
Defining your school's behaviour culture and how it is implemented will ensure a consistent approach that has a positive impact on pupil behaviour.

Top tip
Read your school's behaviour policy with fresh eyes. Is it more about culture or strategy?

---

14 Paul Dix, *When the Adults Change, Everything Changes: seismic shifts in school behaviour*, Crown House Publishing, 2017

#20 **Preventing bullying**

According to the 2018 Teacher Voice Omnibus Survey, around one-fifth of teachers say pupils in their class have experienced bullying.[15] The Department for Education's *Preventing and Tackling Bullying* report[16] says schools that excel at tackling bullying do the following:

1. Involve parents. Keep them up to date with policies and procedures.
2. Involve pupils. Make sure pupils understand the part they can play to prevent bullying.
3. Regularly evaluate and update policies.
4. Implement disciplinary sanctions – this sends strong messages to all pupils.
5. Take the time to openly discuss the differences between people.
6. Teach pupils that prejudice-based language is unacceptable.
7. Draw on the expertise of anti-bullying organisations.
8. Involve staff. Anti-bullying policies are most effective when all school staff know and understand them.
9. Invest in training to help staff understand the needs of their pupils.
10. Ensure that it's easy for pupils to report incidents of bullying.

Why prevent bullying?
Bullying can have long-term effects on young people, such as mental health issues, obesity, unemployment and an inability to form stable relationships.[17]

Top tip
Support the victims of bullying and offer firm guidance to perpetrators of bullying.

15 Robert Smith, Caroline Sharp, David Sims, Sarah Millar, Jo Nossiter, Rebecca Menys and Chloe Rush (National Foundation for Educational Research), *Teacher Voice Omnibus Survey: research report, Department for Education*, 2018, tinyurl.com/ugo9vgx

16 Department for Education, *Preventing and Tackling Bullying: advice for headteachers, staff and governing bodies*, 2017, tinyurl.com/ukrw33b

17 'The impact of bullying', Anti-Bullying Alliance, tinyurl.com/rcl2wt3, accessed 2020

#21 Manners matter: a whole-school approach

Some children don't realise they come across as ill-mannered or don't know why this is a problem (children with autistic spectrum conditions may need additional support with this. Read more in chapter 4). But being polite is a life skill, so try this method to enhance manners in your school.

1. Work with your school council reps to plan and implement a programme for etiquette. Ask them to decide on the manners they expect to see across the school (please and thank you, appropriate use of greetings, small talk, table manners, etc.).
2. The school council can host an assembly or create an instructional film or leaflet outlining the etiquette programme.
3. School council reps could make short presentations to forms or classes, in which they model the expectations, provide scenarios to discuss or host quizzes about manners.
4. Make sure staff place a high value on manners, praising politeness and reminding where necessary. And, of course, staff should set the ultimate example for manners!

Why it works

Building a school ethos that encourages, values and models manners will lead to better working relationships and positive, kind learning spaces.

Top tip

Share the goal with parents and carers by including a feature in the school newsletter.

#22 Manners matter: group interventions

Do you have a core group of ill-mannered pupils, despite a big push on etiquette? Time to enrol them in your very own Conduct Club!

1. Invite pupils to attend a formal meeting.
2. Explain why manners and demeanour are so important in a community like a school. Discuss that, unfortunately, these are things they need to improve and so they have been enrolled in the Conduct Club.
3. As part of the programme of study, pupils learn a variety of skills relating to manners and conduct. Ensure they know what good conduct and manners look like.
4. Take the pupils on a walk around the school, asking them to identify and note good (and bad) conduct and manners.
5. Meet for a short time each week, tackling an issue at a time. For example, in the first week you might cover 'how to respond to something you don't like' or 'how we greet different people'.
6. At the end of the Conduct Club training, set a light-hearted assignment that challenges the pupils to meet and greet a special visitor and show them around the school, using the skills they've gained.
7. When pupils' conduct and manners have changed for the better, they graduate from the Conduct Club.

Why it works
This strategy is a bit tongue-in-cheek, but it gives pupils the chance to develop knowledge, understanding and skills relating to their conduct.

Top tip
Ask the pupils' teachers for brief updates on their conduct and manners, which can be used to inform the weekly meeting.

CONDUCT CLUB

Name		
Skill	Date achieved	Comment
Meeting and greeting		
Greet with a smile		
Welcome with a hello		
Introduce yourself		
Handshake		
Holding conversations		
Active listening		
Contributing equally		
Asking questions		
Opening/closing		
Movement around school		
Walking		
Respectful volume		
Winning and losing		
Congratulate competitors		
Accept the results		
Act gracefully		
Taking feedback		
Listen		
Respect the feedback given		
Explain how you feel		

#23 Tackling rough play at breaktime

Children love rough and tumble at breaktime, but it usually ends in tears. Here's one way for primary schools to banish overly boisterous play.

1. Define what rough play looks like. Discuss this as a staff team, including your lunchtime staff. Invite your school council reps along, too – they'll have plenty of insights.
2. Discuss what types of rough play dominate the playground: pulling coats, head locks, pushing, shoving, pretend fighting?
3. Note whether any groups or individuals keep popping up in conversation.
4. Ask the school council to make a film about the rules of safe play. Keep the film light-hearted but with a clear message.
5. Show the video in an assembly and discuss the issues with this type of play.
6. Provide lunchtime and breaktime staff with red and yellow cards. They can use these as warnings and sanctions against rough play.

Why it works
Pupils might have no idea why rough play is a problem. Telling them straight gives them the knowledge they need in order to make the right choices.

Top tip
Ask your usual suspects to take part in the film, allowing them to feel invested in the cause.

#24 **Troublesome classes**

Undesirable behaviours or attitudes can sometimes gain children a negative reputation across a school. That reputation can lead to a vicious cycle: undesirable behaviours are repeated in order to 'live up' to the reputation – or 'give up' to the reputation. And when a group of unruly students have ended up in the same form or class, how can you handle that troublesome bunch?

1. Divide and conquer. Identify the most influential pupils and the impact they are having on the group's behaviour.
2. Split up key offenders. It's not about dictating friendships, but make sure those pupils are not sat together in class.
3. Knowing the triggers will help you to avoid them. Do issues arise because of covered lessons, a lack of routine, or lessons with too much recording or too much exploration?
4. Tell the pupils they've started to gain a negative reputation, but you want to help turn that around (even if you think you can't) because you believe in them (even if you don't).
5. Develop a strong rapport with individual pupils (see the rapport suggestions in chapter 9).
6. Talk the class up at every opportunity: to them, to others, to anyone who'll listen. Even if it's the fact that they've all opened their books today, give them a win.
7. Keep calm. Be firm but fair. Avoid losing your temper. You know the class are bound to be problematic at times, so be prepared for the worst, yet aim for the best.

Why it works
Often, a tricky class starts out with one or two challenging pupils who, knowingly or unknowingly, mould the class dynamic. This needs to be tackled one pupil at a time, one habit at a time.

Top tip
Reputations are easy to form and difficult to break. Commit to the goal of turning the class around and remember, it won't happen overnight.

#25 Saving the scapegoat

Do you teach a pupil who always seems to get the blame, even if they're not in the room? This strategy helps to stop the blame game and keeps 'that pupil' from being the class scapegoat.

1. Build them up and big them up! Make their positive actions stand out.
2. When blame rears its head, explain the principle of the presumption of innocence and teach pupils what an accusation is.
3. Give all parties a chance to express themselves properly, using restorative justice where necessary.
4. Avoid asking 'Who did this?' or 'Who said that?' when something goes wrong. These questions often lead pupils to unfairly blame the usual suspects.

Why try this?
Research shows that children as young as 14 months are developing an awareness of others' views and that humans have a natural concern about their reputation, thought to be driven by the fear of rejection.[18] Unfortunately, over time one child can become a scapegoat in class and this can lead to rejection. Someone needs to break that cycle.

Top tip
Read the picture book *Edwardo, The Horriblest Boy in the Whole Wide World*,[19] discussing the themes with the class. This is the tale of a boy who constantly behaves badly because he is constantly told how bad he is. When blame occurs, remind the class of Edwardo.

---

18   Philippe Rochat, *Others in Mind: social origins of self-consciousness*, Cambridge University Press, 2009
19   John Burningham, *Edwardo, the Horriblest Boy in the Whole Wide World*, Red Fox Picture Books, 2007

#26 Sharing problems, sharing practice

Is pupil behaviour causing a problem for your team? Dedicate some time to reflecting on behaviour during a staff meeting.

1. Ask staff to come to the meeting with one problem related to negative behaviour in their class and one way in which they positively manage behaviour. Ask them to note these on two pieces of paper.
2. Mix the pieces of paper up, placing them on tables around the room.
3. Ask staff to read the problems and the strategies shared.
4. Everyone leaves the meeting with an idea and, hopefully, a solution!

Why it works
Teachers are great at solving problems but are time-poor, so it makes sense to schedule a time to discuss undesirable behaviours and share good practice.

Top tip
Keep the suggestions and collate these into a 'good practice' document that is sent out after the meeting.

Further resources

Graham Nuthall, *The Hidden Lives of Learners,* NZCER Press, 2007

Sue Cowley, *The Seven C's of Positive Behaviour Management,* CreateSpace, 2013

Paul Dix, *When the Adults Change, Everything Changes: seismic shifts in school behaviour,* Independent Thinking Press, 2017

Jarlath O'Brien, *Better Behaviour: a guide for teachers,* Sage Publications, 2018

Phil Beadle and John Murphy, *Why Are You Shouting At Us? The dos and don'ts of behaviour management,* Bloomsbury Education, 2013

Bill Rogers, *Classroom Behaviour,* Sage Publications, 2011

Tom Bennett, *The Behaviour Guru: behaviour management solutions for teachers,* Continuum, 2010

Igraine Rhodes and Michelle Long, *Improving Behaviour in Schools: guidance report,* Education Endowment Foundation, 2019, tinyurl.com/y2pqq7zt

Ramon Lewis, Schlomo Romi, Yaacov J Katz and Xing Qui, 'Students' reaction to classroom discipline in Australia, Israel, and China', *Teaching and Teacher Education,* 24.3, 2008, tinyurl.com/rmoaabm

Explore the behaviour advice found in the resources section of the Education Support website (educationsupport.org.uk) or call the charity's helpline on 08000 562 561 for confidential support

Chapter 2: Curriculum

The structure, delivery and assessment of a school's curriculum is arguably the foundation of the setting. If children come to school to learn, and teachers come to school to teach and assess the learning, then the 'what' becomes paramount to the outcomes. What is to be taught? What will be learned?

Although maintained schools in England must follow the national curriculum, academies and free schools are not obliged to do so. Despite this, the government still expects all schools to provide a broad and balanced curriculum, and rightly so. I would guess that most free schools and academies follow the national curriculum, using the guidance and structure to map out the coverage and content to be provided. So, when it comes to curriculum content in England, it seems to me that the vast majority of schools are singing from the same hymn sheet. Yet the *implementation* of that content varies from school to school, owing to a wide range of factors (cohort of pupils, catchment area, key priorities of the leadership team, interpretation of the guidance, previous inspection feedback and so on). Furthermore, the content in the national curriculum is vast, so the ways that schools manage the coverage and the focal points also vary. For these reasons, finding one common approach between schools might just be the impossible task. Planning and implementing a school curriculum isn't an exact science.

To me, it seems sensible that schools design their curriculum provision according to their unique circumstances. Schools that buy into generic curriculum planning tools might be in danger of providing a generic education, one that does not support students to develop the knowledge or skills that are relevant to them and their locality. And although some of the lesson plans you can download online are fantastic, some are basic and others are downright flawed. Pre-planned content that has links to the national curriculum can be a real time-saver, but it should be used with caution to avoid a tick-box approach to education.

It can be pretty interesting and exciting to consider the content of your school's curriculum. The richness of the content has a profound impact on the young people we teach. What they learn in their school years will likely affect the rest of their lives, so we have a huge responsibility to make sure that when they leave education, they are armed with the knowledge and skills that they need. In her no-nonsense book *The Curriculum: gallimaufry to coherence* (see idea #27), the education adviser Mary Myatt says, 'Children are entitled to an education which is well-taught, well-resourced and properly funded.' And I couldn't agree more. We, as educators, have a duty to provide children with access to content that will enhance their opportunities.

In recent years, curriculum content has risen up the agenda. I see the subject being discussed more and more on social media such as Twitter or Facebook, where educators flock to express their views and seek the views of others. There has also been an influx of guidance on curriculum content and approaches from the Department for Education and Ofsted. Many of the changes presented in Ofsted's 2019 inspection framework[1] were designed to increase the focus on schools' curriculums and the impact these have upon the learning. In the consultation documents for the inspection framework,[2] Ofsted's chief inspector, Amanda Spielman, wrote: 'The curriculum shapes and determines what learners of all ages will get out of their educational experience. For this reason, the curriculum is at the heart of the proposed quality of education judgement.'

A school's Ofsted grading can be no higher than its quality of education judgement. So, school leaders all over the country will likely be scrutinising their curriculum content as a direct result of Ofsted's increased focus on curriculum. This could have one of two outcomes:

A. Leaders decide their current curriculum diet is strong, suitable for their cohort and well-considered (great news).

B. Leaders decide their current curriculum diet is insufficient, lacks depth or coherence, or has been far too focused on teaching to the test (panic sets in).

If we follow option B, the implications for staff are potentially monumental. The trouble is, accountability on schools and their leadership teams is huge.

---

1   *The Education Inspection Framework*, Ofsted, 2019, tinyurl.com/y2x9xhdx
2   Amanda Spielman, 'Education inspection framework 2019: inspecting the substance of education', Ofsted, 2019, tinyurl.com/y2dve8jq

If a school gets feedback from an inspection that indicates a less than robust curriculum, this could impact the overall grading the school is given and therefore the parental and community support the school receives. This will in turn affect the number of pupils attending the school (which comes with financial consequences) and the attractiveness of employment at such a setting. For this reason, I believe it is vital that school leaders and subject or department leaders take three priority actions when evaluating their current curriculum content:

1. Know the curriculum on offer. (If you lack a deep awareness of the curriculum content on offer at your setting, you are unlikely to feel confident that your pupils are receiving the best possible deal.)
2. Know the impact of the curriculum on offer. (Considering the impact of curriculum content on the long-term learning will put you in a position of confidence when making justifications to the team, governors, parents and other authorities. This is not to say that the only reason to know the impact of your curriculum is in order to prove to others that it is effective. It's about being able to confirm, to yourself first and foremost, that you've got it right, for the kids more than anyone else.)
3. Know how to make manageable and effective alterations to curriculum content for sustained positive outcomes. (If issues around curriculum content arise, the improvement strategies deployed will be the single most important factor in making positive changes. The way changes are handled and implemented could make or break your team, so getting this right is fundamental.)

Senior and subject leaders who make a conscious effort to review and evaluate their curriculum content are likely to have a realistic view of their school's current strengths and areas for development. Like most things in education, a balance is required – if too much or too little change is embarked upon, issues could arise. For this reason, take the time now to consider the current intention, implementation and impact of your curriculum, using these prompts to get you thinking. To keep it simple, answer in no more than 10 words.

1. What is the overarching intention of your curriculum?
2. How do you know that the curriculum is implemented with the intentions in mind?
3. What is the impact of the implemented curriculum?

The likely truth is that no school has the perfect curriculum (at least not for every subject, in every year group). Believing that your school's curriculum is perfectly packaged and tied up with a ribbon could be naive. No school sets out to provide an incoherent, narrow or weak curriculum. Timetables are tight and exam pressure is real; most schools have been doing what they believe to be useful. But now the benchmark has been redefined: in England, curriculum is taking centre stage during the inspection process, so schools need to focus intently on their provision.

The ideas presented in this chapter are intended to assist senior and subject leaders in reviewing and developing curriculum design, and to inspire teachers about the implementation of the curriculum, too. With the rise of education technology, social media, mental health issues, extremism, climate change, remote working and 'influencer' culture, the universal challenge for teachers is to bring what is still a 'traditional' curriculum to life for a more connected generation.

#27 Mary Myatt's brief history of the national curriculum in England

In her book *The Curriculum: gallimaufry to coherence*,[3] Mary Myatt provides a brief history of the national curriculum in England. How much do you know about its development? Inspired by Myatt's book, here's a Q&A to fill you in.

Have we always had a national curriculum?
No. Before the national curriculum was introduced in 1988, local authorities or schools decided the content of their curriculum.

When and why was the national curriculum introduced?
The national curriculum was introduced in 1988 after the Education Reform Act. It is understood that the national curriculum was introduced in order to give all children the same standard of education.

How has the national curriculum changed since 1988?
Since 1988 the national curriculum has undergone a number of revisions. Most of the changes were made with the intention of streamlining the content. In 2011, Tim Oates led an expert panel to report on a framework for the new national curriculum. The new national curriculum was approved by the government in 2013 and schools began to follow it in 2014.

How different is the new national curriculum?
Among other changes, the 2014 national curriculum no longer provides levels for each subject. These had become overcomplicated and were being unnecessarily used for accountability. There is a reduction in content, but also an aim to make content more rigorous.

---

3   Mary Myatt, *The Curriculum: gallimaufry to coherence,* John Catt Educational, 2018

What are the current statutory requirements for schools?

Maintained schools in England are required to teach the content outlined in the national curriculum. Free schools and academies are not currently required to follow the content of the national curriculum (but they are expected to teach a broad and balanced curriculum).

Why this matters

Understanding how reforms have moulded the national curriculum provides further insight into its aims.

Top tip

Read Tim Oates' 2010 paper *Could Do Better: using international comparisons to refine the National Curriculum in England.*[4]

---

4   Tim Oates, *Could Do Better: using international comparisons to refine the National Curriculum in England*, Cambridge Assessment, 2010, tinyurl.com/t6mtpye

#28 Three approaches to the curriculum

In a 2018 article,[5] Ofsted's chief inspector, Amanda Spielman, discusses the three categories identified in a study of schools' curriculum approaches. Here's a summary of those categories.

1. **Knowledge-led approach.** In the schools that take this approach, leaders see the curriculum as 'the mastery of a body of subject-specific knowledge defined by the school', Spielman says. Knowledge is favoured over skills, with skills 'generally considered to be an outcome of the curriculum, not its purpose'.
2. **Knowledge-engaged approach.** Schools that take this approach are 'less reliant on curriculum theory than knowledge-led schools'. They value knowledge, but they also place emphasis on developing skills.
3. **Skills-led curriculums.** A smaller number of schools design their curriculums around skills development. These schools prioritise the delivery of skills that pupils will need in the future and often consider knowledge as 'disconnected facts'.

Why this matters
Spielman's categories might provide food for thought about the curriculum approach taken by your setting.

Top tip
It's worth bearing in mind that just 23 schools were visited for this study. All schools are different and your setting might not fit into any of these categories.

---

5   Amanda Spielman, 'HMCI commentary: curriculum and the new education inspection framework', Ofsted, 2018, tinyurl.com/ycmkn86g

#29 What is a knowledge-rich curriculum?

Knowledge-rich curriculums are a hot topic, but what are they? In an article,[6] the author and education consultant Tom Sherrington suggests that a knowledge-rich curriculum has four components:

1. **Knowledge provides a driving, underpinning philosophy.** In a knowledge-rich curriculum, Sherrington says, 'there is a belief that we are all empowered through knowing things'. Skills and understanding are considered to be forms of knowledge.
2. **The knowledge content is specified in detail.** Sherrington says that, in knowledge-rich curriculums, 'units of work are supported by statements that detail the knowledge to be learned'.
3. **Knowledge is taught to be remembered, not merely encountered.** A good knowledge-rich curriculum takes cognitive science into account, according to Sherrington. Low-stakes testing and spaced retrieval practice are employed in order to optimise the retention of key knowledge.
4. **Knowledge is sequenced and mapped deliberately and coherently.** In knowledge-rich curriculums, thought is given to the sequencing of content in order to build what Sherrington calls 'secure schemas' and create connected learning experiences.

Why consider this?
A knowledge-rich curriculum is about more than just learning facts. When the concept is unpicked, the complexity of the approach is revealed.

Top tip
Read Sherrington's full article online in *Impact*, the journal of the Chartered College of Teaching (tinyurl.com/ycnrfmg8).

---

6   Tom Sherrington, 'What is a "knowledge-rich" curriculum?', *Impact*, 2018, tinyurl.com/ycnrfmg8

#30 **Knowledge organisers**

Many schools use 'knowledge organisers' (see a basic example overleaf) as a way of presenting the minimum knowledge to be learned by pupils in a topic. In an article,[7] the teacher Mark Miller reflects on the purpose, content and pedagogy of knowledge organisers. Here's a summary of some of his thoughts.

Purpose

1. Knowledge organisers aid the construction of schema.
2. They might reduce cognitive load.
3. They may help to develop a teacher's subject knowledge.
4. They can help to guide teaching sequences and direct how the subject should be taught.
5. They can be useful starting points for effectively designing a curriculum.

Content

1. Knowledge organisers are usually restricted to one side of A4.
2. The content needs to be streamlined through careful selection.
3. Teachers should consider which knowledge is most useful in understanding the topic and which is important for assessment purposes.
4. Teachers should also consider the best way to optimise learning through the organisation of information on the knowledge organiser.

---

7   Mark Miller, 'Organising knowledge: the purpose and pedagogy of knowledge organisers', *Impact*, 2018, tinyurl.com/tyxug2g

Pedagogy

1. Knowledge organisers should be routinely used by teachers and students.
2. Teachers should provide regular opportunities for retrieval practice of the knowledge.
3. Teachers should ensure that material on the knowledge organiser is expressed with greater detail by pupils, encouraging them to make links between learning.

Why consider this?
Miller provides useful insights into how to optimise the use of knowledge organisers. If they are going to be created, it makes sense to use them effectively, right?

Top tip
Read the full article on the Chartered College of Teaching website (tinyurl.com/tyxug2g).

KNOWLEDGE ORGANISER: INCREDIBLE EARTH

Key vocabulary	Key knowledge
Earth – the planet that we live on, the world. **Solar system** – the collection of eight planets and their moons in orbit round the sun, together with smaller bodies in the form of asteroids, meteoroids and comets. **Inner core, outer core, mantle and crust** – the layers of the Earth. **Tectonic plates** – the surface of the Earth is broken up into large plates called tectonic plates. **Earthquake** – a sudden violent shaking of the ground, typically causing great destruction, as a result of movements within the Earth's crust or volcanic action. **Seismograph** – an instrument that measures and records details of earthquakes. **Richter scale** – a numerical scale for expressing the magnitude of an earthquake. **Volcano** – a mountain or hill, having a crater or vent through which lava, rock fragments, hot vapour and gas can erupt from the Earth's crust. **Shield volcano, composite volcano, cinder volcano** – these are all types of volcano. **Lava** – hot molten rock erupted from a volcano. **Magma** – hot fluid below or within the Earth's crust from which lava and other igneous rock is formed on cooling. **Water cycle** – the cycle of processes by which water circulates between oceans, atmosphere and land. **Condensation** – the conversion of a vapour or gas to a liquid. **Precipitation** – rain, snow, sleet or hail. **Evaporation** – the process of turning from a liquid into vapour. **Biome** – an area of the planet that can be classified according to the plants and animals that live there, e.g. tundra, grassland, aquatic, desert, forest. **Climate zones** – divisions of the Earth's climates into general zones according to average temperatures and average rainfall, e.g. cold, warm, temperate, tropical.	I know that planet Earth is part of a solar system with seven other planets. I know that Earth has seven continents (Europe, Asia, Australia, North America, South America, Africa and Antarctica). I know that land mass has changed over time due to continental drift. I know that an earthquake causes the ground to shake suddenly and this can have a negative impact on living things. I know that an earthquake is caused by the movement of tectonic plates that are under the Earth's surface. I know that some buildings are specifically designed to be earthquake-proof. I know the features of these buildings. I know that a volcano can be extinct, dormant or active. I know that there are different types of volcano, such as shield, composite or cinder. I know the features of different volcano types. I know that there is an unchanging amount of water on planet Earth and that the water moves around as part of the water cycle. I know the processes of the water cycle. I know that Earth has different climate zones and can name them. I know that Earth has biomes such as aquatic, desert, grassland or forest.

#31 Reviewing your curriculum content

How closely is your teaching content linked to the national curriculum expectations? Review your content to make sure it meets the requirements.

1. Explore the national curriculum expectations for the subject in mind. Reading the overarching aims and programmes of study for the key stage or year group can focus thinking on the end goals.
2. Explore your medium-term or long-term plans. Refer back to the national curriculum guidance to decide how the content taught matches the expectations.
3. Consider whether there is a strong sense of progression through a unit or topic. Daily plans, although important to an extent, should be guided by an overview of lessons that are sequenced in order to achieve long-term aims.

Why try this?
Over time, slight amendments to content and changes in the direction of learning for one reason or another can contribute to a widening gap between content expectations and content taught.

Top tip
Be realistic: the national curriculum content can be very broad and time is limited, so there may be some gaps in coverage.

#32 Overhauling your curriculum

Does your school's curriculum need a makeover? Consider the following before you get started.

1. Do you really need to start over? If you are going to overhaul the content of your curriculum, you need to be confident that you have good reason to do so. Closely review your current curriculum to decide how much needs to change and why.
2. Consider the progression and coherence of each subject/topic. A great curriculum will be progressive across year groups and have coherence, too. Themes and concepts will be repeated and built upon over time, and pupils will be able to make links to previous learning. Spend time mapping out your curriculum's progression and coherence.
3. If you work in a primary school, decide whether you will teach foundation subjects discretely or as part of an overarching topic or theme (if you're not sure, read the next idea).
4. Map out objectives for each subject or topic using the national curriculum to guide you towards the bigger picture.
5. Provide as much support as you can to teachers. Schools must give staff rich resources and time to reflect on the changes being made.

Why this matters
Curriculums can become disjointed and diluted over the years. If you want to rebuild your school's curriculum, you are certainly about to embark upon a journey.

Top tip
One person building a curriculum in isolation might not be effective. This is a very time-consuming project and two (or more) heads will be better than one.

#33 Subjects or topics?

If you're unsure about whether to teach subjects discretely or as part of a topic in your infant, junior or primary school, weigh up some of the pros and cons of each approach.

Teaching topics: the pros

1. Considered to connect learning from different subjects to an overarching theme.
2. Considered to offer creative learning opportunities.
3. Considered to enhance motivation or understanding of content.
4. Considered to enable pupils to use knowledge and skills in a cross-curricular way.

Teaching topics: the cons

1. Might it create forced, tenuous links?
2. Might it dilute content or coverage?
3. Might it blur the identity of discrete subjects?

Teaching discrete subjects: the pros

1. Considered to enhance progression of knowledge and skills in individual subjects.
2. Considered to ensure richer coverage of content.
3. Considered to ensure clarity about the subject being taught.
4. Considered to aid preparation for secondary school, where subjects are taught discretely.

Teaching discrete subjects: the cons

1. Might it create the impression that learning across subjects is not possible?
2. Might it be less motivating?
3. Might it miss opportunities to deepen and connect learning?

Why try this?
Teaching foundation and some core subjects discretely or as topics will greatly affect the way teachers plan at your setting. You might want to use a mixture of both approaches.

Top tip
Different schools and teachers will have different preferences and visions for their curriculum. As long as your approach allows for deep, rich, relevant and cohesive learning, does it matter whether you teach subjects discretely or as part of a topic?

#34 Invigorating your curriculum with minimal impact on workload

Leaders: have you decided on a big shake-up? Making changes to curriculum content or approach can be exciting, but it also has the potential to lead to increased workload for the team. Follow these tips to revitalise the curriculum without overwhelming your staff.

1. **Gather research**. You may be the fount of all knowledge when it comes to curriculum, but keep perspective and remember that others may not have the same level of understanding or passion. Your task is to provide the team with as much information and discussion around curriculum as you can, so everyone is knowledgeable and ready for change.
2. **Create an action plan**. A big change to curriculum can't happen overnight, so set realistic timeframes. You may need to map out key changes over a year or even longer.
3. **Keep the momentum going**. Make the curriculum a regular focus during team meetings.
4. **Celebrate progress and allow experimentation**. You don't want staff to feel afraid of 'getting it wrong' so avoid extreme monitoring, instead favouring reflective and open discussions.
5. **Give teams dedicated time** to unpick new overviews and develop progressive plans.

Why this matters

Even with the best intentions, implementation is likely to fail if your team are not onboard and don't have the right support.

Top tip

If you want staff to read research or theories around curriculum, give them the dedicated time to do so.

#35 Creating a local curriculum

Does your curriculum connect to your community? Consider these prompts to ensure that you make the most of your surroundings.

1. Who are your local artists, authors, singers, scientists, historical figures and so on?
2. What has happened in the past locally?
3. How has your local area changed over time?
4. What are the local career prospects?
5. Are there any local charities or projects to get involved with?
6. What are the local landmarks or physical features?
7. What wildlife and plants live and grow locally?
8. What brings tourists to the area?
9. How does the area compare to other villages, towns or cities?

Why this matters

If young people can't connect with their local area, how can they develop an understanding that goes beyond the local area?

Top tip

Arrange plenty of local visits and visitors throughout the year.

#36 What lesson are we in?

Each school subject is important in its own right. In the past, in some schools, non-core subjects have not received the attention they deserve. In extreme cases, schools have totally disregarded some subjects, leaving huge gaps in the opportunities offered to pupils. But in recent years, curriculums have become more balanced and subjects that were previously neglected are (quite rightly) beginning to regain their status. Use these suggestions to define and express each subject, so that pupils understand the purpose of their learning.

1. **Define the subject**. Create simple, accessible definitions of each of the subjects the pupils are taught. For example: 'Science is the study of life, the Earth and energy through observing, describing and experimenting.'
2. **Consider the purpose and benefits of learning the subject**. Summarise these in a few sentences. For example: 'We take part in science so that we develop a deeper understanding of life, energy and the world around us. Through science investigations, we can answer questions, using our findings to develop understanding or help us improve something.'
3. **Contextualise the subject**. In one or two sentences, write down the types of professions that use the subject. For example: 'People who study science are called scientists. There are many jobs in which science is used.'
4. **Note the word families relating to the subject**. For example: 'Word family – science, scientist, scientific.'
5. **Collate steps 1-4**. Collate your reflections to form an overview of the subject. This can be shared across the school or team to ensure consistent expression.

Why try this?

There is a risk, especially in primary schools, that pupils don't actually understand what the subject is and its purpose.

Top tip

Once the subject definitions and context have been taught explicitly several times, you can begin to ask pupils to offer them at the start of the lesson.

#37 Subject-specific vocabulary

How important is it for pupils to use the correct vocabulary relating to a subject or topic? Without grasping the meaning of key words, pupils are unlikely to fully grasp key concepts. Here are some tips to encourage the use of subject-specific vocabulary in your classroom.

1. **Display the key words**. Initially, all key words for the topic can be displayed in the classroom in a clear, large font.
2. **List subject-specific vocabulary**. Spend a few moments getting pupils to contribute the words they know that link to the topic or subject. Include key words and use misconceptions as teaching points.
3. **Define and contextualise words**. When you first use new words, be sure to define and contextualise them. Don't assume that pupils know the meaning of a word, even if they've heard it before. Pupils often end up guessing the meaning of words, filling the gaps in their understanding, which can lead to misconceptions.
4. **Use the 'listen, say' method**. Allow pupils to hear you saying the word and then ask them to repeat it out loud. Sometimes children will have heard a key term but never actually used it themselves. This method can help with pronunciation and familiarity.
5. **Overuse new words**. When new words are first introduced, using them frequently can help to embed their meaning.
6. **Start each lesson by recapping** some key words from the previous lessons. If you revisit them, they are less likely to be forgotten.
7. **Use synonyms**. When you introduce subject-specific vocabulary, use lots of synonyms (where possible). This should help pupils to make links between the words they know and the words they are learning.
8. **Teach the etymology of words**. Teaching the meaning and origin of words can help pupils to gain a deeper understanding of word families.

Why it works
Understanding and using key words will really help pupils to make connections between key concepts.

Top tip
Don't settle for incorrectly pronounced terms. If a pupil mispronounces a word, correctly pronounce it and ask them to repeat it back to you.

#38 Celebrating subjects

Whether you work in a primary or secondary setting, celebrating different subjects and what they bring to our world is a great way of raising their profile. Here's how.

1. Ensure pupils have a clear understanding of the subject and its aims.
2. Teach pupils about the history and development of the subject over time.
3. Develop pupils' understanding of the subject within the context of the working world.
4. Mark national and international days, such as Science Week, World Book Day or Number Day.
5. Host a subject workshop for parents, led by pupils.
6. Arrange for pupils to lead an assembly or presentation to the school governors about the value and depth of the subject.
7. Make a class list of all the ways the subject is useful to their lives.
8. Make vlogs or mini-documentaries about the subject to share across the school or on the website.

Why try this?
Subjects really are the nuts and bolts of the curriculum – they should be celebrated and enjoyed.

Top tip
Create a display of famous contributors to the subject (ensure you include a diverse range of people).

#39 Enrichment in the curriculum

Is your curriculum all work and no play? It's important to remember that education isn't just about delivering content – children also need enriching, engaging experiences. Here are some ideas for making sure your curriculum is experience-rich.

1. **Trips**. Visit interesting places that will enhance the pupils' knowledge and understanding.
2. **Workshops**. There are some wonderful workshops out there, often run by very knowledgeable people who use hands-on artefacts or resources.
3. **Special visitors**. Inviting experts or workers in the field you are studying to visit your class can really bring the learning to life.
4. **Projects**. Involving your class in a group project can bring together learning and learners.
5. **Record differently**. Asking pupils to present what they know in a different way can boost their motivation.
6. **Connect with other schools**. Local schools are covering similar learning to you. Why not connect pupils to work alongside (or even compete against) one other?
7. **Invite parents or relevant local businesses into school**. Ask your pupils to prepare presentations or work to show to parents or other special visitors.
8. **Get out**. Going outside to learn is just wonderful.
9. **Use music**. There is a song for everything nowadays! And if there isn't, get your pupils to write and sing one.
10. **Present a challenge**. Children enjoy using their learning to solve problems and complete challenges. How could you challenge pupils to use their acquired knowledge and skills?

Why try this?
If enrichment is done right, it is worth the effort for the impact on pupils' wellbeing and outcomes.

Top tip
During the penultimate week of term, plan and map out the enrichment opportunities you have lined up for the following term.

#40 Speak up

Speaking and listening are part of the national curriculum for good reason. Speaking confidently and articulately is a necessity in many jobs, and then there's the importance of being able to hold polite conversations or effectively raise concerns. Try these tips to boost speaking skills in your classroom.

1. Provide opportunities for rich group or whole-class talk. Recording into books often takes precedence over everything else, but the benefits of rich discussion will pay off.
2. Model confident, audible and fluent speaking. Pupils spend a lot of time listening to school staff speak and will pick up the speech that is modelled to them.
3. Provide opportunities for presenting, performing, justifying and debating in front of peers or other staff members. Give constructive feedback on pupils' delivery as well as the content.
4. Explain what effective speaking actually means. It might sound obvious, but many pupils could benefit from a short discussion of this.
5. Tell young people why speaking well is so important to their lives.
6. Provide and display models for discussion, such as 'I agree with what you've said because…', 'To add to this…', 'I have to disagree that…' and 'Have you considered…'.

Why this matters

If young people learn to speak with confidence, eloquence and variation, this will have a profound impact on their lives, boosting their employment prospects and helping them to communicate their views or needs.

Top tip

Discuss the importance of talk as a whole-school team, sharing ideas and strategies to develop oracy across the setting.

#41 Debate and discussion across the curriculum

There is room for debate and discussion in every subject. Ask yourself the following questions to consider how to bring effective debate into your curriculum.

1. **How often have you posed engaging questions for debate?** Think quality over quantity here; giving time for in-depth debate is better than rushing through discussions.
2. **How are children taught to take part in dynamic and well-considered debate?** Debating does require a level of skill. Teach the pupils when and how to interject, how to agree or disagree, and how to build upon each other's comments.
3. **When should debate and discussion take place?** They are often best used when pupils have built up strong knowledge of the topic.
4. **What does good debate look like?** Consider what you expect from debate, and how debate and discussion might vary between year groups.
5. **What is the adults' role during debate?** Make sure the adults in the room know how to interject, leave silence or steer the discussion when needed.

Why it works
Debate and discussion can help to prepare children for the world of work, allowing them the opportunity to be reflective, assertive and curious.

Top tip
Spark debate by providing a thought-provoking statement to agree or disagree with, or by using an open-ended question.

#42 Reading aloud to pupils

Reading is the cornerstone of a good education. Limited reading skills can have a profound impact on pupils' self-esteem and progress across all subjects, so reading should be a key priority for all schools. Here's how to make reading aloud to pupils a success in your classroom.

1. Timetable a slot to read aloud.
2. Protect the time.
3. Create a reading atmosphere. Whether you light a candle or all gather on the floor, make it a special time for the class.
4. Pick the right book, something challenging that you and your pupils will really enjoy.
5. Read a range of texts. Don't neglect non-fiction and poetry.
6. Know when to stop. If you read aloud for too long, children can lose focus. Stop reading after a suspenseful or thought-provoking moment, so pupils are left with something interesting to ponder.
7. Use your voice. When we vary our tone, volume and intonation, this keeps our listeners engaged and models effective reading aloud.

Why try this?
Pupils can learn so much from hearing a text being read aloud (read the next idea to find out more).

Top tip
Provide pupils with the opportunity to read aloud, too.

#43 **Research about reading**

Research conducted by Jo Westbrook, Julia Sutherland, Jane Oakhill and Susan Sullivan sheds light on the power of reading aloud to our pupils. Their report[8] presents the following findings:

1. Reading aloud to adolescents improved the reading of all pupils in the sample by an average of 8.5 months over a period of just 12 weeks.
2. Reading aloud had an even more profound impact on the poorest readers, who were found to make an average of 16 months' progress over 12 weeks.
3. Reading challenging text aloud at a fast pace in each lesson helped 'poor readers' to become 'good readers'.

Why this matters
The benefits of reading aloud to pupils have long been felt by teachers. This research provides evidence to back up what we have seen in our classrooms.

Top tip
Roll with the evidence by reading challenging texts aloud to your pupils (especially those who find reading more difficult) as often as possible.

---

8   Jo Westbrook, Julia Sutherland, Jane Oakhill and Susan Sullivan, '"Just Reading": increasing pace and volume of reading whole narratives on the comprehension of poorer adolescent readers in English classrooms', *Literacy*, 53.2, 2019, tinyurl.com/qrc6alo

#44 Plausible predictions

How confident are your pupils with making plausible predictions about a story? Making predictions is a key skill in developing understanding of a text, so try this simple method to help your pupils make realistic, justified predictions.

1. Pause at a suitable point in the text.
2. Present four predictions for your pupils to explore, three plausible and one unrealistic.
3. Ask pupils to work with a partner to order the predictions from least to most likely.
4. Share the pupils' thoughts, asking them to justify their answers.
5. Finally, ask the pairs to make their own additional prediction, inspired by the discussions.

Why try this?
Some children view making a prediction as 'having a random guess'. Moving pupils towards a reflective model, based on knowledge of the events and characters, will assist them in making more valid predictions.

Top tip
Use the task as an informal assessment tool to see how well pupils understand the story.

#45 Encouraging reading

How can we encourage a love of reading in our pupils? As educators, we know the value of getting children to read, but here's how to help your pupils understand the many benefits.

1. Explain to students that reading is not only fun, but also has a positive impact on the learning.
2. Tell them that fiction and non-fiction both develop knowledge and this helps them to connect ideas.
3. Discuss the fact that reading helps us to learn new words and phrases that we can use in our everyday conversations or writing.
4. Explain that it allows us to explore situations we may not be able to experience first-hand and helps us to develop empathy, too.
5. Tell them that the more they read, the better their comprehension and spelling of tricky words will be.
6. Studies have shown that reading for fun can improve ability in writing and in other subjects like maths. Share this fact.

Why it works
Children truly want to do well. If we are upfront with what research tells us about the benefits of reading, this helps pupils to see reading as an investment in their learning.

Top tip
Give examples of how each reason to read will benefit them later in life. Example: when you have a job interview, using a rich range of vocabulary will help you to stand out and you'll be more likely to get the job!

#46 Improving reading

Try these tips to create a reading-rich culture in your EYFS, KS1 or KS2 setting.

1. Consider how often you read to your class. The more time you dedicate to reading, the more the children are exposed to books.
2. Make reading a priority. Have an action plan for improving and promoting reading.
3. Celebrate books. Make sure your book corner, library and classroom are book-rich. Make books visible and available by displaying a wide range in corridors, on window sills and in baskets.
4. Ensure pupils get the chance to practise comprehension skills, such as retrieval and inference, as they read or are read to.
5. Provide home books that are relevant to individual pupils' ability and interest.
6. Intervene as soon as possible. When a child is notably behind with their reading, offer additional reading support as rapidly as you can.
7. Once a week, invite parents into school to read with their children 10 minutes before the end of the school day.
8. Record staff reading an extract from a text. Videos can be uploaded on to the school website for children to enjoy from home.

Why try this?
The more importance staff place on reading, the better the reading outcomes will become.

Top tip
Talk about yourself as a reader by mentioning the books you are reading at home. The children will see that you practise what you preach.

#47 Every teacher is a phonics teacher

How often do you see common words or subject-specific words spelt incorrectly by your KS2 (or beyond) pupils? Could the problem be a lack of basic phonetic understanding of phonemes, graphemes and trigraphs? Try these three simple ways to improve phonological knowledge beyond KS1.

1. **Flashcards**. Get yourself some grapheme and trigraph flashcards and go through them rapidly every day. This should only take around two minutes. Initially, you might want to practise just five, building on this gradually each day.
2. **Sounds charts**. Ensure that pupils have constant access to a sounds chart that shows graphemes and trigraphs. The chart should also offer examples of each sound within a recognisable word.
3. **'Sound it out' ethos**. When a pupil asks you how to spell a word, always refer to the sounds chart. This applies to every subject, not just English. Model how to use the chart by segmenting the word and identifying familiar graphemes and trigraphs.

Why this matters
Arguably, too many children lack the phonetic skills to spell effectively (or at least make phonetically plausible attempts to spell!). If we rapidly recap sounds each day and always use phonics to aid spelling, we model good practice to our pupils, making phonics for all the norm.

Top tip
Connect with early years and KS1 colleagues to gather further strategies and develop a sound knowledge of phonics (excuse the pun!).

#48 The importance of the arts in education

How can you use the arts to enhance and enrich your curriculum content? The arts are valuable and wonderful subjects, but over the years they have been squeezed out of school timetables. It's about time the arts returned to centre stage, so here are a few tips for including art, drama and music in your teaching.

How can I bring art into my lessons?

1. **Quick, small sketches.** Ask the pupils to make fast (two-minute) sketches on a Post-it note to express their understanding of content coverage.
2. **Display and use artworks that relate to the content.** For example, if covering sound in science, introduce the work of Fabian Oefner, who uses sound waves to create beautiful art.
3. **Plan through drawing.** Whether it's a story, information text or scientific investigation, plans can be created through drawing as opposed to the written word.

How can I bring drama into my lessons?

1. **Role play.** Most subjects will involve significant people, so role play can be used to develop knowledge of historical figures, book characters or famous activists. Pupils can also represent numbers, molecules, blood cells, forces, etc.
2. **Freeze-frames.** Representing a historic moment in a freeze-frame is a quick and simple way to develop an understanding of a key scenario.
3. **Storytelling and mime.** Retelling key events through story or mime is a great way for pupils to express their understanding creatively.

How can I bring music into my lessons?

1. **Learn through singing**. There are many, many songs available online that relate to a huge range of curriculum content.
2. **Create your own songs**. Making up songs that include subject-specific vocabulary and information can be a fun way to build understanding.
3. **Listen to music**. Music that links to the learning can inspire deep thought about content. For example, play Vivaldi's Four Seasons as pupils engage in work about the weather.

Why this matters
Among other benefits, the arts play a vital role in developing pupils' creativity and confidence. Remember that arts subjects have incredible value in their own right, but weaving them into your other subjects is a great way to expand your arts offer.

Top tip
As well as music, drama and art, how could you incorporate subjects such as dance, photography and craft into your teaching?

#49 The Gatsby Benchmarks for good careers guidance[9]

Secondary schools are required to offer independent careers guidance to pupils in Years 8-13. Here are the eight Gatsby Benchmarks for good careers guidance, along with thinking prompts to aid you in preparing your pupils for the future.

1. **A stable careers programme.** What is your school's careers programme? How do you communicate it to parents, staff, employers and pupils?
2. **Learning from career and labour market information.** How do you foster a sound knowledge of future study options?
3. **Addressing the needs of each pupil.** How do you cater to pupils at different stages and provide bespoke support for individuals?
4. **Linking curriculum learning to careers.** How well are all areas of the curriculum linked to careers?
5. **Encounters with employers and employees.** How do you engage pupils through the involvement of employers and employees?
6. **Experiences of workplaces.** Are you maximising opportunities for pupils to experience life in the workplace?
7. **Encounters with further and higher education.** What information do pupils need in order to develop a full awareness of their further education options?
8. **Personal guidance.** Who will provide careers guidance for pupils? How will this be offered?

Why try this?
As well as being a statutory expectation, high-quality careers guidance is vital in helping young people to prepare for a successful future.

Top tip
Appoint a careers leader to ensure that your school's programme receives the time and attention required.

---

9 *The Gatsby Benchmark Toolkit for Schools: practical information and guidance for schools*, The Careers and Enterprise Company, tinyurl.com/vf86gnr, accessed 2020

Further resources

Mary Myatt, *The Curriculum: gallimaufry to coherence*, John Catt
Educational, 2018

Camilla Turner, 'Schools must look beyond "dead white men" to make the
curriculum more diverse, teacher union chief says', *The Telegraph*, 2018,
tinyurl.com/y7rqjgbm

'Welsh education: "Ambitious" new curriculum unveiled', *BBC News*, 2019,
tinyurl.com/ycovd8re

Clare Sealy, 'What's all the fuss about a knowledge-rich curriculum? Part one',
Primary Timery (blog), 2018, tinyurl.com/ycyjzpsp

Lindsay Paterson, 'Scotland's Curriculum for Excellence: The betrayal of
a whole generation?', LSE British Politics and Policy (blog), 2018,
tinyurl.com/yc7wepmg

'What is TOK?', International Baccalaureate Organization, tinyurl.com/
yb3qsbqn, accessed 2020

Closing the Gap: how a narrow curriculum disadvantages the disadvantaged,
GL Assessment, 2019, gl-assessment.co.uk/closingthegap

Frances Brill, Hilary Grayson, Lisa Kuhn and Sharon O'Donnell, *What Impact
Does Accountability Have on Curriculum, Standards and Engagement
in Education? A literature review*, National Foundation for Educational
Research, 2018, tinyurl.com/y9vcgegu

Chapter 3: Engaging parents and carers

Parental engagement in education will always spark debate among teachers and caregivers alike. Where there are children, there are parents,[1] and where there are parents, there is complexity. Effectively communicating with each parent can be somewhat challenging, especially as teachers see them for such a limited time each day (if at all). And parents, who are busy holding down jobs, managing households and raising children, often have little opportunity to become actively involved in their child's education. But parental engagement in education is very, very important.

I could quote research and data to back this up (there is plenty) but I won't, because I don't think we need research to tell us *everything*. Sometimes we just know something, deep down, and parental engagement is the perfect example of this. When you're working on the ground, living and breathing education, you know that parental engagement is hugely significant. You see it and you feel it, every day. If a parent is highly engaged, we usually see a positive impact on the child, and if a parent is totally disengaged, we see a negative impact.

For children to fully reach their potential, we need parents to get involved and value education. The tricky part is figuring out what good parental engagement looks like. Are we talking about helping the child to learn their times tables? Attending the nativity? Helping out at the charity event? Remembering that it's the child's big exam today? Providing breakfast to set the child up for the school

---

1   Throughout this chapter, the term 'parent' extends to any primary caregiver

day? Picking the child up from school on time? Or remembering to pick them up at all? Again, where there are parents, there is complexity.

In her 2017-18 annual report,[2] Ofsted's chief inspector, Amanda Spielman, wrote: 'Parents have the most important role. Rather than expecting educational institutions to pick up the job of parents, parents must step up here.'

Yes, they should. But the trouble is, if parents don't assume responsibility, this leaves educators with little choice but to fill the gap. Raising other people's children becomes part and parcel of the job, whether it's providing day-to-day teaching, emotional support or social etiquette coaching. There is no denying that educators are incredibly important adults in children's lives, but sometimes, for one reason or another, we are *the most* important adults in their lives.

Think about that again: you are potentially the most important adult in a pupil's life. Yes, it's not ideal that the line of responsibility is so blurred in some cases, but if you don't help to meet that child's most basic needs, who will?

It's important to note that engaging parents in education isn't just about engaging the disengaged. The Education Endowment Foundation defines parental engagement as:[3]

- Approaches and programmes that aim to develop parental skills such as literacy or IT skills.
- General approaches that encourage parents to support their children with, for example, reading or homework.
- The involvement of parents in their children's learning activities.
- More intensive programmes for families in crisis.

What does good parental engagement look like in your school community? Is it completing home learning with the child? Attending school events? Supporting the school ethos? Enhancing parents' skills? Sharing the school's values? Ensuring the child's basic needs are met?

Defining what good parental engagement looks like will put you on the path to achieving it; it's the first step in building better relationships between home and school. Try these prompts to get you thinking:

---

2   Amanda Spielman, *The Annual Report of Her Majesty's Chief Inspector of Education, Children's Services and Skills 2017/18*, Ofsted, 2018, tinyurl.com/y89d99wh
3   'Parental engagement: Teaching and Learning Toolkit', Education Endowment Foundation, 2018, tinyurl.com/yarh4ftr

At my setting, good parental engagement is…	To achieve this, I need to…
1	1
2	2
3	3

It rings true that parents of the youngest pupils have the most significant involvement in their child's education. Is this perhaps because at the age of four, your parents are involved in every aspect of your life?

As a parent, one big shift I noticed as my son transitioned to secondary school was that I had far less of a grip over his education. The increase in the number of teachers and the decrease in opportunities for communication made a marked difference to my involvement. Perhaps as young people move into secondary school, their autonomy grows. It becomes almost inevitable that parents must loosen their grip on their child's school life, and this partly includes their learning.

Most parents want to retain understanding of their child's learning beyond primary school, yet simply don't have the know-how. The challenge for secondary teachers and leaders is to find ways to ensure that parents can, wherever possible, maintain enough involvement in their children's education. In this way, parents have the chance to support learning and continue to value their child's personal and academic achievements.

Building those relationships isn't easy. But developing strong home-school links is worth the effort – the positive impact on the child and their education can be immeasurable. In my experience (as a practitioner and a parent), parental engagement is most successful when:

1. Schools communicate regularly with parents.
2. Parents feel welcomed into school.
3. Schools seek and value the views of parents.
4. Parents support the school's values and practices.

The vast majority of parents care deeply about their children, and more often than not this includes their education. If we remember this, we are sure to find success together.

#50 Teacher training for parental engagement

How prepared are your team to talk to a range of parents? A Department for Education review of best practice in parental engagement[4] found that training for staff in working with parents can have a positive impact on engagement. Here are some starting points for staff training.

1. Information about the parental cohort.
2. How to include parents in their child's education.
3. How to express a concern to a parent.
4. How to manage parental concerns.
5. How to defuse parental emotions.
6. How to maintain home-school links with parents.

Why try this?

It is often assumed that staff have the knowledge, experience or confidence to manage relationships with a variety of parents, but in reality this isn't always the case. Provide your staff with a toolkit for working with parents to ensure effective communication and relationships.

Top tip

Most interactions with parents are perfectly pleasant, but it's a good idea to make sure your team have strategies to stay safe in case a conversation with a parent becomes unprofessional.

---

4   Janet Goodall, John Vorhaus, Jon Carpentieri, Greg Brooks, Rodie Akerman and Alma Harris (Institute of Education), *Review of Best Practice in Parental Engagement*, Department for Education, 2011, tinyurl.com/y4xukusp

#51 Fostering relationships early on

According to the Education Endowment Foundation,[5] 'engagement is often easier to achieve with parents of very young children'. The following suggestions can help the parents of the youngest members of your school (whether they are in the foundation stage, Year 3 or Year 7) to feel involved in school life from the get-go.

1. **Check your transitions.** How good are the transitions for your youngest pupils? Make sure transitions enable staff to get to know parents and children alike.
2. **Get them in!** Find a reason to invite parents of the youngest pupils into school.
3. **Know them.** Get to know parents and their children. Start by knowing the child's name!
4. **Address parents' concerns** – they will likely have some. It can be a disconcerting time for parents when their child embarks on a new school journey.
5. **Thank them** for being involved in their child's education and ask them to continue their efforts. A little acknowledgement can go a long way.
6. **Ask for their help.** At the end of the school year, ask parents to be on hand for the next academic year. Invite current parents to offer support and advice at open afternoons for new parents.

Why try this?
Making connections early on will hopefully lead to a long and fruitful relationship between home and school.

Top tip
Towards the end of their first year as parents at the school, ask for a review of your parental engagement efforts. This will help you to consider how to develop parental engagement for the year ahead.

---

5 'Parental engagement: Teaching and Learning Toolkit', Education Endowment Foundation, 2018, tinyurl.com/yarh4ftr

#52 **See and be seen**

What I'm about to say is as simple as it is significant: *be seen!* Children often talk about staff members at home and being visible will help parents to put a face to your name. Your presence will also encourage conversation; it's professional, polite and shows you care. Here are some tips for ensuring you and your team are seen by parents.

1. Be around at key times (drop-off and pick-up).
2. Stand at the door as pupils and parents enter the classrooms.
3. Have a staff photo board in the entrance hall. This will help parents to establish who's who.
4. Keep the school website up to date with the correct staff photos and names.

Why it works
The more visible you are, the more parents see you. The more parents see you, the more familiar you become. The more familiar you become, the better connected parents feel towards you.

Top tip
Don't just be visible in the background – greet and talk to parents as much as possible. In a secondary context, the occasional email (or even video message) can be a great way to make sure parents know who their child's teachers are.

#53 Have you met...?

Looking for a fun way to build parents' knowledge of your staff? Try the 'Have you met...?' method.

1. Tell the team you want to develop parents' knowledge of staff.
2. On the weekly newsletter, reserve a space for the 'Have you met...?' section.
3. In this section, include a photograph of a chosen member of staff alongside their name.
4. Write a short piece of text about the staff member. You could include anything from their subject specialism to their favourite football team or pizza topping!

Why it works
Getting to know staff in this way will help to open up conversations, thus strengthening relationships.

Top tip
Include a range of staff members, from teachers and TAs to site staff.

#54 Welcoming parents into school

Is your setting welcoming for parents? Consider the following to analyse how parent-friendly your setting really is.

1. **Open doors.** Keeping classroom doors open (where possible) is a great way for parents to feel welcome and invited into the learning spaces. Nothing says 'you're not invited' more than a physical boundary like a shut door.
2. **Nice to greet you.** When parents enter the building, is there someone around to greet them? If a parent passes a member of staff in the corridor or school grounds, does the staff member always smile and say hello?
3. **Signposted places.** Are offices, classes and main halls clearly signposted? It's disconcerting to find yourself lost in an unfamiliar building.
4. **Mid-year tours.** How often do you invite parents to tour the school? Why not make a mid-year tour for current parents an annual event – many parents would love to see their child's school in action.

Why try this?
If parents feel welcome, they are more likely to be engaged.

Top tip
Ask pupils to greet visiting parents with a smile and 'Good morning/afternoon'.

#55 Banish the invisible barrier

Is there an invisible barrier in your primary school playground? Often, at pickup times, parents stand on one side of the invisible line and teachers on the other. Here's how to break down the barrier.

1. **Observe.** When you dismiss your class at the end of the school day, observe where parents stand and where teachers stand.
2. **Dismiss differently.** Taking SLT permission and safety into account, could you dismiss your class on the other side of the invisible line?
3. **Cross the line.** Move across and talk to parents!
4. **Invite parents over the line.** Start up conservations that subtly invite parents to cross the line.

Why try this?
Breaking down those invisible barriers will establish better connections with parents.

Top tip
Take five minutes in a staff meeting to discuss other invisible boundaries within your school environment.

#56 'New learning' workshops

Teaching strategies and content can change over time, leaving parents with outdated ways of supporting their children. Keep parents up to date by providing them with 'new learning' workshops.

1. **Write a letter.** Explain to parents that the learning strategies and content have changed, which can make it tricky for them to effectively support their children.
2. **Ask for parent views.** What kind of workshops would they attend? Provide a list of suggestions to make responses simple and focused.
3. **Speak to subject leads**. Ask them to prepare a short workshop (20 minutes max) to dispel myths and teach parents up-to-date methods and content.
4. **Set dates and sell the workshop like mad!** Try texts, letters, posters and prompts on the gates – you want as many parents to attend as possible.
5. **Keep it informal and friendly.** Parents are attending a workshop, not a lesson! Provide tea and biscuits and allow time for discussion and questions.
6. **Reflect and review.** How did the workshop go? Why?

Why do this?

For most parents, their own school days are a distant memory. Introducing them to the content and strategies used in lessons will help them to feel connected to your setting – and help them to help their children!

Top tip

Get the kids involved. Ask pupils from the school council to greet parents, show their learning and present some strategies, too.

#57 Supporting parents with home reading (EYFS, KS1 and KS2)

If we want our pupils to truly excel at reading, we need the time and support of the people at home. Try these tips to support parents with home reading.

1. **Invite parents into school**. Explain to them how phonics and reading comprehension are taught. Stress the importance of reading.
2. **Create and share a list of key stories**, books and poems the children will explore over the academic year.
3. **Create a 'top tips for reading at home' video or leaflet**. Discuss strategies for reading with intonation, how to ask effective questions and which books to use.
4. **Host a book fair**. Book fairs can inspire pupils and parents to discover new books, and often the school can financially benefit from sales.
5. **Create a 'borrow box' for parents**. Poetry and non-fiction books, often the less obvious choice, could be promoted in the box.

Why it works
If books are regularly discussed and promoted, this normalises and encourages reading.

Top tip
Keep a close eye on who is not reading at home – how can these pupils be further supported?

#58 Communication is key

Communication with parents is really important in developing strong home-school links. Which of these communication methods are you making great use of?

1. **Parent texts**. A text system for communication is vital in the smartphone era.
2. **Letters**. Many parents will place letters with key information on the fridge or cupboard door. Keep them simple and clear.
3. **Email**. Working parents in particular might prefer to receive emails, to avoid their children losing/forgetting/denying the existence of any letters that are given out.
4. **Social media**. This can be a wonderful way to show off what has been happening in your school. Be mindful of the dreaded GDPR!
5. **Class blogs.** Updated by teachers or pupils, these can keep parents informed and interested in their child's learning.
6. **Talking face to face**. This is crucial when messages are more personal (concerns, private matters, individual progress conversations, etc).
7. **Praise notes**. Sending home a 'thank you', 'well done', or 'congratulations' note is simple and effective. Parents often really appreciate and treasure these little acknowledgements.
8. **Parent council**. Key parents who represent both the school and the parents can help to bridge the gap between home and school.

Why this matters
Communication is the gateway to understanding on both an organisational and personal level.

Top tip
Ask parents what they think about the modes of communication used. Perhaps the communication is better (or worse!) than you thought.

#59 Parent views

Do you know the views of the parents? Do you seek them? Here are eight ways to ensure you have a strong and balanced understanding of their opinions.

1. Have a suggestion box in the entrance hall resourced with pens and slips.
2. At every event, provide a review box and slip.
3. Simply asking a parent something is a swift way to find out more.
4. Set up and manage a parent council.
5. Have a parent noticeboard.
6. Keep the school website up to date.
7. Create online parent surveys at key points throughout the year.
8. Share staff emails with parents.

Why it works

If you don't seek the views of parents, you are unlikely to get them. Parents often discuss their opinions among themselves, but these often don't make it back to the school. Providing a range of forums will elicit more feedback and ultimately allow staff to reflect and improve.

Top tip

What will you do with parent views? If you gather their opinions, make sure they are acted upon in good time.

#60 **Perfect parents' evening**

Parents' evening can be bustling, unpredictable and, frankly, exhausting! These tips will help to transform it into a tranquil and positive experience for all.

1. **Think about the timings**. For secondary schools or larger primary schools, cramming all the appointments into one evening can result in chaos – appointments don't keep to time and spaces become crowded. If you have a large cohort to see, split the appointments into two or three sessions. But if you have a smaller cohort, spreading out the appointments across a week can drag things out unnecessarily.
2. **Find the right space**. The hall might not be the best place for your parents' evening. Think outside the box (but be sure to consider staff safety).
3. **Plan short breaks for teachers**. Provide 'half-time' snacks and refreshments, delivered to teachers at their table. This will leave them ready to talk effectively about their pupils.
4. **Provide a space for buggies and babies**. Many parents have to bring little ones along to parents' evenings; they will sigh with relief if you provide a small play area with toys and a place to park buggies.
5. **Include pastoral staff**. Parental concerns are often around wellbeing, behaviour or special educational needs. Senior leaders, SENCOs and pastoral staff should be on hand for discussions, too.
6. **Consider privacy**. Put on some calming background music to ensure ample privacy for conversations.
7. **Seek parent feedback**. Provide a 'parent view' review after their appointments. This can be used to plan the next parents' evening.

Why this matters
Parents' evening might be one of the only times a parent actually enters the school building. Make sure they have a positive experience; supporting teachers will help to achieve this.

Top tip
Give a clear breakdown of the evening to parents and carers (e.g. appointments are held in the classrooms, appointments last for up to 10 minutes, toilets are located here, SENCO will be available from...).

#61 Acting on parental concerns[6]

Even when you try your very best, not everything you do will be viewed positively by parents. Sometimes expectations might differ and sometimes we might drop the ball. When a challenging conversation has to take place, being prepared to talk openly and offering parents the chance to air their views are key to getting the home-school relationship back on track. But first you need to unpick their issue to decide how to address the situation.

1. **A parent with a complaint.** Ask them to give you as much information as they can. Make a note of their complaint. Show empathy and explain that you will look into the issue. Promise to get back to them by the end of the day.
2. **A confused parent.** Ask questions to find out what they need help with. If you're able to, give them the information they need. If not, tell them you'll find out more and let them know as soon as you can.
3. **A cross parent**. Keep calm, listen, clarify and ask questions. Show empathy and paraphrase their concerns. Remember: if a parent becomes angry[7] and you feel uncomfortable, tell them you're unable to talk to them when they are not being respectful. Walk away from the situation and straight towards the senior leaders, who should manage the situation for you.
4. **A concerned parent**. Say you can see they are worried and ask questions to unpick the concern. Reassure them that you understand and the school will support them in the best way possible.

Why it works
Responding effectively could make all the difference to the home-school relationship.[8]

Top tip
If a parent wants an immediate lengthy conversation, explain that you want to give the issue the time it deserves and so you need to meet after school.

---

6   Hanna Beech, 'Acting on parental concerns', *Teacher Toolkit*, 2018, teachertoolkit.co.uk/2018/11/28/one-minute-cpd-41
7   John Dabell, 'Angry parents', *Every Day is a School Day* (blog), 2018, tinyurl.com/twgvgnb
8   Hayden Reynolds, 'Building good relationships with parents', *Teacher Toolkit*, 2018, teachertoolkit.co.uk/2018/09/15/relationship-parent

#62 Delivering difficult messages

Do you struggle with phrasing when delivering difficult messages during parents' evening or in written reports? It can be tricky to talk openly without causing offence, so remember these tips.

1. The key thing to bear in mind is that this is someone's child. Whatever has happened (or failed to happen), the parent is more connected to their child than to you, so your approach towards the child is everything.
2. There should be no big surprises. If this is an ongoing issue, the parent ought to have been informed long before parents' evening takes place or written reports are handed out.
3. Get off on the right foot by starting with the positive. There is always something good to say (honestly!).
4. Inform the parent of your concern, but also inform them of your action. For example, if you want to get across that Joey has difficulty following instructions, follow up by explaining how you support him with this. It's likely that the parent will appreciate your efforts and relate to your struggle.
5. Be honest, but not brutal. You want the parent to fully understand what the barriers to learning have been, what you've done about this and how they may be able to provide support.
6. Focus on progress, rather than attainment. Many parents ask how their child is doing in comparison with their peers. With low-attaining pupils, this kind of revelation can really shock and upset parents, so avoid comparisons between pupils.
7. Attendance issues* or home learning often cause difficulties for teachers. Being direct with parents can make a difference.

Why it works
Parents leave understanding the issues, but feeling confident that their child is supported and understood.

Top tip
Ask a colleague's advice about your intended phrasing; two heads are better than one!

Avoid discussing attendance when there is an obvious health concern. The last thing a parent of a poorly child needs is the guilt of a below-average attendance percentage.

#63 Holding honest conversations

Talking to parents about their child's behaviour can be hard. Defensiveness, blame and denial can quickly escalate, causing huge rifts between home and school. This strategy will help you to tackle difficult conversations with parents.

1. **Time.** Think carefully about the best time to approach the parent. If they can't talk at this moment, agree a time slot before you close the conversation.
2. **Approach.** How you approach the parent initially will have a huge impact on how the conversation unfolds. Consider your walk towards the parent, your eye contact as you approach them and your greeting. Keep it casual, yet formal. Explain that you'd like to catch up about their child.
3. **Space.** Avoid getting into the conversation outside an office/classroom space; redirect to a formal location. Thank the parent for coming along for a chat.
4. **Talk.** Explain the issues the school is facing but only talk about the behaviours, not the child ('There was an incident when Joey spoke rudely to …' instead of 'Joey is rude'). Tell the parent what you've already put in place to address the issue. Describe the outcome you want to see. Ask if there is something else they think you could do and explain how they might be able to support the school.
5. **Offer.** Offer the parent the chance to share their thoughts, making a note of any concerns.
6. **Close.** End the conversation by thanking the parent for their support and assuring them that by working together, improvement is possible.

Why it works
Planning a difficult conversation ensures that you get as close as possible to the result you need.

Top tip
Within the next week, follow up with the parent. Whatever the outcomes, keeping the lines of communication open will support improvement.

#64 Supporting separated parents[9]

Separated parents can often feel tension around school, but making sure they feel equally supported and understood can foster strong relationships between home and school. Here are eight tips to get you started.

1. Ensure all contact details are up to date.
2. Establish what the contact order or parental agreements are.
3. Know the pick-up and drop-off routines.
4. Check who has parental responsibility and if there are any residency orders in place.
5. Give two of everything (letters, invitations to events, gifts/work home, praise cards, end-of-year reports). It might take an extra moment of photocopying, but it's worth the effort to stop the child feeling confused about who receives what documentation.
6. Connect with both parents equally and fairly. Avoid having conversations about the other parent – you don't want to be drawn into parental issues.
7. Get to know any step-parents. Being a step-parent can be really isolating when it comes to school, so try to make everyone feel valued and welcome.
8. Offer separate parent meeting times if necessary.

Why this matters
Whether it's parents' evening, end-of-year reports, permission slips or nativities, school can be a place where separated parents are forced to come together in a way they might not usually. Ensuring all parents feel equally supported and connected to the school is vital.

Top tip
Refer parents who can't seem to connect to the family liaison officer or pastoral team, who will be able to offer services and support if needed.

---

9   Hanna Beech, 'Supporting separated parents', *Teacher Toolkit,* 2019, teachertoolkit. co.uk/2019/02/13/one-minute-cpd-48

#65 Parent shout-outs

Parents can be incredible for schools. From raising funds to organising events or simply supporting their child really well, their efforts shouldn't go unnoticed. Give them the acknowledgement they deserve with the following methods.

1. Thank-you letter, card or email.
2. Mention in assembly (their child is sure to let them know!).
3. Social media shout-out.
4. Afternoon tea at school.
5. A good old bunch of flowers.
6. A verbal thank you.
7. A special mention in the newsletter.
8. A note on the parents' noticeboard.

Why it works
A simple thank you can make someone feel really appreciated and even inspire others to step up and help!

Top tip
Consider the parent before you offer a shout-out – would they enjoy public praise or prefer a quiet gesture?

#66 Leading parental engagement

Who leads parental engagement at your setting? It makes sense for something so important to be managed effectively by a member of the team. Roles and responsibilities for the parental engagement lead could include:

1. Ensuring that staff understand the positive impact of parental engagement on learning.
2. Creating a school toolkit of ways to engage parents.
3. Providing staff training in managing and supporting a range of parents.
4. Mapping how parents are engaged across different year groups/departments.
5. Communicating with parents about their involvement and delivering the clear message that being involved is good for their child's education.
6. Managing and leading the parent council.
7. Seeking, monitoring and responding to parent views.

Why try this?
If your school is serious about improving parental engagement, then assigning a person or group to lead the actions will result in positive changes.

Top tip
All actions for parental involvement should have the same clear and consistent goal: improving children's learning.

Further resources

Janet Goodall and Kathryn Weston, *100 Ideas for Primary Teachers: engaging parents*, Bloomsbury Education, 2018

Matthew van Poortvliet, Dr Nick Axford and Dr Jenny Lloyd, *Working With Parents to Support Children's Learning: guidance report*, Education Endowment Foundation, 2018, tinyurl.com/vk4qz3o

Gina Madrigal Sapungan and Ronel Mondragon Sapungan, 'Parental involvement in child's education: importance, barriers and benefits', *Asian Journal of Management Sciences & Education*, 3.2, 2014, tinyurl.com/qwjxobe

Stuart Boydell, 'It's not teacher versus parent – educating children is a shared responsibility', Chartered College of Teaching, 2018, tinyurl.com/ybctgyo3

Anabel Gonzalez, 'Tips for connecting with non-English-speaking parents', *Education Week*, 2015, tinyurl.com/ycvctghb

'Engaging Parents and Families: a toolkit for practitioners', Education Scotland, tinyurl.com/y787mpqy, accessed 2020

Chapter 4: Equality, equity and inclusion

Equality, equity and inclusion are complex topics to tackle, especially in an informal book that attempts to simplify ideas for teachers' ease! I feel it worth mentioning that it is neither possible nor appropriate to simplify issues of such gravitas. But failing to draw any thought and attention to these significant topics would be omitting conversations about vital aspects of our roles. This chapter aims to offer some CPD ideas to ignite interest, thought or action.

To truly pursue CPD in these areas, we must commit to ongoing reading, reflection and improvement. Navigating our way through teaching with these fundamental topics in mind requires dedication and determination. Systemic and deep-rooted societal constructs have meant that often we, ourselves, have been educated through a lens. Did you learn about anti-racism at school? Were people of varying ethnicities, genders, physical abilities or SEN well represented in your curriculum? I would guess that most of us found ourselves steeped in curricula centred around rich, white men. Now we find that it is us who serve up the educational diet and we must reflect deeply to balance the content we offer.

Although society has made great progress towards the understanding, acceptance and celebration of all people, there is still a long way to go. Inequalities linked to gender, race, sexuality, culture, disability and socioeconomic status (to name a few) continue to exist. When we consider the benefits that diversity brings to our world, it's a wonder that there are so many lingering stigmas.

What do you think of when you hear the words equality, equity and inclusion in the context of education? Your response will likely be influenced by your own personal experiences, as well as your school's catchment area and the cohort you teach.

When I hear the words equality, equity and inclusion, my mind is immediately flooded with concerns about a lack of cultural and ethnic diversity in my local area. The results of the 2011 Census revealed that 93.7% of the residents of Kent were classed as white. Is it possible that with such limited diversity in the area, some young people could be at risk of developing unintentional biases or discriminatory views simply through lack of familiarity? As a mixed-ethnicity child (my dad is English and my mum is Iranian), I found myself confronted by overt and covert racism on a regular basis. Name-calling and stereotyping were not uncommon and, looking back, I wonder whether being one of the very few pupils of mixed ethnicity in my primary school contributed to the discrimination I experienced.

This is not to suggest that a lack of diversity always results in discrimination, or that diversity always leads to equity. But ensuring that children in my school setting are familiar with and aware of a wide range of cultures and ethnicities seems an important step in broadening their horizons.

The words equality, equity and inclusion also lead me to reflect on my interest in pinpointing and eliminating gender stereotypes among the pupils I work with. In my view, many of society's outdated conventions for girls and boys are as embarrassing as they are dangerous. Today, we are in a position to begin understanding and amending the approaches that have caused so many social, emotional and mental health issues. If this is of interest to you, the book *Hairdresser or Footballer? Bridging the gender gap in schools*, by Hollie Anderton and my co-author Ross Morrison McGill, unpicks the teacher's role in countering gender stereotypes, offering a range of insights into research and strategies for schools to use to overcome the divide. Two further ambassadors for gender equality are the authors and educators Matt Pinkett and Mark Roberts, who delve into the growing concerns around boys' mental health in their book *Boys Don't Try? Rethinking masculinity in schools* (see idea #73). The powerful work of the campaigner Natasha Devon is also well worth exploring if you are looking to read further about gender and gender identities. In addition, the Stonewall website (stonewall.org.uk/schools-colleges) has a range of suggestions and resources to support schools in tackling homophobia, biphobia and transphobia, which can stem from discrimination and unhealthy stereotypes.

When thinking about the word inclusion, I am initially drawn to consider how educators can ensure that children with autism have their needs met effectively and are treated with equal concern. Children are not carbon copies of one another, they are all different, but some children stand out in ways that others don't. These children can find the world around them confusing, inaccessible and overwhelming. As educators, it's important that we dedicate ongoing thought to the effective inclusion of children who find communication, socialising or accessing the learning more challenging than their neurotypical peers. These children will likely rely on the systems and adults in school to provide a sense of stability. Once again, I have a particular interest in this topic because of my own personal experiences – I have seen first-hand the difference that effective and ineffective teaching can have on learning and wellbeing.

How do your experiences affect your understanding of equality, equity and inclusion? In what area might you like to further develop knowledge? It is my hope that the ideas in this chapter will allow you time to reflect and plan, guiding you towards positive change in your school. One simple question to ask yourself and others is: do we believe in some pupils succeeding or in all pupils succeeding? If it's the latter (which it most likely is!) then we all have much work to do.

#67 Diverse assemblies

Is your curriculum as culturally diverse as our world? Probably not. Diversifying the curriculum and day-to-day school life is a great way to familiarise pupils with different cultures. Many schools hold assemblies every day and they are the ideal opportunity to celebrate cultural and ethnic diversity. Try the following suggestions.

1. Become calendar-aware. Identify key national and international days relating to cultural diversity and key dates for world religions. Map these on to an assembly overview.
2. Share stories about the history and achievements of different cultures and ethnicities.
3. Teach pupils about people who have fought for civil rights (for example, Martin Luther King, Nelson Mandela, Rosa Parks, the Dalai Lama, Ruby Bridges, Mary Seacole, Gandhi, Diane Abbott, Oprah Winfrey).
4. Include a range of ethnicities in your presentations, regardless of the content of the assembly.
5. Teach pupils about the many benefits of living in a multicultural society.
6. Invite diverse visitors into school to lead assemblies relating to ethnicity and culture.

Why try this?
Schools are in a powerful position to spread messages of positivity and equality.

Top tip
Use assemblies to teach and model the correct use of terminology (such as culture, ethnicity, race, religion).

#68 Creating a culturally rich curriculum

A school ethos that embraces diversity isn't just about themed days or one-off events, so how can cultural and ethnic diversity be woven into the curriculum?

1. In English lessons, use varied core texts that represent a wide range of cultures and ethnicities.
2. Use geography to learn about other cultures. For example, when learning about different places, focus on understanding the people who live there.
3. Exploring different time periods in history lessons is an opportunity to consider how cultural diversity has changed over time, and how behaviour towards people of different ethnicities has shifted.
4. Through PE and sport, learn about different cultural sporting traditions and famous sportspeople from the BAME community.
5. Use religious education to develop an awareness of other cultures and ethnicities.
6. Through all subjects, explore key BAME figures in the past and present. For example, when learning about cells in science, discuss Ernest Everett Just, who was well-known for his work on cell structure; when learning about the Second World War, discuss Garrett Morgan, the inventor who patented the first gas mask; and when learning about space, talk about Mae Jemison, the first black woman to travel to space.

Why this matters
If you want your pupils to develop a deep understanding of how society is built by people from a wide range of cultures and ethnicities, then you need to expose them to the facts.

Top tip
Consider these tips in relation to other areas of diversity, such as gender, sexual orientation, disability and age.

#69 Five ways to celebrate diversity

In an article for *Tes*, the academics Shelley McKeown Jones, Amanda Williams and Janet Orchard suggest five simple ways to celebrate diversity in the classroom.[1] Here's a summary of their ideas.

1. **Interaction.** Invite visitors from a range of cultures to allow pupils to interact meaningfully with a diverse range of people.
2. **Learning about differences.** Increase pupils' religious and cultural literacy through subjects like history and religious education.
3. **Challenging stereotypes.** Teach lessons using counter-stereotypical examples.
4. **Empathising.** Encourage pupils to empathise with a range of different people, imagining what life is like for them and walking in their shoes.
5. **Celebrating diversity.** Find ways to embrace difference, such as taking part in a range of festivals, trying a wide range of foods and engaging in rich discussions about the importance and value of diversity.

Why try this?
Our pupils need to see us addressing diversity positively and celebrating difference.

Top tip
Although diversity days or weeks are great, remember that embracing diversity should thread through everything your school does.

---

1   Shelley McKeown Jones, Amanda Williams and Janet Orchard, 'Five ways to celebrate diversity in the classroom', *Tes*, 2018, tes.com/news/five-ways-celebrate-diversity-classroom

#70 Anti-racism in schools

Educators must uphold their responsibility to reject racism and promote anti-racism in all they do. A successful future for our world depends on this. Follow these tips to become an anti-racism school that supports people of black and minority ethnic backgrounds to thrive.

1. Raising awareness and building understanding can be the first step in ensuring that young people act respectfully towards all others. Teach your pupils the difference between prejudice, discrimination, racism and anti-black racism. Use these definitions to guide you:
    *   **Prejudice** is an unreasonable or unfair opinion towards an individual based on their affiliation with a group or because of their characteristics.
    *   **Discrimination** is the unjust treatment of a person or group of people based on their affiliation with a group or because of their characteristics.
    *   **Racism** is hatred or intolerance of another race (or other races) stemming from the belief that one race is superior to the other.
    *   **Anti-black racism**[2] refers to systemic racism that directly excludes and shows prejudice towards black people.
2. Stand firmly against racist acts. Tackle all racism, overt and covert, by following your school's policy. This sends a strong message to all pupils.
3. Support BAME people. Uplift, encourage and celebrate excellence. Be sure to check HR policies and diversity on interview panels.

Why this matters

If we are to create a future where the lives of people of BAME backgrounds are valued and uplifted, we must pledge to tackle racism proactively and rigorously.

Top tip

Log all incidents of racism with senior leaders in a timely and accurate manner.

---

2   Natalie Morris, '"Anti-blackness" is a form of racism that is specifically damaging for black people', *Metro*, 2020, tinyurl.com/yd3em3kl

#71 Reading about role models 1

How well do your library books and core texts reflect a range of cultures or races? Here are some suggestions for reading material.

1. *Noughts and Crosses* series by Malorie Blackman
2. *Boy Overboard* by Morris Gleitzman
3. *Azzi In Between* by Sarah Garland
4. *The Arrival* by Shaun Tan
5. *Tall Story* by Candy Gourlay
6. *High-Rise Mystery* by Sharna Jackson
7. *The Weight of Water* by Sarah Crossan
8. *Amazing Grace* by Mary Hoffman
9. *Imani's Moon* by JaNay Brown-Wood
10. *My Young Adventures: Meet Mya and Family* by Jeannelle Brew
11. *Ramadan Moon* by Na'ima B Robert
12. *The Hate U Give* by Angie Thomas
13. *Handa's Surprise* by Eileen Browne
14. *Mufaro's Beautiful Daughters* by John Steptoe
15. *Preaching to the Chickens: the story of young John Lewis* by Jabari Asim
16. *Mommy's Khimar* by Jamilah Thompkins-Bigelow
17. *Mixed Me!* by Taye Diggs
18. *Max and the Tag-Along Moon* by Floyd Cooper
19. *The Wheel of Surya* by Jamila Gavin
20. *A Dance Like Starlight* by Kristy Dempsey
21. *Planet Omar* series by Zanib Mian
22. *The Youngest Marcher* by Cynthia Levinson
23. *The Mighty Miss Malone* by Christopher Paul Curtis
24. *Red Leaves* by Sita Brahmachari
25. *My Brother Charlie* by Holly Robinson Peete and Ryan Elizabeth Peete

Why try this?

When we look around, it becomes apparent that not all cultures and races are fairly represented in our book corners and libraries. Consider the message this sends to our pupils.

Top tip

Think about ways to raise funds for a large purchase of books with multicultural themes or characters.

 Saving boys from stereotypes[3]

Suicide is the biggest cause of death for men under the age of 45 in the UK. A huge number of men experience extreme pressure to conform to a set of unhealthy stereotypes deemed to be 'masculine' and this can affect their mental health. So, what can be done to free boys from gender stereotypes in the classroom?

1. Highlight positive male role models to the class. Discuss why these men are good role models.
2. Model and encourage the open expression of feelings. Tell boys that it is OK to feel and express emotions.
3. 'Talk up' the boys who challenge stereotypes.
4. Encourage discussion about gender stereotypes.
5. Teach boys how to ask for help. Explaining when, how and who to reach out to could make a huge difference.
6. Have a designated space where young men can talk comfortably and confidentially if they need to.
7. Watch out for increasing signs of distress, low mood or frustration. These can be indicators that boys are suffering and could be at risk of developing mental or emotional health issues.

Why this matters

Many young men grow up believing that being 'masculine' means unfaltering emotional, physical and financial strength. These unrealistic expectations can put boys and men in danger of feeling inadequate when the inevitable happens.

Top tip

Be mindful of the vocabulary and language you use around boys. Ban the phrases 'man up', 'I need some strong boys to move the benches', 'be brave' and 'boys will be boys'.

---

3   Hanna Beech, 'Banish gender stereotypes', *Teacher Toolkit*, 2018, teachertoolkit.co.uk/2018/11/19/one-minute-cpd-39

#73 Three myths about boys' engagement

In their book *Boys Don't Try? Rethinking masculinity in schools*,[4] the teachers Matt Pinkett and Mark Roberts identify three myths surrounding boys' engagement with learning.

1. Boys like competition.
2. We should make learning relevant to boys' interests.
3. Boys have different learning styles.

Why this matters
We need to make sure that the education we provide doesn't back up harmful stereotypes, so bear these myths in mind as you plan and teach your lessons.

Top tip
Read the book – it's fascinating. And be brave in politely challenging others' use of unhealthy gender stereotypes.

4   Matt Pinkett and Mark Roberts, *Boys Don't Try? Rethinking masculinity in schools*, Routledge, 2019

#74 Inspirational women

Teachers can feel almost helpless in the face of deeply rooted gender stereotypes, but through small yet powerful changes we *can* make a difference. How do we raise awareness about gender equality in school? Follow these steps to challenge stereotypes in your classroom.

1. Share some statistics about gender bias and the impact on women.
2. Present your class with some inspirational women – there are plenty to choose from!
3. Discuss how these women had a huge impact on the world.
4. Pose the question, 'Which woman has changed *your* world?' It could be a family member, friend, teacher or anyone, really. Think, pair and share.
5. Task pupils with creating a thank-you card for the woman who has inspired, helped or motivated them. Inside the card, they can write a message telling the woman why she is wonderful.

Why this matters
The facts and figures speak for themselves. It's time to abolish gender inequality, and where better to start than with helping our young people to honour the women in their lives.

Top tip
Explain to the pupils that celebrating inspirational women will help us to tackle gender inequality.

#75 Know your definitions

Gone are the days when your gender was defined by your sex. It is really important that all young people, especially LGBTQ+ pupils, feel understood and represented accurately. Here are some essential definitions.[5]

- **Sex**: the scientific and/or legal classification of a person as male, female or intersex.
- **Gender**: the socially constructed and reinforced divisions between certain groups (genders) in a culture, including social norms that people in these different groups are expected to adhere to and a person's sense of self relating to these divisions.
- **Gender identity**: a person's internal feelings and convictions about their gender.
- **Sexual orientation**: how a person feels sexually about different genders.
- **Bisexual**: someone who is romantically or sexually attracted to people of more than one gender.
- **Gay**: someone who is romantically, emotionally or sexually attracted to people of the same gender.
- **Lesbian**: a women who is emotionally, sexually or/and physically attracted to other women.
- **Transgender/trans**: someone whose gender is not the same as the gender they were assigned at birth.
- **Queer**: an umbrella term used by some to describe members of the LGBTQ+ community.
- **Cisgender/cis**: someone who identifies with the gender they were assigned at birth.

Why this matters
Understanding key terminology is an important part of avoiding stereotypes and accepting people for who they are.

Top tip
There are many other terms and definitions relating to gender and sexual orientation.[6] If you don't know the precise meaning of a term, take a moment to look it up.

---

5   *Terminology Guide: November 2019*, The National LGB&T Partnership and Brook, tinyurl.com/y9c48bpr
6   'Equalities survey and feedback form for events' (page 2), Ross Morrison McGill, 2020, tinyurl.com/yck79yd2

#76 Reading about role models 2

Who are the protagonists in your key texts for each year group? If you fear too many characters in your texts conform to stereotypes, here are some books that break the mould.

1. *Cloudette* by Tom Lichtenheld
2. *Boys Don't Cry* by Malorie Blackman
3. *The Paper Bag Princess* by Robert Munsch
4. *Ballarino Nate* by Kimberly Brubaker Bradley
5. *My Princess Boy* by Cheryl Kilodavis
6. *Pearl Fairweather Pirate Captain* by Jayneen Sanders
7. *Tough Boris* by Mem Fox
8. *Prince Cinders* by Babette Cole
9. *Rosie Revere, Engineer* by Andrea Beaty
10. *The Witch Boy* by Molly Knox Ostertag
11. *I'm a Girl!* by Yasmeen Ismail
12. *Odd Boy Out: Young Albert Einstein* by Don Brown
13. *Ruby's Wish* by Shirin Yim Bridges
14. *George* by Alex Gino

15. *Tomboy* by Liz Prince
16. *William's Doll* by Charlotte Zolotow
17. *You Forgot Your Skirt, Amelia Bloomer* by Shana Corey
18. *10,000 Dresses* by Marcus Ewert
19. *Ruby Redfort: Look Into My Eyes* by Lauren Child
20. *Women in Science: 50 fearless pioneers who changed the world* by Rachel Ignotofsky
21. *Northern Lights* by Philip Pullman
22. *Journey to the River Sea* by Eva Ibbotson

Why try this?

If we only present pupils with stereotypical gender representations, we are limiting their understanding. Pupils are in danger of falling into the constructs that society has created for them. The villains are men, the girls need saving, the heroes are masculine – it's all nonsense.

Top tip

Explore the Let Books Be Books campaign, part of Let Toys Be Toys, which was founded by a group of parents. The website offers a wealth of ideas to challenge stereotypes: lettoysbetoys.org.uk. Don't forget to include representations of LGBTQ+ characters. This will help to improve perceptions and ensure LGBTQ+ pupils feel represented and respected.

#77 Normalising menstruation

Research by Plan International[7] suggests that one in seven girls in the UK have struggled to afford sanitarywear and 49% of girls have missed an entire day of school because of their period. Menstruation is historically a taboo subject, but this can leave girls feeling scared, confused or embarrassed about their cycles. Here are three ways to tackle the taboo and help girls to feel confident about their periods.

1. **Relationships and sex education**. Educating young people on the human body, puberty and periods can normalise the subject of menstruation for girls and boys.
2. **Provide a supply box in the girls' toilets**. Fill it with sanitarywear, spare underwear and a 'Last one' card – whoever uses the last of the supplies can pass the card to office staff, who will arrange a refill.
3. **Put up posters**. Informational posters in the toilets can make periods seem less of a secret and put girls at ease.

Why this matters
If we can normalise periods, we can reduce the stigma.

Top tip
Refer to the statutory guidance document *Relationships Education, Relationships and Sex Education (RSE) and Health Education*,[8] which includes information about the teaching of menstruation at primary and secondary level.

---

7   'Plan International UK's research on period poverty and stigma', Plan International UK, 2017, tinyurl.com/y7vrgs2z
8   *Relationships Education, Relationships and Sex Education (RSE) and Health Education*, Department for Education, 2019, tinyurl.com/y5y76wu8

#78 Avoiding the gender pay and progression gap

Leaders: does your team have gender balance? Ask yourself these questions to consider whether you are paying and promoting with gender equality in mind.

1. How many women and men are there on the team?
2. Does the pay vary for men and women in the same positions?
3. What roles do women tend to have? What roles do men tend to have?
4. Do pupils have a range of gender role models?
5. What gender were the last five members of staff to join the school?
6. Are all genders welcomed for promotion opportunities?

Why try this?
I doubt that any school intentionally contributes to gender inequality within the team, but without consideration, an imbalance could easily occur.

Top tip
Ask these questions once a year as new appointments are being considered.

#79 Social mobility: the facts

The 2020 *Social Mobility Barometer* report[9] from the Social Mobility Commission, based on a survey of around 5,000 people, reveals public attitudes to social mobility in the UK. Here are some of the key facts and figures.

1. 44% of people say that where you end up in society is largely determined by who your parents are.
2. 35% say everyone has a fair chance to get on regardless of their background.
3. 77% say there is a large gap between social classes in Britain today.
4. 77% say poorer people are less likely to go to a top university.
5. 65% say poorer people have less opportunity to get into a professional career.

And the Social Mobility Commission's 2017 *State of the Nation* report[10] presented the following findings:

1. A stark social mobility postcode lottery exists in Britain today, where the chances of being successful if you come from a disadvantaged background are linked to where you live.
2. Disadvantaged young people are almost twice as likely as better-off peers to be Neet (not in education, employment or training) a year after GCSEs.
3. The residents of coastal areas, which make up over a fifth of England's local authority areas, experience extremely poor outcomes for social mobility.

Why this matters
An awareness of social mobility issues will open up conversations about how your school or setting can support social mobility.

Top tip
Consider how you might challenge negative or judgemental views about people from socially deprived areas.

---

9 *Social Mobility Barometer: public attitudes to social mobility in the UK 2019-20*, Social Mobility Commission, 2020, tinyurl.com/yd37xlrp
10 *State of the Nation 2017: social mobility in Great Britain*, Social Mobility Commission, 2017, tinyurl.com/y7k5fdxf

#80 Making the most of pupil premium funding

How does your school spend pupil premium funding and what impact does this have on your vulnerable children? Follow these tips to make sure pupil premium spending has a positive impact on those who need it most.

1. **Interventions**. Using funding to provide additional learning opportunities for pupil premium children is one way to close the attainment gap and boost progress.
2. **Staff training**. Providing teaching, support and pastoral staff with up-to-date training driven by current research findings will ensure that pupils receive the best possible learning experiences.
3. **Attendance**. Using funding to increase the attendance of pupil premium pupils could make a big difference, because if a child isn't in school, other expenditure is redundant.
4. **Therapy**. If your pupil premium children could benefit from mental or emotional support, investing in therapy might be a really good idea.
5. **Speech and language support**. If your pupil premium pupils have speech, language or communication difficulties, these are potentially a huge barrier to their learning.
6. **One-to-one tuition**. If a pupil premium child is in need of intensive support, consider employing a one-to-one tutor.
7. **Develop or strengthen a pastoral team**. If your pupils are experiencing behavioural or emotional problems, building a strong and effective team to provide support and foster stable relationships could help.
8. **Training opportunities for parents**. Supporting parents to help their child at home could boost a pupil's progress.
9. **Ask parents**. What do they think could help their children?

Why this matters

It's a school's duty to spend funding in ways that maximise progress for pupils who are financially disadvantaged.

Top tip

To make spending truly effective, schools should first review their circumstances and priorities.

Raising aspirations: the 10-year plan[11]

Research exploring social deprivation and aspiration has concluded that there is a link between aspiration and attainment.[12] Children from poorer families have much less belief in their own ability than children from richer families; the research also found differences in maternal aspirations, with 81% of mothers from the richest families aspiring for their nine-year-old child to attend university, compared with just 37% of the poorest mothers. Here's one way to inspire pupils with low attainment that could be linked to low aspiration.

1. Hold a meeting with the child.
2. Discuss what aspiration means and why it can help us to stay focused day-to-day.
3. Ask the child if they have any aspirations.
4. Talk about what they don't want their life to be like.
5. Talk about what the child does want for their future.
6. Ask them to imagine where they want to be in 10 years and what they might be doing.
7. Ask how they might journey towards their 10-year aspiration: 'Is there anything you can do from tomorrow to work towards your goal?'
8. Help the child to make an action plan with three simple steps to take this week towards their aspiration.
9. Check in over the week or term to see how progress towards aspirations is unfolding.
10. Connect with parents and carers to discuss next steps.

Why it works
Showing a child that what they do now will affect their future can really open their eyes. Everyone has an aspiration – help pupils to discover theirs.

Top tip
Don't attempt a discussion unless the child is in an open frame of mind. Be sure to respect all aspirations, whether they are vocational, academic or something else entirely.

---

11 Hanna Beech, 'Raising aspirations', *Teacher Toolkit*, 2019, teachertoolkit.co.uk/2019/01/24/one-minute-cpd-44

12 Alissa Goodman, Paul Gregg, Haroon Chowdry, Claire Crawford, Lorraine Dearden, Robert Joyce, Luke Sibieta, Kathy Sylva and Elizabeth Washbrook, *Poorer Children's Educational Attainment: how important are attitudes and behaviour?*, Joseph Rowntree Foundation, 2010, tinyurl.com/trn7qjr

#82 Alex Quigley's seven steps to closing the vocabulary gap

Research[13] shows that children experiencing socioeconomic disadvantage lag behind their more advantaged peers in terms of vocabulary. Alex Quigley, an English teacher and author of *Closing the Vocabulary Gap*,[14] has suggested the following seven steps in order to close that gap.[15]

1. Train teachers to become more knowledgeable and confident in explicit vocabulary teaching.
2. Teach academic vocabulary explicitly and clearly, with coherent planning throughout the curriculum.
3. Foster structured reading opportunities in a model that supports students with vocabulary deficits.
4. Promote and scaffold high-quality academic talk in the classroom.
5. Promote and scaffold high-quality academic writing in the classroom.
6. Foster 'word consciousness' in students.
7. Teach students independent word-learning strategies.

Why try this?
If educators don't work to close the vocabulary gap, disadvantaged children will continue to have fewer opportunities than their better-off peers.

Top tip
Make closing the vocabulary gap a priority on your school action plan next year.

---

13 Whitney Crenna-Jennings, *Key Drivers of the Disadvantage Gap: literature review*, Education Policy Institute, 2018, tinyurl.com/yanspavy
14 Alex Quigley, *Closing the Vocabulary Gap*, Routledge, 2018
15 Alex Quigley, 'How to close the vocabulary gap in the classroom', *Schools Week*, 2018, schoolsweek.co.uk/how-to-close-the-vocabulary-gap-in-the-classroom

#83 Education for life, by Ross

The narrowing of the curriculum is obvious at GCSE, with the emphasis on the 'academic' subjects and the gradual decline of 'vocational' subjects. However, the effect can also be seen at key stage 3 and in primary school, as a child's entire school life is now geared towards getting good exam results in the core subjects. A report by the assessment provider GL Assessment, *Closing the Gap*,[16] suggests that most teachers and parents do not believe this narrowing of the curriculum helps children. They say it prepares children less well for later academic success and life after school, has a negative impact on classroom behaviour, disadvantages students with SEND, and reduces children's wellbeing and their enjoyment of school.

We must transform our practice, so all students can leave school with a range of qualifications. Here's how to make a start.

1. Evaluate your curriculum meaningfully and avoid curriculum fatigue. Get it right the first time, involve all stakeholders and tweak every two years.
2. Raise the profile of the arts in your curriculum offer, not just in after-school activities.
3. Promote literacy and maths as the key priority for parents in all home-learning activities.
4. Encourage all teachers to have the highest expectations. Their expectations matter and do make a difference to outcomes.

Why this matters

If we truly want a world-class education system in which all young people can succeed and be prepared for the workplace, especially in the aftermath of Brexit and Covid-19, we must tweak our current approaches.

Top tip

Find out more about how expectations can improve a person's performance by researching the Pygmalion effect, or reading Simon Burgess and Ellen Greaves' research on whether ethnic minority pupils are subject to low teacher expectations: tinyurl.com/y7camqpq

---

16 *Closing the Gap: how a narrow curriculum disadvantages the disadvantaged*, GL Assessment, 2019, gl-assessment.co.uk/closingthegap

#84 Communicating with children on the autism spectrum

In a survey by the National Autistic Society, less than half of children and young people on the autism spectrum said they were happy at school. Seven in 10 said their peers didn't understand them and five in 10 said their teachers didn't know how to support them.[17] It's clear that although our understanding of autism has improved greatly over the years, there is still progress to be made. Children on the autism spectrum can find sarcasm, irony and figurative language very confusing, so it's vital to choose your words carefully. Follow these tips to make communication clear and concise.

1. Address the child directly by name if you are talking to them.
2. Avoid overcomplicating the instructions or information you want to deliver.
3. Try not to speak too quickly. Give the child time to process your message.
4. Don't demand eye contact. Some children on the autism spectrum find eye contact unbearable.
5. Give simple information and check for understanding by asking the child to repeat it back to you.
6. Use non-verbal communication where appropriate.
7. Avoid asking rhetorical questions.
8. Ask specific, direct, closed questions if you are seeking a specific answer.
9. Avoid confusing phrases such as 'get your skates on', 'you're a good egg' or 'pull your socks up' (unless you have time to explain what they mean!).

Why consider this?
Effective communication will make a huge difference to your relationships with these children.

Top tip
Some children with autism spectrum conditions will talk a lot and others will talk very little. Every child is different, so get to know an individual's preferences for communication.

---

17 *Autism and Education: good practice guide*, National Autistic Society, 2019, tinyurl.com/vahsbk9

#85 Reducing sensory overload

Many young people with autism and ADHD attend mainstream schools, so supporting these pupils must be a key priority for teachers and school leaders. Did you know that many children with autism and some children with ADHD experience heightened senses, and that this oversensitivity to light, sound, touch or smell can cause great distress? Here's how to spot if a child might be experiencing sensory overload.

1. The child covers their ears, eyes or nose.
2. They seem agitated, irritable or stressed.
3. They seem distracted or unfocused.
4. They seem anxious, overexcited or overwhelmed.
5. They might hide under a table, stim (repeat movements) or curl into a ball.
6. They tell you that the noise/smell/visuals/textures are bothering them.

Once you've established that sensory overload is an issue, try these suggestions to help lessen the problem.

1. Offer headphones to block out noise.
2. Allow the child to move away from the room (with supervision).
3. Remove objects that are causing distress (the item with the particular fabric or texture, or the source of a strong smell).
4. Have a plan to help key children identify and communicate when they are experiencing sensory overload, as well as some actions to reduce the overload together.
5. Ensure that all staff understand what sensory overload is and how problematic it can be.

Why this matters
Including children with autism spectrum conditions and ADHD, and making reasonable adjustments to their learning, is part and parcel of the job.

Top tip
Predict which situations (visitors, parties, trips, pantomimes) are likely to cause sensory overload and discuss this with the pupil beforehand.

#86 Social interactions

Children on the autism spectrum can find it challenging to connect to others on a social level. They may appear withdrawn, isolated or lonely. They might be overly friendly, lacking awareness of how to hold a two-way conversation. Or they might have no desire to interact socially, being quite content in their own company and reluctant to work collaboratively at all. Here's how to support children on the autism spectrum to develop their social skills.

1. Connect them with others who have similar interests.
2. Encourage them to join a club or social group relating to their special interest, if they have one.
3. Teach their peers about autism and encourage acceptance, raising awareness about the social challenges experienced by some people with autism.
4. Have a plan for unstructured times such as child-initiated learning times, breaks or free periods.
5. Provide the child with opportunities to ask an adult about how to interact socially.
6. Use 'social stories' (a concept introduced by Carol Gray in 1991[18]) to develop an understanding of how social interaction works in different situations.

Why try this?
Feeling socially isolated can negatively affect a child's mental health.

Top tip
Don't force children on the autism spectrum to socialise.

---

[18] 'Social stories and comic strip conversations', National Autistic Society, tinyurl.com/ydhjqxgx, accessed 2020

#87 Stable routines

Children on the autism spectrum often enjoy predictability and routine. Try these tips to help them feel secure and safe about the day's events.

1. Ensure you have a visual timetable for the child that accurately reflects the events of the day.
2. Look ahead each term to consider which events might take the class off-timetable and how this might affect the child. You might need to discuss these events with the child or their parents well in advance.
3. Consider the impact of breaktimes, child-initiated play or free periods. How can these times be given a bit more structure?
4. Think about when the timetable changes, such as Christmas or exam time. Ensure that the child has a timetable to reflect what is happening.
5. Have a plan for unpredictable events or emergency situations, such as unexpected fire alarms, which can cause extreme distress. A termly discussion to remind pupils of the plan if something unexpected happens will help to keep the child as prepared and safe as possible.

Why this matters

Children on the autism spectrum will rely on timetables, routines and rules to get them through what can be an overwhelming day. It is good inclusive practice to make sure that organisational strategies are in place.

Top tip

Particular attention might need to be paid to routine during 'back to school' periods or after long periods of absence from school.

#88 Getting organised

Although many children with autism spectrum conditions (or other conditions such as ADHD) prefer routines and predictability, it is not uncommon for a highly functioning child to lack organisational skills. They may need additional support to get organised – here's how you can help.

1. Offer additional verbal reminders about trips, homework and equipment.
2. Provide notes or emails home so that parents can assist with equipment, homework or resources.
3. Ask the child to repeat instructions back to you, so you can be sure they have understood.
4. Don't punish the child for forgetting equipment or resources. Instead, find ways to ensure they have the support they need to be fully prepared.
5. Encourage the child to write down key instructions or deadlines in their planner or diary.

Why this matters
Children with autism can feel upset, frustrated or ashamed if they believe they have failed to remember something. Educators must support them in the best possible ways.

Top tip
Enlist the help of the child's class peers to deliver reminders.

#89 Appreciating and understanding disabilities

Educators in mainstream schools can feel a little daunted when they work alongside a physically disabled pupil for the first time. The responsibility and duty of care can feel enormous, and it's vital to develop the confidence and knowledge to handle physical disabilities with the utmost care and precision. According the charity Scope, there are 13.9 million disabled people in the UK, so how can your school help young people to appreciate and understand disabilities?

1. Share stories of achievement. Many people with disabilities have experienced great success – ensure that their stories are shared and celebrated.
2. Talk about a range of disabilities. There is no reason to treat disabilities as taboo – talking about them can aid pupils' understanding and acceptance.
3. Have a disability-friendly environment. Consider how your environments suit the needs of all people.
4. Invite inspirational people with disabilities to your setting to give talks or lead workshops.
5. Use images of people with disabilities on your teaching presentations, as opposed to always using non-disabled people.

Why this matters
Schools have a duty to encourage equality for all.

Top tip
You might have young people at your school who have a disability. How can they be emotionally and physically supported?

#90 Accessible opportunities

Pupils who have a disability deserve to be included in as many opportunities as children without disabilities. Consider the following events carefully to make sure all children are considered and catered for.

1. **Sports day, sporting events and PE**. How might children with disabilities partake in sports day and PE sessions?
2. **Drama performances**. How accessible is the stage? Are all children offered the same opportunities for lead and other roles?
3. **School trips**. What provisions need to be put in place so that children with disabilities can engage safely in trips?
4. **Parties, proms and discos**. What amendments need to be made to allow all children to fully enjoy celebratory events?
5. **Music and dance lessons**. Do any special arrangements need to be made regarding access to music or dance lessons?
6. **Art lessons**. Do children with disabilities need additional support to use the resources?

Why try this?
Having a disability ought not to limit the lessons and events that a child has access to. There are often simple and effective ways to make reasonable adjustments.

Top tip
Safety should always come first.

#91 Inclusion for children with physical disabilities, by Ross

Twenty years ago, local authorities were generally ill-equipped to meet the complex and varied needs of children with physical disabilities who wished to attend their local state school. However, this has changed significantly over the past decade. Education providers now have a duty to make 'reasonable adjustments' to ensure that disabled students are not discriminated against. This has been supported by the political narrative used for admissions: 'parental choice and access to a good school.' All schools need to consider these four key aspects of inclusion:

1. **Safeguarding**. All schools must consider safeguarding in their day-to-day practice, as part of due diligence and care for each child.
2. **Education, health and care plans or support plans**. Every child may be entitled to SEN support, and an EHCP may be available for young people who have more complex needs.
3. **Training for staff, particularly teaching assistants**. Training should be well mapped-out, regular and sustainable. Specialist training may be needed to meet the needs of individual students.
4. **The curriculum, and teaching and learning**. Once safeguarding procedures are in place and training is matched to individual pupils and teacher needs, then the curriculum, including timetabling, can be matched to suit teaching and learning strategies.

Why this matters
We need to make sure that disabled pupils are not left behind. Communication is key to success, so keep in regular, face-to-face contact with these children and their families.

Top tip
Seek specialist help and support if you lack the necessary knowledge or resources. And ensure that all teachers are equipped with the safeguarding knowledge and curriculum expertise to meet pupil needs.

Further resources

Hollie Anderton with Ross Morrison McGill, *Hairdresser or Footballer? Bridging the gender gap in schools*, John Catt Educational, 2018

Matt Pinkett and Mark Roberts, *Boys Don't Try? Rethinking masculinity in schools*, Routledge, 2019

Vivienne Porritt and Keziah Featherstone, *10% Braver: inspiring women to lead education*, Sage Publications, 2019

Chandrika Devarakonda, *Diversity and Inclusion in Early Childhood: an introduction*, Sage Publications, 2014

Neil Humphrey and Sarah Lewis, 'What does "inclusion" mean for pupils on the autistic spectrum in mainstream schools?', *Journal of Research in Special Educational Needs*, 8.3, 2008, tinyurl.com/rfp5yd8

National Autistic Society: autism.org.uk

June E Downing and Kathryn D Peckham-Hardin, 'Inclusive education: what makes it a good education for students with moderate to severe disabilities?', *Research and Practice for Persons with Severe Disabilities*, 32.1, 2007, tinyurl.com/wv9j94m

Paul N'Dri Konan, Armand Chatard, Leila Selimbegovic and Mugny Gabriel, 'Cultural diversity in the classroom and its effects on academic performance: a cross-national perspective', *Social Psychology*, 41.4, 2010

The Teacherist: teacheristblog.wordpress.com

Stonewall: stonewall.org.uk

The National LGB&T Partnership: nationallgbtpartnership.org

Chapter 5: Feedback

If you ask me, feedback is the most valuable tool we have as educators. But over the years, education seems to have developed a narrow view of what feedback is – it's not just about adults feeding back to children. The term 'feedback' encompasses a range of methods that enhance not only the learning undertaken by children, but also the learning undertaken by staff. It is often branded as 'marking', giving the impression that all feedback is visible in pupils' books.

What else does feedback mean? To begin answering this question, we can first go back to basics with the dictionary definition of the word: 'Information about reactions to a product, a person's performance of a task, etc. which is used as a basis for improvement.'[1]

With this in mind, let's consider feedback in a broader and deeper way. Feedback in educational settings can include staff-to-staff feedback, staff-to-parent feedback, staff-to-pupil feedback, authority-to-staff feedback, staff-to-governor feedback and more, plus all those examples reversed! The reason I love (effective) feedback is because it leads to improvement, and that is something to embrace. The examples above begin to reveal the many layers of potential improvement that can stem from effective feedback.

I don't want to get into an inspection-bashing rant, but the undeniable impact of pressure on schools that have been denounced as 'inadequate' or 'requiring improvement' has meant that the education world has developed an unhealthy relationship with feedback. After years of grading teachers in ways that promote fear, as opposed to reflection, feedback has become more about what label you receive after an observation and less about how to make positive

---

1   en.oxforddictionaries.com/definition/feedback

changes to the learning. I hope that this culture of grading lessons and teachers is beginning to fade away, but I can almost guarantee that you know of a school, maybe even your own, that continues to grade individual lessons or teachers.

In Ofsted's defence, the abolition of grading individual lessons in 2014, and various clarifications on this point since then, have been a step towards ending this unproductive and ineffective practice. Yet the message (although repeatedly communicated by Amanda Spielman and other Ofsted inspectors) struggles to be heard over the ingrained view from some school leaders that grading lessons is what Ofsted wants. I can only hope that leaders who are yet to cease this practice eventually receive the message loud and clear from those in charge of the inspection processes. Perhaps those leaders will then reflect on the detrimental impact such gradings have on teaching and learning, as well as teacher wellbeing.

According to the assessment guru Dylan Wiliam, evaluating teachers' effectiveness is far more complex than observing a few lessons here and there. In his book *Creating the Schools Our Children Need*,[2] Wiliam expresses concern over the methods traditionally used by schools to assess the effectiveness of teachers. He suggests that rather than trying to figure out who the 'good' and 'bad' teachers are, leaders should instead focus on developing a school culture that allows all teachers the scope to improve. With this in mind, leaders ought to consider if grading teachers is really a valuable tool for driving improvement.

The writer Matthew Syed, who has a special interest in the science of high performance, comes to similar conclusions. His books *Bounce*[3] and *Black Box Thinking*[4] both offer interesting anecdotal examples of learning from feedback and many useful approaches. The following quote, from *Black Box Thinking*, sums up why grading lessons is inferior to giving useful and direct feedback: 'If we interpret difficulties as indictments of who we are, rather than as pathways to progress, we will run a mile from failure.'

The message rings true in education. When we grade lessons, we inadvertently grade teachers. When we grade teachers, the feedback is about a label rather than about improvement. It shuts down opportunities to reflect. And it's not just poor gradings that have that result: I've seen teachers who were graded as 'outstanding' become defensive and hostile when the label changes in a subsequent observation.

---

2   Dylan Wiliam, *Creating the Schools Our Children Need*, Learning Sciences International, 2018
3   Matthew Syed, *Bounce: the myth of talent and the power of practice*, Fourth Estate, 2011
4   Matthew Syed, *Black Box Thinking: marginal gains and the secrets of high performance*, John Murray, 2016

Yet, regardless of these lingering unproductive approaches, I'm convinced that feedback can be the most effective method for driving improvement. That's why I want educators to reclaim feedback and extract every ounce of its power to become more confident and reflective practitioners. Educators know the benefits of giving effective feedback to pupils, so we need to take advantage of these benefits for ourselves, too. School leaders have tremendous influence over how feedback is delivered and received, and are accountable for ensuring that the feedback culture in their setting optimises development.

In reclaiming feedback, I suggest we have distinct responsibilities depending on our roles:

- **Senior leaders** must work to create environments where feedback is used as a means of strengthening practice, not as a means of labelling staff. Leaders should themselves be open to feedback from all school stakeholders.
- **Teachers** must be open to genuine feedback, letting go of the idea of lesson feedback being about *them*, because it's really about strengthening their practice.
- **Teachers and support staff** must give feedback to children in ways that promote reflective thinking and enhance the learning.
- **Inspection teams** must reflect deeply on the negative consequences of branding schools and consider how giving schools precise feedback could lead to better outcomes.

What one thing could you do in order to reclaim feedback as a tool for improvement? The ideas in this chapter are a good place to start. I hope they help you to establish a culture of openness, cooperation and reflection in your school.

#92 Honest, effective feedback

If you are in the position of offering feedback to a colleague, getting the balance right can be tough. You want to make sure your messages are direct and useful, while ensuring that your colleague has the opportunity to express their views, too. Follow these tips to give feedback that makes a difference.

1. **Know your audience.** Some people prefer direct, concise feedback, while others respond well to a coaching approach with prompts to guide them in their reflection. Consider the personality of the person you are giving feedback to.
2. **Focus on the learning or performance of the pupils.** All lesson observations ought to be about the outcomes and what helped or hindered these. Building the conversation around outcomes helps to keep the feedback focused.
3. **Give the feedback in a timely manner.** The longer the gap between the lesson and the feedback, the harder it will be for everyone to reflect purposefully.
4. **Listen.** If the person you are giving feedback to has the chance to express their views or ask questions, the feedback becomes more like a valuable conversation about teaching and learning.
5. **Relax.** If you are tense when giving feedback, this can make the recipient tense, too.
6. **End with actions.** Ensure the recipient leaves the conversation feeling confident about their successes and aware of the actions they need to take to improve further.
7. **Keep feedback short.** In my view, 5-10 minutes is optimal. Less than five minutes indicates that the conversation has not received sufficient time, but more than 10 minutes could leave the recipient feeling overwhelmed or confused.

Why this matters
If you are going to observe colleagues, then getting the feedback right is the best way to ensure that the observation was purposeful and meaningful.

Top tip
To make sure the recipient has understood the feedback, end by summarising your main points.

#93 Structuring feedback conversations

We've all heard of the 'feedback sandwich', but this approach is pretty dated and can make conversations feel contrived. Here are the five components of a constructive feedback conversation with a colleague.

1. **Purpose.** Unpick the purpose of the lesson in the context of the bigger learning picture.
2. **Content.** The content of the lesson is really important, so talk about its impact.
3. **Delivery.** Discuss the successes of the instruction and delivery. Focus on any parts of the delivery that need adjusting to optimise learning.
4. **Outcomes.** Talk about the outcomes of the lesson as a result of the purpose, content and delivery.
5. **Summarise**. Highlight the elements that strengthened the learning. Identify ways to improve the purpose, content and delivery.

Why try this?
Following this model will ensure that core elements are discussed and keep the conversation concise and useful.

Top tip
Remember that feedback should always be personalised, but never personal.

#94 Giving difficult feedback

No one wants to give negative feedback to a co-worker, but sometimes a clear message needs to be delivered. Consider these points before you embark on giving difficult feedback.

1. **Plan your feedback**. Know when and where the conversation will take place. Decide exactly what the message needs to be and keep this in mind.
2. **Predict the reaction**. Might the recipient be in agreement, surprised or defensive? What might they say?
3. **Open the conversation kindly**. Say that, on this occasion, the feedback is going to be difficult to give and receive. Explain the issue and its impact. Avoid blame and don't get personal – be matter-of-fact.
4. **Listen**. Offer an opportunity for the recipient to respond.
5. **Say it again**. If necessary, repeat the feedback.
6. **Define next steps**. End the conversation with a summary and the next step. Let the person know they are supported and valued.
7. **Keep it short and simple**. Avoid being drawn into further conversation or debate. If more needs to be discussed, allow time for emotions to settle. Say that you want to talk further, but now isn't the right time.

Why try this?
Thorough preparation for difficult conversations will mean that messages get through and staff wellbeing is unaffected.

Top tip
It might be necessary to invite a third party to sit in on a difficult feedback conversation – perhaps a person with whom the recipient has a positive relationship.

#95 Fair feedback

Being fair with your feedback can make all the difference to outcomes and progress. So how can you ensure that your feedback to a colleague is just?

1. **Be clear about expectations**. If someone doesn't know what the benchmark is, very specific feedback can feel unfair. Be sure to fully explain what is expected.
2. **Provide a model**. Offer your colleague the chance to observe the teaching or outcomes of others as a model of practice.
3. **Allow time**. Always give the team member sufficient time to learn, practise and embed skills or knowledge before you review their practice again.
4. **Ask for a second opinion**. Checking your expectations with a senior colleague is a good way to ensure that you are being fair.

Why this matters

No one sets out to do a bad job. Giving the person every chance to succeed is fair and allows for a win-win situation.

Top tip

Ask the person in question if they feel the feedback is fair. You might not like the answer, but listen to what they have to say.

#96 Giving difficult feedback to the SLT

How often do you offer your senior leaders valuable and honest feedback? Try this approach to get difficult feedback across effectively and fairly.

1. **Schedule an informal meeting**. Briefly describe what you'd like to discuss. For example: 'I'd like to have a chat about the cover timetable. Could we please meet on Monday?' This makes it very clear that your discussion needs a little time and focus, while giving the leader a heads-up about the topic.
2. **Be matter-of-fact**. Use the time effectively, making sure your views are expressed clearly and your feedback is explicit.
3. **Show empathy**. Senior leaders often spend a lot of time considering and preparing initiatives, so be careful not to talk personally or too harshly about these.
4. **Only speak on behalf of yourself**. Discussing others' views or comments can backfire!
5. **Have an outcome in mind**. Offering a solution is a good way to show that you have thought carefully about the issue. Be aware, however, that senior leaders might not take on your suggestion, or may have just reasons for continuing with their plans.
6. **Thank them for their time**. A good leader will make time to listen to the views of their staff (even if they don't always act on them).

Why it works

Allowing dissatisfaction to fester can lead to resentment or frustration. Opening up a dialogue with leaders is a good way to build a connected and open team.

Top tip

Don't rush into feedback. Take a little time to gather your thoughts before you arrange a meeting. You never know, you may well change your mind after some reflection.

#97 Giving yourself feedback

Many teachers spend time reflecting on the lessons they teach, often considering the elements that didn't go so well. Try this method for a more well-rounded reflection on your lessons.

1. **Reflect on the planning.** A good lesson starts with a good plan. Ask yourself, 'Was the learning intention purposeful? Did the planning lead us to the learning intention?' If you answer no to either question, consider how the lesson planning needs to be amended.
2. **Reflect on the delivery.** The delivery of the lesson through effective instruction and explanation has a big impact on the outcomes. Ask yourself, 'Did I explain and instruct clearly and effectively?' If you answer no, decide how to improve your explanation and instruction.
3. **Reflect on the pupils' behaviour and engagement.** If pupils are engaged and behaviour is good, the lesson is more likely to be a success. Ask yourself, 'Did the pupils behave well? Were they involved in the learning?' If you answer no to either question, consider what action you need to take to improve the situation.
4. **Reflect on the lesson outcomes.** If pupils make efforts to complete the work and many succeed, this can be a good indicator of learning. Ask yourself, 'Did the majority of pupils perform well during the lesson?' If you answer no, consider what the barriers were.

Why it works
With reflection comes improvement.

Top tip
For each step, also ask yourself, 'What were the successes?' We can learn from positives as much as from areas for development.

#98 **Accepting feedback**

How can you get the most out of feedback given after a lesson observation?

Scenario 1: the observer asks how you think the lesson went

1. This can leave you trying to second-guess them. What you think: 'You tell me!'
2. What you often say: 'I think it went OK…'
3. What you could say instead: 'I've jotted down some strengths and areas I'd change for next time.'
4. Why it works: you take ownership of your feedback and show self-awareness.

Scenario 2: the observer advises you to try something that you actually did after they left the room

1. What you think: 'I do that!'
2. What you often say: 'I always do that' or 'I did that when you left'.
3. What you could say instead: 'I've often used that approach and you're right, it can work really well' or 'I love that approach – I did actually use it later in the lesson and this was the impact…'
4. Why it works: you show understanding and don't come across as defensive.

Scenario 3: the observer makes a comment or suggestion that you don't agree with

1. What you think: 'You're wrong.'
2. What you often say: 'I don't agree' or (worse) 'OK…'
3. What you could say instead: 'I have a different view, so can we come back to this point once I've had some time to think about it?'
4. Why it works: you come across as open-minded.

Why it works
An open attitude towards feedback will benefit your teaching practice.

Top tip
View your feedback as an opportunity for everything to be about you! Embrace the time to talk about yourself and your class.

#99 Grading or degrading?

Since all UK school inspectorates stopped grading individual lessons as part of the inspection process, giving lesson gradings has been considered dated practice in most schools. If you are still grading individual lessons, here's how to shift from degrading labels to useful feedback in five simple steps.

1. Immediately stop grading lessons and teachers. Avoid using labels.
2. Consider your current lesson feedback form. Do the headings and structures provide valuable opportunities for feedback? What do the team think about the form? Remove all trace of grading words such as 'outstanding', 'good', 'requires improvement' or 'inadequate'.
3. Create and trial a new and improved feedback form. Use staff reflections and your school ethos to build the form; keep it as simple and concise as possible. Trial the feedback form during your observations of staff.
4. After the trial, reflect on the form's effectiveness and ask staff for their feedback, too.
5. Make any amendments to the form, before creating a final draft.

Why this matters
When we grade lessons, teachers feel branded. This is poor practice that can be detrimental to wellbeing and stress levels. Feedback ought to be about success and improvement, not labelling.

Top tip
Remember the gradings are not the feedback – the feedback is the feedback. If the feedback is effective, people will quickly understand what needs improvement, without being told that they 'require improvement'.

#100 The impact of written marking

In 2016, the Education Endowment Foundation published a review of evidence on the impact of written marking, entitled *A Marked Improvement? A review of the evidence on written marking.*[5] Here's a summary of the findings.

1. Careless mistakes should be marked differently to errors resulting from misunderstanding. The latter may be best addressed by providing hints or questions that lead pupils to underlying principles; the former by simply marking the mistake as incorrect, without giving the right answer.
2. Awarding grades for every piece of work may reduce the impact of marking, particularly if pupils become preoccupied with grades at the expense of teachers' formative comments.
3. The use of targets to make marking as specific and actionable as possible is likely to increase pupil progress.
4. Pupils are unlikely to benefit from marking unless time is set aside to enable them to consider it and respond.
5. Some forms of marking, including acknowledgement marking, are unlikely to enhance pupil progress. A mantra might be that schools should mark less, but mark better.

Why this matters
Reviewing the evidence can help schools to move practice in the right direction.

Top tip
Debate and discuss these findings with your team during a staff meeting.

---

5   Victoria Elliott, Jo-Ann Baird, Therese N Hopfenbeck, Jenni Ingram, Ian Thompson, Natalie Usher, Mae Zantout, James Richardson and Robbie Coleman, *A Marked Improvement? A review of the evidence on written marking*, Education Endowment Foundation, 2016, tinyurl.com/tjvuxxy

#101 Creating a feedback ethos

Does your school have a feedback culture to be proud of? We all respond differently, but you can get a sense of your school's culture by observing how people generally react to the feedback they are given. How well is feedback received among staff in your school? Follow these steps to make your school a place that is open to feedback.

1. Drop gradings.
2. Use coaching.
3. Pair all staff with a mentor.
4. Host a staff meeting about the value and benefits of feedback.
5. Ask staff for feedback about the school systems or leadership approaches (practise what you preach!).
6. Avoid approaches such as the 'feedback sandwich'.
7. Provide opportunities for staff to react to feedback. If feedback is not acted upon, it becomes meaningless.
8. Make feedback about genuine discussions of teaching and learning, as opposed to the one-way delivery of information.
9. Embrace people's mistakes or areas for development as opportunities for progression. Lesson observations should be about reflection, not perfection.

Why try this?

In Matthew Syed's book Black Box Thinking,[6] he writes: 'You can build motivation by breaking down the idea that we can all be perfect on the one hand, and by building up the idea that we can get better with good feedback and practice on the other.'

Top tip

Eradicating the perceived threat of feedback takes time and consistency, so stick with it.

---

6   Matthew Syed, *Black Box Thinking: marginal gains and the secrets of high performance,* John Murray, 2016

#102 Building pupil feedback guidance

Schools often use a marking policy in place of feedback guidance, implying that all feedback to pupils arrives through written marking. But feedback is so much more than marking, so build strong guidance that focuses on the power of feedback.

1. Decide on your ethos for feedback. Why do you give feedback to pupils? What is the intention?
2. List the multiple ways in which feedback is given to pupils at your setting – for example, staff-to-pupil one-to-one verbal feedback, group feedback, whole-class feedback, peer-to-peer feedback, written feedback, etc. Outline the methods and their impact.
3. Consider the expectations for written feedback in different subjects and different key stages. These expectations have considerable impact on staff workload and wellbeing. The Education Endowment Foundation report *A Marked Improvement? A review of the evidence on written marking*[7] may help to inform your thoughts.
4. Trial and embed the use of the feedback guidance.
5. Finalise expectations and ensure that any monitoring of feedback fairly reflects the guidance. For instance, if you've decided that written comments are not necessary in English books, don't give feedback that is contrary to this.
6. Share the guidance with all staff, governors and parents.

Why try this?
Feedback is a huge part of the teacher's role, so it's helpful to define what effective feedback looks like at your setting.

Top tip
Include your team at every stage of building the guidance. Your teachers are the ones who will follow the guidance, so their views and investment are vital to its success.

---

7   Victoria Elliott, Jo-Ann Baird, Therese N Hopfenbeck, Jenni Ingram, Ian Thompson, Natalie Usher, Mae Zantout, James Richardson and Robbie Coleman, *A Marked Improvement? A review of the evidence on written marking*, Education Endowment Foundation, 2016, tinyurl.com/tjvuxxy

#103 Seven ways to give better feedback to students

An article published by *The Guardian* in 2016[8] suggests the following seven ways to give better feedback to students. Which suggestion could you embed to improve your verbal feedback?

1. Don't go overboard.
2. Correct quietly.
3. Don't compare.
4. Be specific.
5. Focus on process, not natural ability.
6. Combine open and closed questions.
7. End with clear action points.

Why try this?
Effective feedback can have a positive impact on learning.

Top tip
Read the full article online (tinyurl.com/ycpyf9z7).

---

8   Bradley Busch, 'Seven ways to give better feedback to your students', *The Guardian*, 2016, tinyurl.com/ycpyf9z7

#104 Dylan Wiliam's feedback that moves learning forward

Feedback is such a powerful classroom tool, so make the most of your time in class by offering rich and positive feedback that helps pupils to develop. In a video,[9] the assessment guru Dylan Wiliam offers his thoughts on how to give feedback to pupils that moves learning forward. Here are his key points.

1. Avoid feedback that is 'backwards looking' and states only what should have been done.
2. Instead, talk about what comes next in the learning.
3. Create feedback that is specifically designed to move learning forward.

Why it works
Wiliam echoes Douglas B Reeves' idea that feedback ought to be more like a medical than a post-mortem.

Top tip
Ask yourself, 'Did that feedback give the child an idea of what to do next time?'

9   Dylan Wiliam, 'Strategy 3: providing feedback that moves learning forward' (video), Learning Sciences International, 2018, youtu.be/vdIk9ysWJXQ

#105 Live marking

Live marking can be a great way to give feedback on pupils' work as they create it, allowing them to respond instantly. Follow these tips for successful live marking.

1. Move around the classroom. Getting stuck with one child limits your ability to support others in the room.
2. Have pens around the room and on your person, so that live marking is easy and accessible.
3. Couple the live marking with decent verbal feedback. Remember that your aim is not just to get the books marked, but to offer useful written notes alongside verbal prompts.
4. Avoid writing long or detailed comments in books. Live marking should be used as a tool to scaffold improvement.
5. Tell the pupils that you'll be moving around to mark their work. This makes them aware that feedback is likely and you expect them to listen and act upon it.
6. Ask support staff to complete live marking, too.

Why try this?
Live marking has obvious benefits, such as giving the pupils instant feedback to act upon and reducing the workload of distant marking later on.

Top tip
At the end of the lesson, scan the pupils' books to find any work you didn't see during the lesson. Make notes about this to form your whole-class feedback (read more about this in idea #107).

#106 Giving verbal feedback that sticks[10]

Do you find yourself repeating the same feedback to the same pupils? Use this strategy to give, repeat and consolidate feedback.

1. When you notice something specific, let the pupil know that you're about to give them some very important feedback, and you'd like them to listen carefully because it will help to make their work better.
2. Give the feedback in the simplest terms: 'I want you to make better vocabulary choices. This will impact your work by making it sound more appealing to the reader. Use the thesaurus to replace these words.'
3. Ask the pupil to 'bounce' the feedback back to you, repeating what you have said.
4. Leave the child to act on the feedback.
5. When you return to the pupil, bounce the feedback back to them once more.
6. Ask the pupil to explain what they did.
7. They can show their peers the improved work, explaining how they acted on the feedback they were given.

Why it works
Bouncing the expectation back and forth allows pupils to gain clarity on what they're being asked to do.

Top tip
Remember to refer to the impact on the pupil's work, asking them to identify how their work has improved. Ask how they might use this feedback again in the future.

10 Hanna Beech, 'Verbal feedback that sticks', *Teacher Toolkit,* 2018, teachertoolkit.co.uk/2018/01/03/one-minute-cpd-12

#107 Whole-class feedback

Have you tried whole-class feedback? If not, follow these simple steps to get you started.

1. At the end of a lesson, scan the outcomes in books. As you do this, make notes under headings such as 'Shout-outs', 'What went well', 'Even better if' and 'Revisions'.
    *   Under 'Shout-outs', list a couple of children whose work could be shared as an example of success.
    *   Under 'What went well', note common successes.
    *   Under 'Even better if', list common themes for developing outcomes.
    *   Under 'Revisions', note what you would like the pupils to rapidly revise – for example, 'Include a justification for your response to question 3' or 'Check calculation for question 4'.
2. During the first 5-10 minutes of the next lesson, give your whole-class feedback, allowing pupils time to reflect and revise if prompted.
3. Summarise by telling pupils what you would like them to do next in light of the whole-class feedback.

Why try this?

This effective method of giving feedback allows pupils to learn from their peers, reflect on their own work, act upon feedback, celebrate successes and know their next steps, all while reducing unnecessary teacher workload.

Top tip

You likely have a school policy or approach to marking and feedback. Before you embark on whole-class feedback, it's worth discussing the idea with your SLT.

#108 Feedback with coaching

Teacher feedback is great, but sometimes it's possible to prompt pupils to reflect on their work, creating their own feedback. Here's how.

1. As the lesson progresses, explore the pupil's work with them.
2. Ask the pupil which of two pieces of feedback is more relevant to them and why it is likely to improve their work. For example: 'Do you think I'd like you to next include more expressive language or add more dialogue between characters?' Use the success criteria to scaffold the content of the feedback.
3. Prompt the child to revisit their work.
4. Return to the child and ask them how they improved their work.

Why it works
For some pupils, coaching them towards self-improvement is more effective. It allows them to be autonomous and make meaningful reflections about their work in a scaffolded way.

Top tip
Inspire others by sharing the child's journey towards improvement through feedback coaching.

#109 Giving honest feedback to pupils

If you want your feedback to pupils to be purposeful, you have to be honest. Try these three suggestions for giving honest feedback that is well-received.

1. **Keep growth in mind**. Growth mindset approaches have been all the rage and for good reason. Be sure to use words such as 'yet' and phrases that praise effort and outcome, rather than the individual. Use praise with caution – pupils can sense insincerity. Remember that growth mindsets are not about telling children they can 'do anything' or 'do your best and you will get there', so avoid these hollow phrases.
2. **Know your audience**. If you are unsure how a child might take honest feedback, don't give it. Instead, spend time questioning the pupil, coaching them to their own conclusions. This is better than giving feedback that could damage their motivation or self-esteem.
3. **Fair warning**. Tell your pupils from the outset that you are going to be honest with them about their outcomes and their efforts. Explain that this will help them to understand how they are doing and how to improve. Feedback should be personalised, not personal, and pupils should be ready to receive honest feedback as part of the class ethos.

Why try this?
Giving honest feedback to children can build trust and encourage a culture of openness.

Top tip
We all know a teacher's time is precious. If you doubt that honesty is the best policy, remember, honesty saves everyone's time.

#110 How to reduce marking

Written feedback has been a hot topic in education for many years, owing to the amount of time consumed by excessive marking expectations. Follow these tips to make sure marking doesn't result in unmanageable workload for teachers.

1. Remove expectations for next-step comments.
2. Remove expectations for teachers to write what went well in the lesson or if the learning intention was met.
3. Reduce the scrutiny of marking in books, favouring exploration of the learning outcomes seen in work.
4. Stop expecting children to respond to teachers' comments (deemed 'meaningless exchanges' by the education writer David Didau[11]).
5. End the expected use of coloured highlighters or pens to indicate a range of cryptic messages to pupils.
6. Do not ask teachers to 'evidence' when verbal feedback has been given via a stamp or jotting 'VF'. This type of evidence-gathering creates a feeling of mistrust and wastes time. Of course teachers are giving verbal feedback to students.

Why consider this?

Excessive marking increases teacher workload and there is little to no evidence that any of the actions above have positive impacts on learning outcomes.

Top tip

If you are still convinced that these strategies work, why not trial abolishing excessive marking strategies in one class to explore the impact for yourself.

---

11 David Didau, 'Why "triple marking" is wrong (and not my fault)', *Learning Spy* (blog), 2014, learningspy.co.uk/leadership/triple-marking-wrong-not-fault-2

#111 The power of feedback, by Ross

A new meta-analysis of empirical research,[12] published by researchers including the *Visible Learning*[13] author John Hattie, shows that 'feedback cannot be understood as a single consistent form of treatment'. According to the researchers, their findings 'suggest that feedback has rightly become a focus of teaching research and practice'. They also 'point toward the necessity of interpreting different forms of feedback as independent measures'.

The research is a follow-up to another Hattie paper published in 2007,[14] which argued that there were three key forms of feedback:

1. **Feed-up** – comparison of the actual status with a target status.
2. **Feed-back** – comparison of the actual status with a previous status.
3. **Feed-forward** – explanation of the target status based on the actual status.

One of the most consistent findings about the power of feedback is the remarkable variability of its effects. Although Hattie's research on feedback is welcome, my travels to schools across the world have shown me that, as with all research, it is important to translate both theory and practice for your own context. At present, we don't have any robust research about the effects of different types of feedback in different contexts. So, what *do* we know?

1. Feedback must be recognised as a complex and differentiated practice.
2. Feedback comes in many forms that can have quite different effects on student learning.
3. The more information feedback contains, the more effective it can be.

Why this matters
When you understand the various forms that feedback can take and their potential effects, you can tailor your feedback to your school and your individual students.

Top tip
Remember, feedback in a class for visually impaired students in an alternative provision provider will be very different from feedback in a maths classroom in an inner-city state school.

---

12 Benedikt Wisniewski, Klaus Zierer and John Hattie, 'The power of feedback revisited: a meta-analysis of educational feedback research', *Frontiers in Psychology*, 10, 2020, tinyurl.com/y79g34n2
13 John Hattie, *Visible Learning*, Routledge, 2008
14 John Hattie and Helen Timperley, 'The power of feedback', *Review of Educational Research*, 77.1, 2007, tinyurl.com/hbtcsd7

#112 The downsides of peer feedback

Peer feedback certainly has its benefits, but consider these three cautions before you embark on pupil-to-pupil feedback.

1. **Pupils don't know how to give effective feedback**. Often, during peer feedback, pupils are unsure of what to say. The result is that the feedback focuses on presentation of work instead of the substance of the learning.
2. **Pupils are not expert enough to offer effective feedback**. Unless they are extremely confident in the learning, they might actually do more harm than good when giving feedback.
3. **Pupils might end up damaging self-esteem**. Children can be tough critics and their feedback can be delivered in a way that unintentionally harms their peers' self-worth.

Why consider this?
Without careful consideration, peer feedback can end up being a waste of time.

Top tip
Before you try peer feedback in your classroom, teach pupils how to offer feedback effectively. Guide the feedback by asking pupils to use the success criteria for the lesson.

#113 Verbal feedback, by Ross

As any teacher will tell you, one of the greatest challenges is managing the marking burden. One of the most effective strategies I have seen on my travels to schools around the world is the use of effective questioning techniques to regularly assess pupils' learning. Verbal feedback is a huge victory for teacher workload.

In 2019, I published the results of my Verbal Feedback Project, conducted with University College London. The project explored the impact of verbal feedback approaches on outcomes for disadvantaged students in Years 7 and 8. After a one-year trial, all teachers reported a significant difference in pupils' outcomes. The findings suggest that verbal feedback, when applied well, has a positive impact on the engagement of all students, and may also lead to gains in progress and achievement.

Why this matters
Verbal feedback has the potential to reduce the marking burden for teachers, as well as improve student outcomes.

Top tip
Read the Verbal Feedback Project research report and its resources at bit.ly/VFFindings

Further resources

Ross Morrison McGill, *Just Great Teaching: how to tackle the top ten issues in UK classrooms*, Bloomsbury Publishing, 2019

Benedikt Wisniewski, Klaus Zierer and John Hattie, 'The power of feedback revisited: a meta-analysis of educational feedback research', *Frontiers in Psychology*, 10, 2020, tinyurl.com/y79g34n2

John Hattie and Helen Timperley, 'The power of feedback', *Review of Educational Research*, 77.1, 2007, tinyurl.com/hbtcsd7

Chapter 6: Leadership

There is a strong case to argue that all teachers are leaders. Teachers spend much of their time leading the learning, personal development and emotional wellbeing of their pupils, and if they are lucky enough to have support staff, they lead them, too. In some ways, teachers also have to lead parents and carers, guiding them with resources and offering support and strategies. In fact, many transferable leadership skills (effective communication, organisation, long-term vision, delegation, creativity, integrity) can be developed through teaching.

Whether you're a classroom leader, a middle leader, a senior leader or an aspiring leader, spending a little time reflecting on your leadership is likely to enhance and improve it. But before you explore the ideas and research in this chapter, I would like to offer you some of my own personal leadership lessons.

Lesson 1: what makes *you* a good leader?

My own journey to leadership was a slow and steady progression over about 11 years of teaching. I was in no rush to steam to the top and I'm really proud to have taken the time and space to develop as an educator. I think the saying goes 'always the goal, never the role' and that about sums my journey up.

About two years into my teaching career, my role was extended and I was asked to manage and lead 'pupil voice' across our school, which at the time was a new and undefined role. I was really keen to contribute to the school in some way, and I felt quietly confident that I had developed some of the skills required to manage school initiatives through my classroom teaching practice. The challenge for me was to develop a deep understanding of all things pupil voice – an area in which I had little knowledge. And with no predecessor's footsteps to follow in, I felt unnerved. This feeling led me to the internet, to do as much research as I could. What was interesting about this was that the more I found out about pupil voice, the more passionate I became about it. I immersed myself in reading and soon implemented some successful initiatives.

My leadership role was subsequently expanded to 'pupil voice, wellbeing and involvement'. To learn about wellbeing and involvement, I read and I read and I read. And as I read, my confidence and passion grew. I put my learning into practice and led some huge whole-school initiatives that had a really positive impact on pupils and staff. Then my leadership role evolved again: 'wellbeing, involvement, teaching and learning'. The cycle continued. In 2018, I accepted a role as deputy head, and I've continued to stretch and deepen my knowledge of leadership and my specific areas of leadership in particular (curriculum, teaching and learning, and pupil mental health). Each time I've been given an area to lead, I've learned as much as I can about it, in order to be really good at leading it. Of course, the leadership skills I gained in my classroom practice came into play at all stages of my wider leadership. I used my time-management, planning and communication skills, and applied these to the projects and initiatives I led. I took the time to get to know the people I was leading and meticulously planned my projects with clear goals in mind.

The point of this story is to stress something I believe to be really significant. In order to lead something successfully, you need to have three things: knowledge, passion and drive. I've known colleagues who were immensely driven to lead, but lacked the depth of knowledge or passion for their leadership area. They would lead anything just for the status of leading. I've also known leaders with incredible knowledge and passion in a particular area, but they had absolutely no drive or desire to extend their expertise beyond their own practice.

When you get the right balance of knowledge, drive and passion, great and profound things can happen in leadership. With knowledge, you are equipped to implement initiatives and make progress. With drive, you are relentless in your aims, organised and time-aware; you are determined to achieve the highest results. With passion, you are inspiring and you spread excitement about your leadership areas. Of course, communication, time management and creativity are necessary skills but, for me, knowledge, drive and passion are key. Perhaps there are three different leadership attributes that *you* value greatly?

Lesson 2: the importance of people

Another vital aspect of leadership is the ability to understand and connect with others. If you can develop a deep understanding of what drives, motivates and unsettles the individuals you lead, you are already halfway there. Leading a wide range of people, all with different lifestyles, approaches and skills, truly throws you into leadership at its best and worst. Some of my proudest leadership moments have been those where I've connected with, supported and empowered my colleagues, but some of the most challenging and confusing moments have come from feeling disconnected from team members who have, for one reason or another, felt disempowered or unsupported. Leading and managing extremely difficult people has taught me some of the most important lessons about leadership (and some pretty important lessons about myself, too). I'm lucky to able to say that 99.9% of my interactions with colleagues have been positive, inspiring and fun, but leading others can be hard!

Lesson 3: find the balance

In my experience, good leadership relies upon balance. It requires a strong vision, yet an open mind. It requires a drive towards goals, but an awareness of workload and pace. It requires confidence and also modesty. It requires you to be present and distant all at once.

Lesson 4: reflections

School leadership is a really important job, so there is a great deal to be achieved by reflecting on your leadership experiences. Through reflection can come either self-assurance ('I'm sure I made the right choice') or self-improvement ('Next time I won't repeat that'). To reflect on your own leadership, take the time to consider the following thinking prompts.

Current leaders
- What is your proudest leadership moment?
- What leadership moment challenged or unsettled you?
- What would others say about your leadership?

Aspiring leaders
- What aspect of leadership are you most looking forward to?
- What are your potential concerns?
- What sort of leader do you aspire to be?

Lesson 5: back yourself

I've spent some time reflecting on my own leadership and what I'm about to say is a bit embarrassing and a bit brave, too.

I can be really good at leadership.

There, I've said it. It isn't very British to compliment oneself in one's own book, but I do so in order to make an important point: if you don't back your own leadership, no one will. Undoubtedly, competence is crucial to leadership, but so are confidence and trust in your own ability. How much confidence do you have in yourself? How might this affect the way your team perceive your leadership?

I've learned that I won't always get leadership right and I've stopped beating myself up about it. That's not to say that I won't reflect on or learn from my mistakes, but leaders are human beings, too. These days, I know that my desire to steer a team towards success is far greater than my fear of failure. This is a good place to be, but I haven't always felt this way. Like many educators, I've felt in the past that I lacked capability, despite experiencing much success in my aims. You've probably heard of impostor syndrome, that feeling that you're unworthy of your role and you're going to be 'found out'. This persistent, crippling feeling of inadequacy can have huge negative effects on wellbeing and mental health.[1] In a study, students experiencing impostor syndrome saw their symptoms lessen when they reached out to others, but the benefit came less from talking about their feelings and more from *who* they chose to talk to.[2] When the students spoke to a person from a social group outside their course, their feelings of inadequacy were reduced compared with when they 'reached in' by speaking to others on their course. If you find yourself battling with an internal dialogue that tells you that you aren't good at your job or you're about to be discovered, try talking to someone outside school who can help you to see the bigger picture.

There is no one route to leadership success. Whatever your role – whether it's leading pupil voice, maths, key stage 1 or the entire school – there are plenty of leadership principles out there. The trouble is, there is almost *too much* leadership advice. Sifting through thousands of books, blogs and articles can lead to confusion, so this chapter offers an overview of some popular leadership approaches, along with some of my own ideas and tips that I've picked up along the way. I hope they will help you to discover the kind of leader *you* want to be.

---

1   Pauline Rose Clance, *The Impostor Phenomenon: overcoming the fear that haunts your success*, Peachtree, 1985

2   Richard G Gardner, Jeffrey S Bednar, Bryan W Stewart, James B Oldroyd and Joseph Moore, '"I must have slipped through the cracks somehow": an examination of coping with perceived impostorism and the role of social support', *Journal of Vocational Behavior*, 115, 2019, tinyurl.com/reocgfz

#114 Ready for leadership?[3]

How do you move up the leadership ladder? And how do you know when you're ready? Ask yourself these questions to decide if the time is right to make the leap.

1. **Do you have something to lead?** It sounds obvious, but you need to be confident about what you want to lead: a subject, a team, a group of pupils?
2. **Are you passionate?** In leadership, you are most likely to succeed when you have true passion for your aims.
3. **Are you knowledgeable?** Even with all the passion in the world, if you don't have enough expertise in the area you wish to lead, you may end up feeling ill-equipped to support others effectively.
4. **Do you have time to commit?** Leadership of any form requires a time commitment. Great senior leaders will allow you adequate time away from class to develop your area of leadership, but this isn't always an option.
5. **Are your managerial skills up to scratch?** If you are organised and keep to deadlines, this will help you in leadership.
6. **Are you good with people?** Every aspect of leadership involves working for and alongside people. Much of leadership is about managing people, showing empathy and being able to have difficult conversations when necessary.

Why it works
Leadership is a wonderful step to take, but there are challenging aspects. Thinking carefully before you take the leap will drive you forward with confidence.

Top tip
If you were put off by any of your responses, don't be! Just find systems and people to help you address your areas for development.

---

3   Hanna Beech, 'Ready for leadership?', *Teacher Toolkit*, 2019, teachertoolkit.co.uk/2019/03/06/one-minute-cpd-50

#115 Highly effective habits

Looking for the core features of leadership? Stephen R Covey's 1989 book *The 7 Habits of Highly Effective People* has stood the test of time – his leadership guidance remains popular and well-cited. Here's a summary of the seven habits he attributes to highly effective people.

1. **Be proactive.** Get things done, do what is necessary and make things happen.
2. **Begin with the end in mind.** Imagine what you want the outcomes to be, then regularly reflect to understand how close to these outcomes you are.
3. **Put first things first.** When doing something, remember to ask, 'Does this have a bearing on the long-term goals?'
4. **Seek to understand, then be understood.** Listening is a powerful tool that allows you to reduce assumption and gives you accurate information to work with.
5. **Think win-win.** When it comes to interactions with other people, find ways for both parties to benefit.
6. **Synergise.** Remember that two people can disagree and neither are wrong. Combining efforts and ideas to generate better results leads to success.
7. **Sharpen the saw.** Blunt saws don't cut wood. You are the saw. Renew yourself mentally, socially, spiritually and physically to ensure you are as effective as you can be.

Why it works

These simple approaches help us to remain focused as we work towards complex goals, alongside complex people.

Top tip

Consider how to use these seven approaches to evaluate your leadership each term. Jotting down your reflections for just one minute per habit could mean you make significant headway in under 10 minutes.

#116 Transformational leadership traits

The political scientist James MacGregor Burns first introduced the concept of transformational leadership (when 'leaders and followers raise one another to higher levels of motivation and morality') in 1978.[4] The academic Bernard Bass then extended Burns' work and released a 1985 book that highlighted the essential traits of transformational leaders.[5] According to Bass, the transformational leader:

1. Is a model of integrity and fairness.
2. Sets clear goals.
3. Has high expectations.
4. Encourages others.
5. Provides support and recognition.
6. Stirs the emotions of people.
7. Gets people to look beyond their self-interest.
8. Inspires people to reach for the improbable.

Try the following four methods to reflect on how you demonstrate those traits.

1. **Weakest link.** Order the traits from your strongest to your weakest. Set yourself the goal of focusing on your weakest areas in order to raise your leadership game.
2. **Pick and mix.** Choose two traits and aim to use them as much as possible over a set period of time, reflecting on the impact this has on your leadership.

---

4   James MacGregor Burns, *Leadership*, Harper Torchbooks, 1978
5   Bernard M Bass, *Leadership and Performance Beyond Expectations*, The Free Press, 1985

3. **Show and tell.** Present how you demonstrate the traits in your day-to-day leadership to members of your SLT or wider team.

4. **Tell me how it is.** Ask your team to give you feedback on each trait. You might want to do this anonymously to gain truly useful responses. A word of warning: don't ask if you don't want to know. You need to be ready and willing to accept personalised feedback.

Why try this?

These admirable traits ooze a common-sense approach to leadership, but as we all know, what is right isn't always what is easy! Taking the time to think about your traits might be all the leadership CPD you need.

Top tip

Reflection begets perfection.

#117 Listening leader

Listening is a powerful leadership tool. Try these tips to become a listening leader.

1. **Don't interrupt**. Be sure your team member has finished what they are saying before you respond. If you accidentally interrupt, apologise and ask them to continue.
2. **Ask questions, hear responses**. Asking careful questions and listening intently to the response is the best way to find out more.
3. **Nod and paraphrase**. Confirming that you understand someone's ideas or responses will help them to feel heard and supported.
4. **Eyebrows and arms**. Think about what you do with your eyebrows and your arms while you listen. These body parts can give away a lot about what you are thinking.
5. **Concentrate**. If your mind wanders while someone is talking, it's more apparent than you think. Maintain focus by reminding yourself how important it is to listen to this person.

Why listen?
If you don't listen, you miss key insights into your team's feelings, thoughts, ideas or wellbeing. This could be detrimental to progress.

Top tip
If you are not in a position to listen fully, let your colleague know and set a time to come back to them.

#118 Learning leader

How often do you take onboard the views and ideas of the team around you? When given a leadership responsibility, it's easy to assume that you make all the decisions. But the direction in which you take your subject or team will have a huge impact on people's lives, and your success also depends on those people, so why not find out what they have to offer? Be a learning leader by taking these approaches.

1. Ask questions you think you already know the answers to. Sometimes, seeking clarification where you feel most confident is a great way of establishing where you're at with your subject or leadership goal.
2. Ask staff to offer one way to make your leadership area more manageable.
3. Poll or quiz your team members, from support staff to SLT, to gather a range of ideas or views. Just don't do this too often!
4. Use a subject suggestion box or staff suggestion box to allow colleagues to submit their views at any time.
5. Read blogs and articles about your area of leadership to gather a range of strategies or resources.
6. Make links with local leaders in your field to share ideas and practice.
7. Ask the pupils. They often have insightful and unique ways of reflecting on areas of school life.

Why try this?
No man is an island.

Top tip
Develop confidence in asking for ideas or support by practising it often.

#119 The GROW model for coaching

Acting as a coach or mentor is an incredibly rewarding aspect of school leadership. By sharing ideas and helping someone to reflect, you provide them with key opportunities to develop and grow. Although the roles are often combined, they are distinctly different: in the simplest terms, a mentor *shows* you how and a coach *asks* you how. The GROW model[6] was developed by the business coaches Graham Alexander, Alan Fine and Sir John Whitmore in the 1980s; here's a quick summary of how to use this simple yet effective model.

G is for goal. Meet with your coachee and work with them to set their goal.

R is for current reality. Use questions to establish how the current reality is different from their goal.

O is for options and obstacles. Ask about the options your coachee has to help them make progress towards their goal. Ask them to identify any obstacles that might occur on the way and how they might overcome these.

W is for way forward. The final step is to establish what your coachee will do next. Use questioning to help them decide the way forward.

Why it works

The GROW model gives structure to a coaching conversation, enabling the coach and coachee to make progress through the discussion.

Top tip

Avoid slipping into a mentoring role by telling your coachee what to do or sharing your views or experience. Coaching is about supporting someone to set their goals and actions for themselves.

6   John Whitmore, *Coaching for Performance: the principles and practice of coaching and leadership*, Nicholas Brealey Publishing, 2017

THE GROW MODEL

Developed by Graham Alexander, Alan Fine and Sir John Whitmore

Comments	Potential questions	Key points to note from coaching discussions
GOAL	• What is your goal? • Why is this important? • What do you really want? • Who might benefit from this goal? • What is the ideal outcome?	
REALITY	• What is the current reality? • How close is your goal to the current reality? • What might need to change? • Have you already taken steps to achieve your goal? • How urgent is your goal? • How long might your goal take?	
OPTIONS & OBSTACLES	• What are your current options? • What might happen if you did this? • Which option do you prefer? Why? • What obstacles might you face? • How could you overcome these? • What if the plan doesn't work?	
WAY FORWARD	• What is your first step? • How will you achieve this? • When will this be achieved? • How will you know if you've been successful? • What will come next?	

#120 The quick coaching method[7]

Coaching is a powerful tool and it doesn't have to be time-consuming. This quick coaching technique gives your coachee something important to consider but only takes up three minutes of your time – and theirs. First, tell your coachee that you will occasionally send them an email with the subject 'Quick coaching'. The email is intended to encourage them to think independently about a particular issue; it doesn't require a response and they need only discuss their thoughts with you if they really feel it will be of value. Here's how you both use your three minutes.

The coach

1. **Minute 1**: Consider what is going on for your coachee at this time.
2. **Minute 2**: Think of three questions that might guide them into thinking around the issue or event, such as, 'What are your goals for the coming term?', 'What professional development might benefit your practice?' and 'What guidance might your team need as parents' evening approaches?'
3. **Minute 3**: Choose one question that you feel will generate interesting thought for your coachee. Email this question to them.

The coachee

1. **Minute 1**: See the subject 'Quick coaching' and decide whether you can spare three minutes now or not.
2. **Minute 2**: Open the email and read the question. Jot down three responses.
3. **Minute 3**: Choose one response and decide on an action or strategy you will use to help you solve the problem.

Why it works
Coaching has multiple benefits. To encourage someone to reflect deeply, sometimes all it takes is a quick question.

Top tip
Only send up to three of these emails a term. The last thing you want to do is overload your coachee, filling up their inbox or mind with additional pressures.

---

7   Hanna Beech, 'The quick coaching method', *Teacher Toolkit,* 2018, teachertoolkit.co.uk/2018/07/11/one-minute-cpd-31

#121 How to effectively mentor an NQT

Being an NQT can be a difficult and overwhelming experience. Here are 10 ways to effectively support an NQT at your setting.

1. Ensure that you, as an NQT mentor, feel well trained and prepared to provide support. If you are unsure about anything, speak to your SLT.
2. Provide your NQT with a school handbook and a bank of any must-have resources.
3. Schedule a weekly meeting with your NQT. Keep this as a protected time.
4. Ensure that your NQT has sufficient time outside the classroom for planning, preparation and assessment.
5. Map out the support you plan to provide over the coming year and share this with your NQT.
6. Build in opportunities for your NQT to observe practice across the school. Observing the practice alongside them will aid the reflection.
7. Check in with your NQT every day, even if it's just for a two-minute chat. You never know when they might need to ask a question or see a friendly face in the morning.
8. Keep up to date with your NQT assessments. Make sure they are given the time they deserve.
9. Praise your NQT for the progress they make. Trainees are often very hard on themselves, so a little positivity from you will go a long way.
10. Be aware of flash points throughout the year, such as parents' evening, report-writing terms and assessment weeks. Be available to discuss expectations and provide support where necessary.

Why this matters
Great mentors can produce great teachers.

Top tip
Keep your SLT up to speed with your NQT's progress.

#122 Unpicking an issue

From time to time, every leader comes across a person who is very hard to lead. They might ignore requests, miss deadlines, act superior or behave unprofessionally. Whatever the issue, leading difficult people can be exhausting, physically and emotionally. Before you spring into action to address an issue, take 10 minutes to unpick your concerns.

1. **What is the issue?** Identify precisely what the issue is and if it really needs addressing.
2. **When is the issue?** Is it temporary, periodic or constant?
3. **Why is the issue?** Think empathetically and logically, removing your own personal views or emotions from the equation.
4. **Who might be able to help?** Perhaps you need guidance from a fellow leader or a colleague of the person in question.
5. **How much do I know?** Decide whether you have the whole picture, part of the picture or if you have no idea why the issue is occurring. Deal only with facts and avoid assumption or hearsay. With a little thought, you can usually separate the facts from the fiction, which helps when planning a blunt discussion.
6. **Plan your time and place of approach**. This will be vital in ensuring that a manageable discussion can take place. Avoid transition times or breaktimes, and spaces that include children or colleagues who might overhear the conversation.

Why this matters
A little thought before responding to an issue can make a huge difference to how events unfold.

Top tip
Read the next idea for tips on how to structure the conversation.

#123 How to say anything to anyone[8]

In difficult conversations, it can be easy to beat around the bush and avoid the real concerns (and even easier to avoid the conversation completely!). But if you do that, nothing really changes. Instead, try Shari Harley's eight-step approach from her book *How to Say Anything to Anyone*.

1. Introduce the topic for conversation. Describe what you want to talk about and why.
2. Say, 'This is difficult for me to say and it might be difficult for you to hear.'
3. Describe the issue, starting with the words 'I've noticed'.
4. Share the impact of the behaviour discussed.
5. Ask them, 'What are your thoughts?'
6. Make a request or suggestion about what should happen next.
7. Build an agreement.
8. Thank the person for their time, saying, 'I know this conversation was difficult. Thank you for having it with me.'

Why it works
Preparation for difficult conversations is key. This straightforward approach avoids discomfort and ambiguity.

Top tip
Stick to two minutes for this feedback. Any longer allows the feedback to become lost or altered.

---

8 Shari Harley, *How to Say Anything to Anyone: a guide to building business relationships that really work,* Greenleaf Book Group, 2013

#124 **Managing a toxic colleague**

The vast majority of educators are driven, caring individuals, but as in any job, you sometimes find yourself working with a colleague who goes out of their way to cause upset or create trouble. According to Amy Morin, the psychotherapist who wrote *13 Things Mentally Strong People Don't Do*, these are the four ways to deal with a 'workplace psychopath'.[9]

1. Don't act intimidated.
2. Stay calm.
3. Refuse to buy into their stories.
4. Turn the conversation back on them.

Why try this?
Working with a toxic colleague can take a toll even on the most confident and strong person. Knowing how to disarm them could help you to minimise their negative impact.

Top tip
Communicate your concerns about a toxic colleague with members of the SLT or a governor. Avoid one-to-one interactions with the person as much as possible.

---

9   Amy Morin, 'How to deal with a workplace psychopath', *Psychology Today*, 2017, tinyurl.com/usts9yy

#125 Servicing school systems

Using the same old systems, resources or approaches can stifle or slow progress towards goals. Be a leader who advocates a review-and-renew approach. Here's how.

1. **List key areas of your leadership**. If you are a senior leader, these will be broad, but might include assessment, planning, feedback, curriculum, appraisal, lunchtimes and so on. If you are a subject leader, your key areas might be planning, instruction, lesson content, policy or resources.
2. **Identify one area to 'service'**. For example, if you focus on marking, you might service the current policy. Ask yourself, 'Does this need updating? Is the policy functioning optimally?'
3. **Replace or renew** the parts that have served their purpose and now require an upgrade. Ask yourself, 'How could this aspect be improved?'
4. **Seek to find ways to improve parts that need fixing**. Research, read and revitalise. Gather the views of stakeholders and seek to trial amendments.
5. **Shore up and embed the changes to be made**, introducing them to all staff with justifications.

Why try this?
If you change nothing, nothing changes.

Top tip
Remember the old saying 'If it ain't broke, don't fix it'. Be sure you are not advocating change for change's sake. Changes must produce positive impacts for staff and pupils.

#126 Developing a school improvement plan

Creating a school improvement plan that leads to success in key areas is an important part of school development. But what should be on your SIP and, more importantly, why? Here are some suggestions for developing an effective SIP.

1. Start by gathering the views of all stakeholders, including pupils, parents, staff and governors. Look for areas of common interest.
2. List your own priorities for the coming year. How do these align with those of other stakeholders?
3. Explore what the data tells you about progress and attainment, and use this to identify the school-wide strengths and areas for development.
4. Reread your previous inspection report or any school monitoring feedback.
5. Consider how any changes in statutory requirements might form a key priority.
6. Ensure your priorities consider the impact on a range of pupil groups – for example, disadvantaged pupils, EAL and SEN pupils, all genders.
7. Make sure any priorities for improvement have realistic timeframes.
8. Consider how progress towards actions can be measured.
9. Follow your gut instinct. Leaders know their schools well and there are often areas for development that keep you up at night. How can these be included in your SIP?

Why try this?

To stop your SIP becoming another piece of pointless paperwork, use it as an opportunity for deep reflection and improvement. Make it a valuable document that drives the school in the right direction.

Top tip

Make an 'easy to digest' version of the SIP priorities and display this in school. Remember to build in evaluation points throughout the year.

#127 Ethos in mind

Your ethos is key to providing you with an overarching goal and a bigger picture to reflect on from time to time. Use this strategy to build a three-part leadership ethos in less than 10 minutes.

1. **Minute 1**. Fill the gaps below with three adjectives.
   We will work with _____, _____ and _____...
2. **Minutes 2 and 3.** To complete the sentence, fill the gaps with two core aims.
   ...to _____ and _____.
3. **Minutes 4 and 5.** Decide how you will achieve this with three simple actions.
   We will achieve this by _____,
   _____ and _____.
4. **Minutes 6 and 7.** Decide what the impact of those actions will be.
   As a result, _____.
5. **Minutes 8 and 9.** Read your ethos statement, ensuring you believe in what you've written.

Why it works
Developing a simple ethos for your area of leadership will keep you outcome-focused.

Top tip
Share the ethos with the team. Make sure it is to hand for you to review when you lose direction or focus.

#128 Stop, look, listen, list

Leadership sometimes feels like a tsunami of interruptions from pupils, parents and colleagues. One surefire way to make someone feel unwelcome is to continue with your task when they visit your office, so follow this method to make sure visitors leave feeling satisfied.

1. Stop what you're doing.
2. Look up at the person who is visiting you.
3. Listen to them.
4. List back to them the things they have told you.
5. Let them know when you will get back to them if their query can't be handled right now.

Why try this?

As all Spider-Man fans know, with great power comes great responsibility. Leaders are responsible for making sure their teams feel heard and valued.

Top tip

If your Spidey-senses tell you the conservation is going to take longer than you have, simply say that you want to give the issue the time it deserves. Arrange a more convenient moment to talk before the person leaves your office.

#129 Three key things

Are you a senior leader? Are you busy? If the answer to the first question is yes then I'm sure the answer to the second is yes, too. This approach will keep you focused on your primary aims when the volume of work threatens to distract you.

1. List your three key drivers as a leader – for example, pupil outcomes, engaging parents and staff wellbeing.
2. Consider three key things you can do each day to keep you focused on these drivers – for example, visiting classrooms to see teaching in action, being present on the playground at drop-off times and checking in with staff each day.
3. Every day, attend to your drivers by completing your three key things.

Why try this?
Senior leaders can easily become swamped in tasks and emails, leaving them stuck in an office or in meetings for far too long.

Top tip
On some days, achieving your three things might be impossible. Forgive yourself and find a way to make them a priority throughout the rest of your week.

#130 Avoid creating an inspection-driven school

How often do you talk about inspections at your school? Leaders who make their schools all about inspection are in danger of harming wellbeing, directing staff attention away from children and towards inspections, creating a culture of scrutiny and fostering a fear of judgement. Avoid making inspection the driver for your school's improvement by:

1. Talking about teaching and learning in relation to children.
2. Embedding initiatives with a clear purpose.
3. Referring to outcomes for pupils, rather than outcomes for departments or year groups.
4. Providing effective CPD to ensure a love of learning and progress towards mastery for the team.
5. Refusing time-consuming and irrelevant paperwork driven by what the school down the road says about its inspection.
6. Doing what is right for your staff, pupils and parents.

Why this matters
Schools should do what they do for the young people they serve, not for inspections.

Top tip
Leaders absolutely do need to consider the expectations of the inspectorate, but keeping staff focused on the pupils will ultimately lead to better inspection outcomes.

#131 Reducing staff workload

With workload the word on every educator's lips, leaders have a duty to ensure that all practices in school are worthwhile. Try these top tips for keeping an eye on workload across your school.

1. Ask your staff about workload. You might get more honest responses if they can be submitted anonymously.
2. Keep track of subject leaders' plans. Leaders at every level want to achieve great things, but plans need to be monitored with the bigger picture in mind.
3. Avoid last-minute observations or scrutinies. Any necessary monitoring ought to be scheduled evenly across the year.
4. If something 'pops up', make sure you drop something else. It's inevitable that events or tasks will arise unexpectedly, but adjusting expectations elsewhere will help to maintain the balance.
5. Be aware of workload flash points such as exam times, report-writing terms or parents' evenings.
6. Out with the old, in with the new. For every new initiative, ask yourself which old one can be dropped.
7. Ensure workload appears on the agenda at termly SLT meetings. That way, it remains a priority throughout the year.

Why it works
Leaders have the best view of the bigger picture and therefore have the insight to monitor and improve workload. Staff perform best when they have work-life balance.

Top tip
Don't forget to keep an eye on your own workload, too!

WORKLOAD REVIEW

I have a good work-life balance

| Completely disagree | Disagree | Somewhat agree | Agree | Completely agree |

Comments

Senior leaders take workload into consideration

| Completely disagree | Disagree | Somewhat agree | Agree | Completely agree |

Comments

Work I am asked to complete is reasonable within my role

| Completely disagree | Disagree | Somewhat agree | Agree | Completely agree |

Comments

If I felt there was unnecessary or excessive workload, I would speak openly to leaders about this

| Completely disagree | Disagree | Somewhat agree | Agree | Completely agree |

Comments

I feel that workload could be reduced

| Greatly | Somewhat | A little | Workload can't/doesn't need to be reduced |

Comments

Any other comments?

#132 Going beyond the specialism

How often are secondary teachers expected to teach subjects outside their specialism? This can be daunting and time-consuming, so if you, as a leader, must ask them to go beyond their specialism, here's how to make sure they are supported to do so.

1. Provide CPD. Sending the teacher on training sessions is necessary if they are expected to teach an unfamiliar subject.
2. Create a teacher's pack including a list of key knowledge and skills to be taught, a list of websites, books and a range of relevant resources.
3. Provide additional planning time.
4. Provide a mentor. The teacher should have someone to support them on a regular basis.
5. Allocate time for the teacher to observe good practice and explore pupils' books.

Why try this?

Teaching outside your specialism can feel intimidating and create additional workload pressures. And without the right support, there could be a negative impact on pupil outcomes.

Top tip

Being highly supportive of teachers who teach outside their specialism and thanking them for their efforts will have a positive impact on how they work.

#133 Preparing to interview

Conducting interviews that are purposeful and positive is a great way to make sure the school and the candidates all benefit from the process. The interview process might be the only opportunity to get to know a candidate before you sign them up to work with you. Try this interview preparation method to design questions that give you the information you really need.

1. Decide on the personal qualities you need on your team. For example, if you have a team full of extroverts, perhaps you need a more introverted personality to bring a bit of balance.
2. Decide on the professional qualities you need on your team. For example, perhaps the team is lacking forward-planning skills.
3. Decide what type of teacher the class or cohorts in mind might respond best to. Perhaps you have a group of disengaged pupils, a very able cohort or a group displaying challenging behaviour.
4. Use your thoughts about steps 1, 2 and 3 to identify the questions that will give you the information you want.
5. List your questions under the following section headings: personal qualities, professional qualities, cohort qualities.

Why it works
This method allows you to avoid using generic interview questions, which won't help you to find the team member you truly need.

Top tip
Make sure you ask important questions about safeguarding. For creative interview questions, read the next idea.

#134 Mixing up interview questions

Interviewing potential staff can quickly become dull if you use the same old questions. Choose a selection of these thought-provoking questions to get the best out of your candidates.

- What do you think about lesson gradings?
- What do you think about marking?
- What do you think about parental engagement?
- What do you think about the national curriculum?
- What makes you angry?
- Who has inspired you in education?
- Who gets on your nerves?
- Who do you think should be accountable for progress?
- Who do you go to for help?
- Would you rather close the school to pupils an hour early every day or on a Friday all day?
- Would you rather plan all lessons four weeks in advance or plan each lesson the day before?
- Would you rather go on a school trip to London Zoo or to the local woods?
- Would you rather work at a school with an unlimited budget but challenging behaviour, or little budget but impeccable behaviour?
- If you could change one thing about education, what would it be?
- If you had to ban one object from the classroom, what would it be?
- If you use one phrase in class all the time, what is it?
- If you want to get the attention of the class, what do you do?

Why try this?
Choosing questions to find out about a candidate's views and approaches can help you to make the right appointment.

Top tip
Avoid preconceived ideas about the answers. Everyone has different views on education and these questions will simply provide an insight into the candidates' thoughts.

#135 How to pitch a new idea[10]

Trying out fresh approaches can feel like a risk or even a waste of time, but when they work, they can have an incredible whole-school impact. It isn't always easy to pitch to those in charge, so try this 'hear me out' method.

1. Don't be tempted to talk to anyone about your idea straight away. Let it rest for two days. If you're still as excited after the wait, you know your idea has some staying power.
2. Research and read. Think it through. Be thorough.
3. Be prepared to talk in-depth about why your idea is good.
4. Think about the impact it could have on pupils' learning, teaching staff and parents.
5. All ideas have downfalls, limitations or sticking points. Predict these and plan ways to overcome them to help you argue your case.
6. Consider the feedback. How might people react to your idea? Plan your responses.
7. Request a 30-minute slot to discuss your idea with the relevant person. Don't be tempted to run into their office and share the idea on *your* schedule – no one likes an idea being sprung upon them and your efforts might be wasted if you catch the person at the wrong time.
8. Present your idea confidently. Ask for a chance to trial the initiative in your class.
9. Trial it properly. Give your idea the best shot you can and teach what you preach.
10. Book another meeting with the SLT explaining how the trial went and what might need to be amended.

Why it works
If your idea is truly good, prove it by knowing it, living it and adapting it to perfection. The proof is in the pudding!

Top tip
Keep communication open throughout your trial so that the idea is fresh in the minds of your SLT.

---

10 Hanna Beech, 'How to pitch a new idea', *Teacher Toolkit*, 2018, teachertoolkit.co.uk/2018/11/14/one-minute-cpd-38

#136 Adopting staff initiatives

Do your team often approach you with fresh ideas? It's exciting to hear their thoughts, but when you have to keep an eye on workload and ensure good progress for the pupils, how do you choose which initiatives to adopt? These tips will help you to decide.

1. When someone comes to you with an idea, make sure they are ready to express the aim, actions and impact of their initiative before you agree to move forward with anything.
2. Do your research. Make sure you know what the initiative fully entails before you give it the go-ahead.
3. Ask yourself these two vital questions: how will this idea affect the children? And how will it affect the staff?
4. Decide if you will move forward with the idea.

Why it works
If an initiative is presented, it's worth making sure it will have a positive impact on all stakeholders before you give it the green light.

Top tip
If you do go ahead with the initiative, what 'old' process could be removed to balance the workload? If you don't go ahead with it, explain to your colleague why the idea can't be implemented at this time.

Further resources

Diana Osagie, *Courageous Leadership*, 2019

Andy Buck, *Leadership Matters: how leaders at all levels can create great schools*, John Catt Educational, 2016

Gary Jones, *Evidence-Based School Leadership and Management: a practical guide*, Sage Publications, 2018

Stephen R Covey, *The 7 Habits of Highly Effective People*, The Free Press, 1989

Julia Steward, *Sustaining Resilience for Leadership: stories from education*, John Catt Educational, 2018

Sonia Gill, *Successful Difficult Conversations in School*, John Catt Educational, 2018

Ken Blanchard and Spencer Johnson, *The New One Minute Manager*, Harper, 2015

Rob Carpenter, *A Manifesto for Excellence in Schools*, Bloomsbury Education, 2018

Chapter 7:
Learning environments

We spend so much time in the grounds of our schools: in the classrooms, the bustling corridors, the playground landscapes and the staffroom (actually, not *that* much time in the staffroom!). Children also spend a large proportion of their lives in school. So, it seems sensible to think carefully about the impact the school environment has on us all.

It's obvious that working in a cramped, dark and cluttered space for eight hours a day, five days a week, would have an impact on our wellbeing, stemming from discomfort, overstimulation or understimulation, poor light conditions or lack of adequate ventilation. A study commissioned by the Department for Business, Innovation and Skills[1] suggested that low subjective wellbeing in workers could have a detrimental impact on workplace performance. My first-hand experience (and common sense) tells me that this is certainly the case in classrooms and other school spaces. To put it simply, environment affects wellbeing, and wellbeing affects performance. If we are seeking to optimise teaching performance, which should lead to good progress for pupils, then we need to optimise our learning spaces.

When it comes to turning classrooms into fantastic learning environments, the educators I've worked with so far in my career tend to either do the bare minimum or go all out. But to really maximise the potential of our classrooms, we need to look beyond displays, working walls and interactive surfaces and

1   Alex Bryson, John Forth and Lucy Stokes (National Institute of Economic and Social Research), *Does Worker Wellbeing Affect Workplace Performance?*, Department for Business, Innovation and Skills, 2014, tinyurl.com/ttdvdet

think in broader terms: structure, accessibility, ambience and layout. Look at the words in the table below and score your setting from 0 to 5 against each one (0 – doesn't describe my setting at all; 5 – describes my setting perfectly).

Drab		Bright		Inspiring	
Clean		Spacious		Overstimulating	
Spotless		Natural		Unchanging	
Modern		Clear		Ever-changing	
Dirty		Messy		Child-focused	
Inspiring		Light		Stuffy	
Dark/dimly lit		Dusty		Noisy	
Cluttered		Cramped		Tranquil	
Accessible		Comfortable		Welcoming	
Shabby		Sparse		Considered	
Secure		Safe		Airy	

Next, consider the strengths and weaknesses of your school or classroom environment. Choose three words that you wish described your school or classroom and ask yourself what changes you can make, within the physical and financial limitations, to help your space fit that description. A simple reflection such as this helps us to see our surroundings with fresh eyes, and with a little thought often comes inspiration.

It's strange how you only see your surroundings clearly for a short time. The sights, smells and structures soon fade into the background. My current school is housed in a brand-new building, whereas my previous school was in a well-maintained but far older building. When I first moved settings, I was awed by the shiny, modern premises. I noticed something new every day. But as I learned which doors led to rooms and which led to stock cupboards (not embarrassing at all), I thought less and less about the space I was in. According to neurologists, our brains sift out unnecessary information through a process known as sensory filtering. Rather than attempt to direct our attention to everything that surrounds us (which would be a bit overwhelming), the brain selects the information in the environment that it deems to be useful. In my case, once I had become accustomed to my new setting (and stopped trying to walk into cupboards), my brain started to perceive the space in a different way. I only noticed *new* changes to the school: a fresh art display in the entrance hall; a plimsoll on the stairs; a new role-play area in the Reception classroom.

For this reason, changes to a classroom environment need to be handled with great care. Imagine a classroom that looks different every day: the pupils would be perpetually distracted by their surroundings, trying to re-establish an understanding of the space. On the other hand, never changing anything could leave the room feeling uninspiring and unloved, and it could go unseen by pupils. If children's brains are drawn to novel visual stimuli, why don't teachers exploit this by regularly constructing useful working walls and displaying vocabulary prompts and images?

Because we're busy, that's why.

Frankly, creating an all-singing, all-dancing working wall isn't always going to be top of the priority list (and probably shouldn't be). So why even include a chapter on learning environments? Well, making classroom and school spaces feel and look good, while optimising their use, doesn't *have* to be the thorn in the educator's side.

Take three things into account when designing and organising your teaching space: your school policies, your personal preferences and the needs of your pupils. Different schools have different expectations – and different pupils, too – so what works in one setting doesn't always translate to the next. It's not always about time-consuming wall displays. Just a few carefully considered changes could create spaces that enhance our teaching and the pupils' learning, having more of a positive impact than we might have thought possible.

#137 Wall displays

Make displays quick for staff at your school to create, yet effective and aesthetically pleasing for pupils.

1. **Pupil work:** exhibiting children's work can enhance pride in learning and offer good examples for others to learn from.
2. **Learning-led displays:** less is more, so only put up what is useful for learning. We need to keep a handle on our workload – don't waste time creating overloaded displays.
3. **Word walls:** key vocabulary for topics or core texts can be useful for teachers and pupils to refer to during lessons.
4. **Hessian backing:** using hessian means you don't have to change the backing for every display. It doesn't tear and no unsightly staple holes are left behind, so it's a cost-effective option. And the neutral colour means pupils can focus on the displayed work rather than a garish background.
5. **A balance of beige and bright:** research has found that too much or too little colour can negatively affect learners.[2] Try to have light-coloured walls and add flashes of colour in wall displays or even a painted feature wall.

Why try this?
You may think displays are a waste of your time, but it's likely that your school has some expectations. You can use research to ensure your efforts don't go to waste.

Top tip
Classroom displays can quickly become wallpaper, so take the time to update them. If leaders can allocate time or support to update displays, this could reduce workload concerns.

---

2   Peter Barrett, Fay Davies, Yufan Zhang and Lucinda Barrett, *Clever Classrooms: summary report of the HEAD project*, University of Salford, 2015, tinyurl.com/rnok7pw

#138 **Surface displays**

Fed up of the clutter on the surfaces in your classroom? Make better use of these areas by creating surface displays.

1. Consider your current foundation topic, maths focus or English core text.
2. Create a quick list of props, artefacts and books that link to the topic. For example, if you're studying *Charlie and the Chocolate Factory*, you might include other Roald Dahl texts, a Wonka bar, an everlasting gobstopper and Willy Wonka's top hat. If your maths topic is fractions, try fraction fans, wooden pizza or cake role play, an egg box with different coloured eggs and so on.
3. Source the objects on the list, or use your (or your teaching assistant's) creative skills to make models of the props or artefacts.
4. Display the objects on the surface, along with a label or question prompts.

Why try this?
Displays are often two-dimensional, but surface displays keep things interesting.

Top tip
If you're a leader who wants teachers to go the extra mile with surface displays, make sure you give them a dedicated time to prepare these (such as a staff-meeting slot).

#139 Classroom layouts[3]

The debate about seating arrangements is a big one, so we won't go down that road! All I will say is: how teachers structure their classrooms ought to be their choice. Here are some of the options.

1. **Rows.** They can be considered more traditional or 'old school', but rows are the first choice of many teachers. A study of the effects of seating arrangements indicated that pupils were more engaged in their task when seated in rows.[4]
2. **Horseshoe/semi-circle.** This allows pupils to look towards each other or the teacher. Research has shown that this arrangement generates a higher number of questions from pupils,[5] but it can take up a fair amount of space.
3. **Pairs.** Seating pupils in pairs on their own table is a variation on row seating and is traditionally used for testing, although it's not uncommon in day-to-day lessons. It also allows for focused paired collaboration.
4. **Groups.** Group seating is common in primary settings and is useful when you want pupils to work as a collective. The disadvantages include more off-topic talk and less focus.

Why this matters
How you position pupils in your classroom can affect their learning, so it's worth thinking about.

Top tip
Remember, seating arrangements are not final. You can always mix it up, moving the tables around to suit particular tasks.

3 Hanna Beech, 'Table arrangement choices', *Teacher Toolkit*, 2019, teachertoolkit.co.uk/2019/02/27/one-minute-cpd-49
4 Nigel Hastings and Joshua Schwieso, 'Tasks and tables: the effects of seating arrangements on task engagement in primary classrooms', *Educational Research*, 37.3, 1995, tinyurl.com/taz5e7b
5 Alexandra Marx, Urs Fuhrer and Terry Hartig, 'Effects of classroom seating arrangements on children's question-asking', *Learning Environments Research*, 2, 1999, tinyurl.com/vs94zv5

#140 Who sits where?

Deciding where to seat pupils can feel like an impossible task. Personality clashes, peer influences, motivation for learning and special educational needs should all be taken into account. Use these reflection prompts to help you get started.

1. **What space is available?** Sketch out the seating layout in your classroom before you decide where pupils will be seated.
2. **Who must be placed near the front?** Pupils with visual or hearing impairments often need to be closer to the teacher. Children with autistic spectrum conditions might prefer to sit at the front where there is less sensory information to absorb (read more about autism in chapter 4). And pupils who are highly disruptive or easily distracted might also be better placed at the front.
3. **Who must be seated near the door?** Some pupils might need to leave the room regularly, and pupils who are often late to class might appreciate being seated by the door so they can make a more discreet entrance.
4. **Who works well together?** If you know the pupils already, you will have a good idea of successful pairings. You will also be aware of which children are unlikely to work well together.
5. **Is ability a consideration?** Research has highlighted the benefits of mixed-ability seating compared with ability groupings.[6] It's worth considering which pupils will help one another and which might be so far ahead that they won't benefit from mixed groups.

Why try this?
Think carefully about seating arrangements and you will save yourself the challenge of having to move pupils around during lessons.

Top tip
Mix up the seating positions throughout the academic year, so that pupils get to experience working with each other. In primary settings, the subject being taught is also a consideration.

---

6   Antonina Tereshchenko, Becky Francis, Louise Archer, Jeremy Hodgen, Anna Mazenod, Becky Taylor, David Pepper and Mary-Claire Travers, 'Learners' attitudes to mixed-attainment grouping: examining the views of students of high, middle and low attainment', *Research Papers in Education*, 34.4, 2019, tinyurl.com/wk2pu6b

CLASS SEATING

Sit near the front	Work ineffectively together	Sit near the door
Work effectively together		Special considerations

#141 Organising your desk[7]

Research suggests that working in a cluttered space can produce anxiety.[8] With a non-stop stream of things going on, it's no wonder teachers' desks become overloaded, so try this method to make your workspace as clear and clutter-free as possible.

1. Source a set of five desk drawers or in-trays.
2. Label them:
   - To do – things that need action from you, e.g. forms, letters, lists.
   - To read – things you need to cast your eye over, e.g. policies, research, articles.
   - To keep – important documents that you will need soon, e.g. parents' evening times, risk assessments.
   - To file – things that need to be filed away, e.g. notes from a meeting, data analysis.
   - To store – keepsakes or things you want to throw away, but not in front of people, e.g. pictures from pupils, cards.
3. Once a week, set aside 10 minutes to sort through each tray/drawer.

Why it works
Having specific areas for different documents saves you having to hunt through a huge pile of paperwork when you need something, and makes clearing a backlog of paper far easier. In addition to this, keeping documents out of sight is important for data protection purposes.

Top tip
Always find time to tidy your desk before the end of the day. There's nothing worse than starting a new day with a messy desk.

7 Hanna Beech, 'Organise your desk', *Teacher Toolkit*, 2018, teachertoolkit.co.uk/2018/10/17/one-minute-cpd-35
8 Lenny R Vartanian, Kristin M Kernan and Brian Wansink, 'Clutter, chaos, and overconsumption: the role of mind-set in stressful and chaotic food environments', *Environment and Behavior*, 49.2, 2017, tinyurl.com/r9kh5tj

#142 Clutter-free classrooms

When you share your working space with 30 young people, clutter can accumulate – and fast. Here are some quick-fix ways to make your classroom a mess-free zone.

1. Spend five purposeful minutes assessing your space. Note the red zones (extreme clutter), amber zones (some clutter) and green zones (no clutter).
2. Start with the red zones. What is creating the clutter?
3. Share your findings with the class – after all, the classroom doesn't belong to one person, but many.
4. Explain that you need everyone to make an effort to ensure all spaces are clutter-free, talking about the positive impact this will have.
5. Allocate your pupil councillors or other children to keep an eye on clutter zones. They should report to the adults when clutter begins to build.

Why try this?
Clear spaces are calmer spaces.

Top tip
At the end of each term, spend 10 minutes clearing the classroom. You will begin the next term with a clear space and therefore a clear mind!

#143 Streamlining your space

Furniture, resources and even possessions can contribute to clutter. But what should you keep, what should you rehome and what should you chuck?

1. **Tables and chairs.** Count the number in your classroom. I once found that I had three unnecessary tables and six unnecessary chairs – these take up a lot of space. Get them moved out of the classroom by liaising with the grounds team.
2. **Storage.** Explore the tray units and any cupboards in your classroom. Could any be removed, thus making more space for the pupils?
3. **Unused resources.** Classrooms often collect resources over the years, with each teacher leaving a legacy behind as they move on. Sift through the resources in your classroom and ask the pupils which they have never used. Unwanted resources can be rehomed with colleagues or taken to charity shops.
4. **Books, games and other items.** There's no sense in keeping torn books or games with half the pieces missing, so go through the books, games and trinkets you have in class. You may well uncover some treasures that have been hiding under a pile of old resources or shoved in a cupboard. If you find something interesting as you clear away the junk, be sure to place it in a visible location and make it accessible.
5. **Send things home.** Holding on to too much work can contribute to mess. Work that has been created and celebrated in class can be taken home by pupils.

Why it works

Streamlining your classroom makes way for important resources and allows furniture to be used effectively.

Top tip

It would be wise to check with senior and subject leaders before you get rid of resources or furniture, just in case.

#144 Better book corners

Is your book corner just a pile of cushions and a stack of books? Here's how to revamp these spaces.

1. **Create a cosy spot.** Use cushions, bean bags, draped fabric or a small sofa to make a comfortable, cave-like area that invites readers inside.
2. **Get decent books.** This sounds obvious, but without good books that interest your class, a book corner is not going to work. School leaders may need to provide a budget for this, or you could ask parents or book shops for donations.
3. **Basket swaps.** Place a selection of books into a basket and arrange a basket swap between classes each term to keep the reading material fresh. You might want to label all books with the name of their home classroom and keep a list of books in your basket, so they don't get mixed up.
4. **Book trailers.** Each week, read an extract or blurb from a great book. Place the book on a stand in the book corner, inviting pupils to read it if they were inspired by the 'trailer'.
5. **Keep order.** Group genres or authors together in a way that makes sense to you.
6. **Sound blockers.** Reading in a noisy environment is hard. Keep a basket of headphones in the book corner for pupils to put on when they want to get lost in a book.
7. **'Read me' cards.** Choose a few books you think pupils might like. Create 'read me' cards by writing a sentence or two about each book's characters or events. Slip these into the books' front covers.
8. **Reviews.** Leave a reviews sheet (see opposite) on a clipboard, asking pupils to rate the book they read in the book corner.

Why try this?
If you are going to have a book corner, make it enticing and effective.

Top tip
Assign two children as 'book corner bosses'. They can ensure order is maintained, choose texts for book trailers and keep an eye on who is reading.

BOOK REVIEWS

Book title/author	Star rating	Reviewed by

#145 Making the most of desks

Desks are obviously great for sitting at and for resting books on, but what else could pupils do with them? Try these alternative ways of using classroom desks to enhance learning.

1. **Draw on the desks.** Most school desks can be drawn on in whiteboard pen, which easily rubs off when needed. Pupils can make notes, calculate answers or draw angles and shapes on their desks.
2. **Cover the desks in paper.** If you're not keen on drawing directly on to the desks, throw some backing paper over them. Your pupils can make notes without being restricted by size.
3. **Stand at the desks.** For certain lessons, standing up at desks is far more convenient. Interestingly, I've taught a fair few pupils who prefer to stand rather than sit at their desk. If it works for them, I say let them do it.
4. **Tape across the desks for maths.** Using masking tape to create lines can be handy for identifying and measuring angles, calculating the area and perimeter, or exploring types of lines.
5. **Tape to clarify boundaries.** When pupils share a desk, this can sometimes cause distress. Taping off the desk to create boundaries can help.

Why try this?
These ideas will help you to mix up the ways in which learning unfolds.

Top tip
Consider what you keep on your desks. Pupils might need resources, but large quantities of these just get in the way.

#146 Open doors

Do you teach with your classroom door open? Although noise pollution is an obvious concern, there are multiple benefits to teaching with an open door.

1. Colleagues will feel welcome to enter your classroom.
2. Visitors can enter discreetly, so your pupils won't feel fazed.
3. When senior leaders want to visit the classroom, they don't feel they are interrupting the lesson.
4. You won't be disturbed by the constant opening and closing of the door as pupils, leaders or colleagues come and go.
5. The classroom and corridor become fluid spaces, allowing pupils to learn in the corridor with ease.

Why it works

Of course, open-door cultures are not born from simply keeping classroom doors open. Senior leaders have much work to do in order to build school cultures that foster openness and trust. Leaders must consider the systems for monitoring and appraisal, asking themselves how these might affect their staff on a team and individual level. Yet perhaps physically open doors can help towards creating an open-door culture. Read more about this in an article I wrote for *Tes*.[9]

Top tip

Keeping the door open might not be an option if you have fire doors, or if you have a pupil with a hearing impairment in your class.

---

9   Hanna Beech, 'Why you should keep your classroom door open', *Tes*, 2019, tes.com/news/why-you-should-keep-your-classroom-door-open

#147 Corridors as learning spaces

How often do you use the corridor as an additional learning environment? If you want to use your corridor for learning, here's how.

1. **Be prepared.** Make sure you have a learning space set up for corridor work. You will need all necessary resources for the lesson, including seating and surfaces to write on.
2. **Inform and select the pupils.** Some children will be really keen on the idea of working in the corridor – just make sure they are keen for the right reasons! Only send them to work in the corridor once you have completed your direct instruction.
3. **Keep a close eye on them.** Leave the door open and monitor the learning regularly.

Why try this?
Classrooms can become cramped and sometimes stale places to learn, and the noise and bustle might give some pupils a desire to retreat to a quieter space. As a leader, I love to see pupils learning in all areas of the school environment.

Top tip
Choose your timing wisely. Using the corridor as an extension of the classroom won't always work.

#148 Green spaces

Do you have any plants in your school or classroom? Multiple studies have shown that potted plants have positive effects on workforces, including fewer health complaints, increased attendance and higher productivity.[10] Go green by trying these quick suggestions.

1. Decide which type of plants you want. Jade plants, African violets, snake plants, cacti, weeping figs or spider plants are good choices – they look nice and are easy to keep!
2. Provide each class with a potted plant to get them started.
3. Add large potted plants to corridors and office reception areas.
4. Share research on the benefits with the staff team.

Why try this?
Research aside, plants make a space look and feel good.

Top tip
Allocate some pupils to water the plants each week.

---

10 'The positive effects of office plants', *Nursery Papers*, 6, 2010, tinyurl.com/wxrsfqu

#149 Bright and breezy

Can fresh air and natural light really make that much difference to learning? Research indicates that they can.[11] With outcomes such as higher levels of concentration, better behaviour and improved exam
results, this no-cost approach really is worth trying.

1. Keep the blinds and curtains open.
2. Keep the windows open.
3. As long as noise won't be problematic, keep the
   door open to allow airflow.

It's that simple.

Why try this?
Low levels of sunlight have been linked with increased cortisol (stress hormone), while a lack of fresh air has been connected to low wellbeing.

Top tip
Get into the habit of opening windows and blinds when you arrive in your classroom.

---

11 Steven Edward Higgins, Elaine Hall, Kate Wall, Pam Woolner and C McCaughey, *The Impact of School Environments: a literature review*, Centre for Learning and Teaching, School of Education, Communication and Language Science, University of Newcastle, 2005, tinyurl.com/sfugu25

#150 Teaching and learning outside

Learning environments can extend beyond the four walls of the classroom and working in a different space can boost pupils' motivation. Most schools have some outdoor space and some are fortunate enough to have wonderful green areas to enjoy. Here are some great reasons to take teaching and learning outside, provided by the Children & Nature Network.

1. Inspire pupils and improve their creativity.
2. Get fresh air and enjoy nature, while improving academic achievement.
3. Improve pupils' focus and attention.
4. Increase pupils' enthusiasm for learning.
5. Increase pupils' impulse control.

Why this matters
Multiple research studies have shown the benefits of spending time in nature on academic performance; find out more on the Children & Nature Network website (childrenandnature. org). Additionally, so much of the curriculum links to the outside world.

Top tip
While planning lessons, ask yourself how you can (meaningfully) include outdoor learning.

#151 Role-play areas

Need some inspiration for successful role-play areas for your Reception class? Here are six suggestions.

1. **Rope the parents in.** There might be parents or carers who can contribute to creating role-play areas. Carpenters or gardeners might have props or be able to make something special for you!
2. **Make links to reading, writing and maths.** For example, in a cafe role-play area you might provide a till and 'money' for front-of-house staff, notepads for waiters/waitresses, and even make your own menu templates.
3. **Keep it real!** Using real objects, props and tools (as long as it's safe to do so) will mean you don't have to buy or make resources.
4. **Get creative.** Try pet-grooming parlours, space stations, garden centres, cafes, sweet shops, factories, castles, forests, bakeries, beaches, gyms and fire stations. You might want to try deconstructed role-play areas, which have no theme but offer a wide range of materials to help children build their own scenarios.
5. **Model the play.** Often Reception pupils engage in role play relating to their real-life experiences, but if the role-play space is totally unfamiliar (let's face it, not all four-year-olds have been to the hairdresser or beach) they will have limited experience to draw upon. To alleviate this problem, tell them stories or anecdotes about the place and model the play to them.
6. **Show us all.** If you spot some great role play taking place, either film it or ask the children if they will re-enact it in front of their peers. This modelling of good practice embeds effective ways of using the role-play area.

Why try this?
Children enjoy pretend play, learning much about the real world as they use their imaginations.

Top tip
Take photos of your role-play corners, briefly reviewing how successful they were as a reminder for future creations.

#152 Outdoor learning

The outdoor environment is often considered to play a significant role in early education. So, how can you enhance your early years outside spaces?

1. **Create book-rich spots.** Make sure you display a wide range of books outside. These might link to current themes or concepts being learned, and can be strategically placed in key areas.
2. **Ignite curiosity through exploration.** Placing something mysterious or intriguing outside for children to explore can boost motivation and encourage enquiry and play. Remember, anything that goes into the learning space should have a purpose.
3. **Provide varied opportunities.** It's easy to offer the same activities to develop the early learning goals. Keep things fresh by regularly sharing ideas about how the outside space can maximise learning potential.
4. **Go green.** Bring as much greenery to the outdoor environment as possible. You could set up a growing area for pupils to observe the growth of herbs and other plants.
5. **Be gender-blind.** Don't always put the trucks and diggers in the sandpit or just dolls in the dolls' house – mix things up with some dinosaurs in the house and fairies in the mud kitchen. That way, all children feel invited to play with all the toys in all areas (read more about banishing gender stereotypes in chapter 4).

Why try this?
Reflecting on how to keep the outside learning space fresh and exciting could revitalise child-initiated learning.

Top tip
Pinterest (pinterest.co.uk) can offer you far more ideas for your outdoor environments than I ever could.

#153 Sharing ideas

Teachers often have unique styles and interesting ways of setting up their classrooms, but time constraints mean it is rare to have the chance to explore colleagues' classrooms with the intention of sharing practice. If you need inspiration, why not request a classroom exploration session as part of a staff meeting and see what you can learn from your colleagues. Use the following prompts.

1. How is work celebrated?
2. How has the environment been used to enhance the learning?
3. What books or resources are available?
4. Are there any interactive areas?
5. How does the classroom layout contribute to the feel of the environment?
6. What ideas can I take away to try?

Why it works
Learning from colleagues is a powerful yet somewhat untapped tool. All the inspiration and motivation you need might be just down the corridor!

Top tip
Remember that everyone is different. Use the experience as an opportunity for inspiration, not comparison.

#154 Artwork for walls

How much art does your school have on display? Here are four ways to make the most of artwork in your corridors and learning spaces.

1. Ask staff to vote for famous artworks to display. Choose 6-8 pieces by a diverse range of famous and undiscovered artists. You could include the work of local artists, too.
2. Decide where the artwork can be displayed around the school. Liaise with the site manager about this.
3. Purchase the art as posters or prints, buying some simple frames, too. Large A2 posters look striking.
4. Ask staff or pupils to write a brief review on a display card that can be placed next to the piece.
5. Host an assembly to promote the new artworks. Show each piece and challenge children to spot them across the school. Discuss the content and contexts of the works, and share information about the artists.

Why it works
Exposure to well-known or undiscovered artists and their work is a great way of promoting art as a subject and growing pupils' knowledge.

Top tip
Classes could each vote for their favourite artwork, creating their own work inspired by the piece and displaying this around school.

211

#155 **First impressions**

What might it feel like to enter your school as a first-time visitor? Use this 'reflect, connect, respect, react' strategy to consider the first impression you are making.

1. **Reflect.** Write down the ideal experience you want a visitor to have at your school. Consider what you would like them to see, hear, smell and think when they arrive. Perhaps you'd like them to see lots of pupil work, some media coverage or staff photos. Create a 'Welcome to our school' questionnaire for a visitor with questions such as 'What is the first thing you notice as you enter the school?', 'How welcome did the office staff make you feel?', 'Did you see any pupil work?' and 'Was there a clean and clear feeling upon entrance?'
2. **Connect.** Ask an educator from a local school to pay a visit, explaining that you want to get a second opinion about how your school appears to a first-time visitor. Share your 'Welcome to our school' questionnaire with them, asking for their honest views.
3. **Respect.** Thank the visitor for their views and effort. Reflect on their responses and offer to return the favour if they would like a review of their space.
4. **React.** Take the feedback and react accordingly. Whether you get some art on the walls or reduce the amount of clutter in the entrance area, make sure you use the experience to improve your environment.

Why try this?
Because first impressions really do count. It's easy to become numb to your environment.

Top tip
Make sure the staff who welcome visitors do so in a genuine, friendly and helpful manner. See the next idea for more on this.

#156 A warm welcome

Who welcomes visitors into your school? Even if you've got the cleanest, most appealing space in the universe, it's the people who set the tone. Ensure the reception staff are as much an advert for your school as the entrance area.

1. **Greetings.** Visitors should be greeted quickly and politely. There's nothing more unwelcoming than standing in front of a desk while the person behind it stares at their computer screen as if you don't exist. A smile and a 'Hello, please give me one moment' can go a long way.
2. **Helpful heroes.** People who arrive at reception often want something. Make sure the office team help in every way possible, even if they simply pass on a message or find someone else who might be able to assist. No job is too big or too small (within reason!).
3. **Familiar faces.** Ask the office team to make sure that regular visitors to the school are treated with familiarity. Knowing their name and the reason for their visit creates a good impression.
4. **Open the hatch.** Sliding hatches at an office are a physical barrier that can be very unwelcoming. If there has to be a hatch, keep it open, at least during high-traffic times.
5. **Phone calls.** Ensure that phone calls are answered, but only if the conversation is not going to be abruptly interrupted. If there is a phone call that *has* to be answered, ask if the person doesn't mind waiting for one moment.

Why try this?
Reception staff are often the face of the school. The team should embody the school values as they encounter parents, potential staff or visitors.

Top tip
Remember to show appreciation to the office team; they are so vital to the running of the school.

#157 **Delightful dining**

Fed up with noisy or chaotic dining spaces? Try these ideas to create a lunchtime haven that offers a sense of community and is easier to keep clean.

1. Offer training to the meal supervisors – their role is key. Lunchtime will be far calmer if they feel well-prepared and supported.
2. Play background music. This creates a calm ambience in the dining space.
3. Don't expect silence. It's unrealistic and unenjoyable.
4. Have clear rules in place and make sure everyone is aware of these. Decide on some dining expectations and share these among staff and pupils, so that any behaviour issues can be addressed by referring back to the expectations.
5. Enjoy lunch with the pupils. This allows you to build rapport and model good dining etiquette.
6. Create a top table. This table can be reserved for pupils who have made great achievements during the week. Dress the table with place settings, flowers and a jug of squash.
7. Expect pupils to clean up after themselves. They should always clear their plates and wipe down their tables.
8. Purchase some menu holders. Place the dining expectations and some healthy eating prompts inside and position on each table.

Why try this?
Because it's easy for a dining space to become chaotic.

Top tip
Ask your school councillors to drum up pupil ideas on how to improve the aesthetics of the dining hall.

#158 Safe spaces

Where might your vulnerable pupils go if they don't feel safe? A safe space ensures every child has a place to retreat to when they feel upset, overwhelmed or worried. Here's how to make the most of your safe space.

1. **Assess the space.** Is the room accessible, welcoming and comfortable?
2. **Is the safe space resourced?** Provide a range of distractions (games, books, wordsearches, etc).
3. **Staff the area.** How can you ensure that when a child goes to the safe space, an adult is available to help them?
4. **Is it safe?** This sounds obvious, but always ensure that cupboards are locked and there is nothing dangerous in the room. Young people should be supervised.

Why try this?

Even the most supportive, ordered schools can be scary for some children. Every child deserves to be and feel safe in school.

Top tip

Make sure pupils (especially those who are vulnerable) know there is a safe space. Show them the space and explain how it is to be used.

#159 Staffroom spaces

Is your staffroom in need of a spruce? Here are some suggestions to keep it fresh, fun and friendly.

1. Ensure there is little clutter in the staffroom. Get rid of old tat that no one claims or wants.
2. Keep it clean to make it a place everyone actually wants to use.
3. Create a photo board for staff special events or social gatherings.
4. Keep it as a social space. Don't be tempted to display too much work-related material or managerial information unless totally necessary. People come to the staffroom to relax and escape for half an hour, not to worry about workload.
5. Create a 'book borrow' shelf. This can be a mixture of fiction and non-fiction for staff to share at their leisure.
6. Provide comfy and sociable seating.

Why try this?
A welcoming and pleasant space for staff to enjoy some child-free time can be a lifesaver.

Top tip
Placing a few biscuits and some fruit in the staffroom every so often will make it even more inviting. Oh, and good coffee!

Further resources

Marlynn K Clayton with Mary Beth Forton, *Classroom Spaces That Work*, Northeast Foundation for Children, 2001

Todd Finley and Blake Wiggs, *Rethinking Classroom Design*, Rowman & Littlefield, 2016

Peter Barrett, Fay Davies, Yufan Zhang and Lucinda Barrett, *Clever Classrooms: summary report of the HEAD project*, University of Salford, 2015, tinyurl.com/rnok7pw

Peter Barrett, Fay Davies, Yufan Zhang and Lucinda Barrett, 'The impact of classroom design on pupils' learning: final results of a holistic, multi-level analysis', *Building and Environment*, 89, 2015, tinyurl.com/ws5oyfl

Angela Ford, 'Planning classroom design and layout to increase pedagogical options for secondary teachers', *Educational Planning*, 25, 2016, tinyurl.com/ru2cupx

Chapter 8: Mental health and wellbeing

Talking about mental health can bring up feelings of fear, discomfort and even shame. For so long, issues surrounding mental wellbeing have been shrouded in taboo, but mental health issues don't just affect some people all of the time. Arguably, they can affect all people, some of the time. One in four adults experiences at least one diagnosable mental health issue in any given year.[1] But what does the research say about teachers? The Teacher Wellbeing Index 2019[2] found that 78% of education professionals had experienced behavioural, psychological or physical symptoms due to their work, 34% had experienced a mental health issue in the previous academic year and 84% of senior leaders were suffering from work-related stress. On top of managing their own mental health and wellbeing, school staff must also support the mental health and wellbeing of the young people in their care (and sometimes their families, too). That's a lot of pressure.

Despite big changes in the public perception of mental health issues, it is undeniable that some stigma persists. According to a 2014 research report, 39% of adults in England think people who are mentally unwell are prone to violence.[3] This type of entrenched stigma takes a long time to unravel, and this won't happen without public education and increased support for those in need. After years of underinvestment in mental health services, it seems that

---

1   *The Five Year Forward View for Mental Health*, Mental Health Taskforce to the NHS in England, 2016, tinyurl.com/gvc4or3
2   *Teacher Wellbeing Index 2019*, Education Support, tinyurl.com/yx56d88l
3   *Attitudes to Mental Illness: 2014 research report*, Time To Change, 2015, tinyurl.com/yafwhbjp

mental health is becoming more of a priority. By 2023-24, the NHS in England will have ringfenced funding of at least £2.3 billion a year, which will help an additional two million people to access high-quality, evidence-based mental health services. Children and young people's mental health services will grow faster than overall NHS funding and total mental health spending.[4] Meanwhile, campaigns such as Time To Change, run by the charities Mind and Rethink Mental Illness, are working to shift perspectives and end discrimination against people with mental health conditions.

One way for individuals to help lessen the stigma is to think more carefully about the language they use. How often do we hear 'Are you mad?', 'He went psycho', 'Are they mental?' or 'She's insane' in the classroom and beyond? These terms, although often not intended to cause offence, perpetuate harmful stereotypes and make people suffering from mental illness feel as though their condition is something to be ashamed of. We all need to commit to avoiding these terms.

Think about a society in which we can openly discuss the factors that contribute to mental health issues. For example, adverse childhood experiences (ACEs) are known to have a lifelong impact on health and behaviour; they can include domestic violence, parental abandonment, being a victim of neglect or abuse, and having a parent with a mental illness.[5] Although poverty itself is not considered an ACE (and it's important to remember that mental illness is not financially selective about who it strikes), it can make managing ACEs significantly more challenging. Evidence shows that children from low-income households are up to three times more likely to develop mental health problems than children from high-income households.[6] This extract from a blog post[7] by Dr Morag Treanor of Stirling University makes some points about the links between poverty and ACEs that I think all schools should consider:

> 'While the majority of children living in poverty are not affected by multiple ACEs there is a significant proportion of families with multiple ACEs who experience poverty. And when poverty and ACEs coincide they become more than the sum of their parts. When a child lives with ACEs, and also lives in poverty, the conditions are ripe for long-lasting

4   *NHS Mental Health Implementation Plan 2019/20 – 2023/24*, NHS, 2019, tinyurl.com/y4fnoqq3
5   'Adverse childhood experiences', NHS Health Scotland, tinyurl.com/vea7bcy, accessed 2020
6   Michael Marmot, *Fair Society, Healthy Lives: strategic review of health inequalities in England post-2010*, The Marmot Review, 2010, tinyurl.com/y93feycd
7   Morag Treanor, 'Poverty and adverse childhood experiences', Children 1st, 2018, tinyurl.com/yx5pwtnb

trauma, or toxic stress, which is devastating to children in childhood, and which continues on into adulthood. The trauma associated with the combination of ACEs and poverty makes it more likely for children to experience deeper and more prolonged levels of poverty throughout their lives and on into future generations.'

Communities have an important role to play in helping young people to overcome ACEs. If we as a society are to successfully address these issues, we have to interrogate the systems that may exacerbate them. In schools, for example, we need to reflect deeply on the ways in which we measure progress. We need to consider the effects of the reduction or complete lack of arts in some schools. We need to understand why schools feel such immense pressure that they narrow their curriculum or off-roll pupils. We need to explore why behaviour is sometimes so challenging that staff feel afraid of pupils. We need to investigate why 72% of education professionals describe themselves as stressed and 60% would not feel confident in disclosing mental health issues or unmanageable stress to their employer.[8] And we need to discuss why some schools overlook the fact that some of their approaches might be contributing to mental health problems in their staff and pupils.

I'm not suggesting that any school *intends* to contribute to mental health issues. However, in some educational settings, there might be practices that are less than adequate if we are seeking to improve the mental wellbeing of pupils and staff. We need to look beyond the decisions that some settings have to make, and instead consider the reasons *why* those choices were made. And when we begin to examine those reasons, we may discover that many decisions are being made in response to external pressures beyond the school or trust.

Talk about opening a can of worms.

Most teachers recognise the importance of being able to support pupils' mental health, but a lack of adequate training, alongside staffing issues, means many educators feel ill-equipped to identify and support mental health problems in schools. This adds more pressure to an already incredibly challenging job. What should I look for? What if I don't notice when mental health is a concern? What if I can't support them? What if I say something wrong? With little to no training in many schools, it's no wonder some teachers view mental ill health as a minefield.

If you want to develop your understanding of mental health in young people, training courses are available. There are incredible people out there, doing

---

8   *Teacher Wellbeing Index 2019*, Education Support, tinyurl.com/yx56d88l

incredible things, and the courses run by Mental Health First Aid England[9] are a great starting point. It's also worth seeking out the wonderful work of the mental health campaigner Natasha Devon (see idea #182) and the mental health specialist Dr Pooky Knightsmith. If you're a school leader, consider whether you could facilitate whole-team training, nominate someone as a mental health first-aider or improve the resources your staff have access to.

If we can develop, adopt and teach approaches to improve wellbeing, we will be better able to protect ourselves and our pupils against the effects of mental health issues. The trouble is, positive wellbeing doesn't just happen. Looking after our mental health takes work, yet we don't always make the time or effort to invest in our wellbeing – even though we know how important it is. Why is this? The psychology professor and behavioural economist Dan Ariely has studied the reasons why we make 'irrational' choices relating to our lives, our health and our wellbeing, despite knowing right from wrong when it comes to self-care. His work provides fascinating and salient insights into human behaviours and motivations; if you have time(!), it's well worth taking a look at his TED talks or reading his book *Predictably Irrational.*[10]

Another important message, which comes from the teacher Adrian Bethune via the charity Education Support, is that we must approach wellbeing and mental health in the same way we would a plane crash: put your own oxygen mask on first.[11] If you don't take the necessary steps to look after yourself, you won't be able to support the children in your care. Protecting your own mental health and wellbeing is not an indulgence or a luxury. It is a must.

Society knows that teachers are under pressure, but I'm not always sure it understands. For this reason, we are the ones who need to take charge of staff wellbeing. This isn't just about reducing workload, and it goes far deeper than yoga sessions and free cakes. It's about creating a culture where staff feel genuinely supported, understood and valued. It's the corridor conversations and moments of comradeship. It's facing the fact that we can't do it all, not for every single child, every single day. It's letting go of perfection and embracing reflection. It's knowing that if you say, 'I'm really not OK today', the people around you will be OK with that.

In this chapter, ideas #160-173 are about teacher wellbeing; don't skip them in favour of gathering inspiration about helping others. The other ideas will help

---

9 mhfaengland.org
10 Dan Ariely, *Predictably Irrational: the hidden forces that shape our decisions*, HarperCollins, 2008
11 Adrian Bethune, 'Teacher wellbeing: put your own oxygen mask on first', Education Support, tinyurl.com/ulen99k, accessed 2020

leaders to foster a culture of positive mental health in their schools, and help educators to support pupils' mental health and wellbeing.

To get you thinking about your mental wellbeing, write down two things that positively affect your mental health and two others that have a negative impact.

Impacts my mental health positively (e.g. time with friends, exercise)	Impacts my mental health negatively (e.g. working late into the evening, too much time on social media)
1	1
2	2

Consider how often you find yourself experiencing these things and the impact this has on you. Personally, I'm very aware of the factors that positively and negatively affect my mental health, but I need to exert a huge amount of self-discipline to engage in those things that make me feel good and avoid those that make me feel bad. I'm sure I can't be alone in this. I therefore offer the following mantra: self-awareness is the first step, taking action is the biggest one. Without keeping a check on your wellbeing, you are at risk of emotional and physical burnout. Don't wait for that before you act.

#160 Go hard and go home

Finding a balance between working as a teacher (or school leader) and living your life can be very challenging. Work lures you in, and when it comes to improving the lives of young people, there always seems to be more that you can do. If you feel your work-life balance going awry, try this quick and easy way to adjust the scales.

1. Choose a day of the week that doesn't have a scheduled meeting.
2. At the start of the day, make a list of up to five two-minute tasks for you to complete at the very end of the day. Keep these tasks short and easy – for example, 'Tidy my desk. Reply to the email. Set out the morning's books. Make a to-do list for tomorrow.'
3. At the end of the day, set a 10-minute timer once the children have gone.
4. In this time, go hard by moving through your tasks as quickly as you can.
5. When the timer goes off, it's time to go home – even if there are still things on the list!

Why it works

You'll be surprised how many 'quick jobs' you can steam through in a focused 10 minutes. You tick off some easy-win tasks and you get to leave early.

Top tip

Tell your colleagues that on this day, you'll be going home early. That way, if you linger too long, they'll likely remind you that you should have already left.

TWO-MINUTE TASKS

Date:			
	Task	Done	Roll on
1			
2			
3			
4			
5			
HOME TIME			

#161 **Working at home**

Do you often find yourself working into the night? We don't need to go into detail about the negative impact this has on you, your family and your teaching, but we do need to find ways to switch our brains out of work mode. There is no use in pretending that educators will never have to work from home, but until significant changes in workload occur, try these tips.

1. Jot down three things that take you the most time to do at home. Find ways to work these into your PPA or school time. Restructure your time at school to reduce the amount of work you take home.
2. Speak to your line manager or team about tasks that consume a disproportionate amount of your free time. Is this an issue for others, too? What might need to change?
3. Get tips from colleagues by asking, 'How do you manage marking/planning/reports?' You might find you're missing a trick or two!
4. Before you go home, make a list of priorities for the next day or upcoming week, with approximate timings for each task. Decide which task needs to be completed before tomorrow and take this one home.
5. Define a time limit for work and stick to it. Set an alarm – what isn't finished will have to wait.
6. Have at least one weekday where you don't complete any work at home.
7. Make a list of three things you'd love to do at home that relate to your personal life – for example, phone your best friend, visit Dad, read with the kids, paint your nails, walk the dog. Treat these things as a priority, ticking them off your list as you complete them (see the next idea for help with this).

Why this matters
In the Department for Education's Teacher Workload Survey 2019,[12] teachers and middle leaders reported working a weekly average of 12.8 hours during weekends, evenings or other out-of-school hours. For senior leaders, the average was 12.3 hours. That is far, far too much.

Top tip
If you regularly work late into the night, you need to speak to your senior leadership team. Burnout is a real thing. Ask for help.

---

12 Matt Walker, Jack Worth and Jens Van den Brand (National Foundation for Educational Research), *Teacher Workload Survey 2019: research report*, Department for Education, 2019, tinyurl.com/ruykqzk

#162 Prioritising your personal life

When someone asks you about the most important things in your life, you're likely to talk about your family, friends and loved ones. Despite this, we often fail to put those people top of our priority list, because our thoughts are full of work-related tasks and projects. Turn this around with a 'priorities planner'.

1. List between one and six important people who you feel are a priority in your life.
2. For each person, list one weekly wish relating to the two of you. This could be anything from a quick text to a weekend away. For example, 'This week, I wish to spend some time building Lego with my son and I wish to meet for a catch-up coffee with my friend.'
3. Consider the impact of fulfilling this wish on you and the other person.
4. Plan a day and time when you can fulfil the wish. This may require coordination with the person in question.
5. Write the wish into your school diary. Prioritise this wish over other tasks that might arise during the week, keeping it as a protected time.
6. Honour the wish, even if you feel busy or your thoughts are with work-related tasks.
7. Reflect on how fulfilling the wish has made you feel and what you might do next week.

Why it works
As with work-related goals, if we don't plan and justify our personal priorities, they are unlikely to happen. Taking a couple of minutes a week to plan will force you to actually prioritise your priorities.

Top tip
Don't forget yourself as a priority! That haircut, dentist appointment, quiet walk or reading time needs to be planned into your life, too.

#163 Saying no[13]

Do you find yourself saying yes when you really want to say no? Sometimes, saying no (or at least 'let me think about it') is more productive in the long run. In a podcast,[14] the education professor Doris Santoro has talked about this being the main reason why teachers leave the profession – not being able to say no and thus becoming demoralised. Here are seven moments when you ought to say no.

1. When you're on your way to a meeting and someone wants to 'have a minute'.
2. When you don't have the time to commit to a request without it impacting negatively on your mental health.
3. When you don't have the necessary skills to complete the job.
4. When you feel a request goes against your moral code.
5. When you're asked to do something beyond your physical capabilities (lifting, moving, trekking, etc).
6. When you're asked if you are 'OK' with something and you're not.
7. When you're asked if you've completed something that you haven't had time to do.

Why this matters

Saying yes when you mean no is either unfair on you or on the person making the request. More often than not, when colleagues ask something of you, their intention is good, so being honest is vital if there is any reason the request can't be fulfilled.

Top tip

If you're unsure whether your answer is yes or no, ask for a reasonable amount of time to think about the request. Remember, saying no doesn't have to mean a blanket refusal: say 'I really can't, I'm afraid' or 'Let me get back to you' to soften the blow.

---

13 Hanna Beech, 'Seven times why you should say no', *Teacher Toolkit*, 2019, teachertoolkit. co.uk/2019/07/03/one-minute-cpd-59

14 'Podcast 51: teacher ethics, burnout and demoralisation', *Teacher Toolkit*, 2019, teachertoolkit. co.uk/2019/06/15/podcast-51

#164 Put a pin in it: self-focus

Have you ever found yourself overthinking an incident that happened at work? When an interaction or experience bothers you way past home time, it can leave you feeling overwhelmed, frustrated and anxious. Try the 'put a pin in it' method to move on.

1. Set aside 15 minutes to reflect on the incident.
2. Think about what happened that led you to feel disheartened. Jot it down in one sentence.
3. Ask yourself why this bothered you so much. Write this down in one sentence.
4. Ask yourself what you will do next. Think of three steps. Write them down, one sentence per step. Include any stakeholders you might need to involve.
5. Read the steps over to confirm you're happy with the action you intend to take.
6. Fold the piece of paper and leave it in your coat pocket for tomorrow.
7. Distract yourself for the evening by engaging with friends, your favourite TV show or a great book, knowing that you will handle the situation at the next opportunity.
8. If your brain returns to the thought, allow yourself to reread your action plan and tell yourself it's all in hand.

Why it works
Research has found that rumination is a significant contributor to depression and anxiety.[15] Trying to block out something that is bothering you without planning your next steps is unlikely to be successful. Instead, face your worry, reflect on it and then put a pin in it until you can take positive action.

Top tip
Talk it over with a friend or colleague, if possible, but limit yourself to five minutes.

---

15 Peter Kinderman, Matthias Schwannauer, Eleanor Pontin and Sara Tai, 'Psychological processes mediate the impact of familial risk, social circumstances and life events on mental health', *PLoS ONE*, 8.10, 2013, tinyurl.com/reoe4rg

#165 Exercise to improve mental health and wellbeing

How often do you get active? It's not groundbreaking news that exercise is good for us physically and mentally, but how often do we find ourselves prioritising work? Try this strategy to keep active.

1. Timetable a routine for exercise, whether it's a brisk walk, jogging, badminton, a gym class, a swim or yoga at home.
   Decide which days you can fit in one (or more)
   sessions and block out some time.
2. Tell everyone you can, especially your boss and your colleagues, that on those days you will be leaving at the given time to go and exercise.
3. Set an alarm on your phone or watch. When the alarm rings, stop what you're doing and remind yourself that the task can be completed another time.
4. Have your activewear at work so you can get changed before you leave. This is the crucial part: get changed, even if you would rather go home and sleep/work/watch TV.
5. Go and exercise, knowing that when people ask how it was, you don't have to tell them you bailed!

Why this matters
The benefits of exercise are well known. The problem is not our understanding of those benefits, but the willpower to do what we need to do when other tasks demand our attention. Fight the urge to neglect your health and wellbeing and lace up!

Top tip
Put the commitment first. Imagine the exercise as a special appointment you need to keep. After all, you wouldn't fail to show up to a big meeting or an important hospital appointment.

#166 Three good things: self-focus

Educators often have 101 things to do and this can potentially lead us to feel low and overwhelmed. Take control of your thoughts by recognising the good in each day; there are always good things, we just need to look for them! Try the 'three good things' exercise by the positive psychologist Martin Seligman.[16]

1. Before you go to sleep, think about three things that went well in the day.
2. Write each of them down.
3. Reflect on *why* those things went well.

Why it works
According to Seligman, this exercise boosts happiness and reduces the negative feelings that can lead to depression.

Top tip
Try this for a minimum of one week to feel the full benefits.

16 Martin E P Seligman, *Learned Optimism: how to change your mind and your life,* Vintage Books USA, 2006

#167 Learned optimism and cognitive distortions

The more negativity you allow into your thoughts, the more you'll have in your life. The good news is that you *can* change your perspective. Martin Seligman explores the differences between optimistic and pessimistic 'explanatory styles' in his book *Learned Optimism*.[17] Here's a summary of the aspects of explanatory styles.

1. **Personalisation.** Seligman suggests that optimistic people tend to lay blame on external forces or circumstances. For example, if a lesson observation were to go wrong, they wouldn't blame themselves or others, but would instead consider the other forces or actions at play. They might think 'The planning was not so strong this time', as opposed to 'I must be a terrible teacher, this is all my fault'. But be careful not to slip into the habit of denying your share of responsibility; the fine line between optimism and delusion has been noted in Seligman's work, too!

2. **Permanence.** Seligman says optimistic people tend to see problems as temporary rather than permanent. For example, 'This poor behaviour will settle after Christmas.'

3. **Pervasiveness.** Seligman says that when optimistic people experience failure in one area, they do not necessarily extend this to other areas. The opposite can be said of pessimists, who may experience failure in one area and feel as if they will therefore fail in other areas. For example, 'My maths planning was weak so my English planning must be weak, too.'

Other interesting ideas stem from the work of the psychiatrist Aaron T Beck, who laid the groundwork for the theory of cognitive distortions in the 1960s. Cognitive distortions are irrational thought patterns: our minds convince us of things that are just not true. Here are five common cognitive distortions.

1. **All-or-nothing thinking:** those times when you feel that things 'always' or 'never' happen. For example, if your boss rejects an idea, you might think 'My boss *never* listens to me!' even though this is unlikely to be the case.

---

17 Martin E P Seligman, *Learned Optimism: how to change your mind and your life,* Vintage Books USA, 2006

2. **Overgeneralisation:** the times when one-off or isolated events lead to sweeping generalisations. For example, 'I've had one bad lesson observation – they are all bound to be bad now!'
3. **Disqualifying the positive:** those times when negativity takes over and you decide positives 'don't count'. For example, if a colleague presents a positive solution to a problem you face, you reject it by saying, 'Yes, but…'.
4. **Jumping to conclusions:** making negative assumptions and then seeking evidence to back up these assumptions, as opposed to seeking evidence and then forming more rational conclusions.
5. **'Should' and 'must' thinking:** believing that there are conditional behaviours that you should or must fulfil in order to be successful. For example, 'To be a great teacher, I must always mark every book.'

Why this matters

Our thoughts form our words and our words create our persona. Additionally, research[18] has found that more optimistic people live longer! If you always feel negative about your work, perhaps there is a deeper issue to unpick.

Top tip

Reflecting on the psychology of thinking is useful, but if something is constantly getting you down, maybe it's time to move on. You don't deserve to feel unhappy or face unfair workload demands.

---

18 Lewina O Lee, Peter James, Emily S Zevon, Eric S Kim, Claudia Trudel-Fitzgerald, Avron Spiro III, Francine Grodstein and Laura D Kubzansky, 'Optimism is associated with exceptional longevity in 2 epidemiologic cohorts of men and women', *PNAS*, 116.37, 2019, tinyurl.com/urlrcsd

#168 Imagine working in a school..., by Ross

Imagine working in a school where teacher wellbeing is placed at the bottom of the priority list. A school where anything less than your everything means you're not fit to be a teacher. I used to work in that type of school. I was so surrounded by that ethos that I soon started to live, breathe and impart it on to everyone I line-managed. In schools like this, deadlines are ill-considered, meetings overrun and all aspects of line-management are top-down.

However, there is another way! Imagine working in a school where professional development is a weekly occurrence. A school where the newly qualified teacher's ideas are heard and shared. A school where the headteacher talks publicly about what they are learning, and is the first person to arrive at staff wellbeing events or the first to go home at the end of the day. These schools do exist and I would encourage you to visit them.

Why try this?
This is the first tip we experienced teachers give to new teachers: visit as many schools as you can. Often we visit only one or two, are offered a job and then settle down into the rhythm of life and work. In my career, I would visit four or five schools every academic year, attending CPD events or leadership meetings as part of a common agenda.

Top tip
Networking with other teachers is a great way to find out about different schools. Set yourself the challenge of visiting one school each term.

#169 Working with bullies, by Ross

Sadly, even within the teaching profession, you may find yourself supporting colleagues who are being bullied. You may even experience bullying yourself. In his book *The Asshole Survival Guide* (2017), Robert I Sutton quotes a pithy sentence that went viral on Twitter: 'Before you diagnose yourself with depression or low self-esteem, first make sure that you are not, in fact, just surrounded by assholes' (attributed to @debihope).

If you believe you're working with a bully, my first piece of advice would be to speak to the person concerned in a direct and professional manner. If you don't get a positive outcome, seek advice and, if necessary, professional support. In serious cases, talk to colleagues or your manager, focus on tasks that will make a difference to the relationship, make sure communication with the person takes place when others are around and take time to reflect on your relationship.

Here are some questions to help you prioritise your mental health. If you answer yes to at least one of these questions, you've experienced some form of bullying behaviour.

1. Does the person shout at or frequently interrupt you?
2. Does the person display aggressive behaviour towards you?
3. Do they deliberately ignore you?
4. Do they respond with impatient remarks (e.g. 'About time!').
5. Do they make fun of you?
6. Do they ask for your time at inappropriate moments?
7. Do they make snide comments about you with other people, loud enough so you can hear?
8. Do they smile with other people, but never with you?
9. What do other people say about the person? Have you spoken to enough sources to determine whether others are experiencing the same behaviour?

Why this matters
In our challenging profession, we will all struggle at some point to deal with a difficult relationship. This can blur our priorities and affect our wellbeing.

Top tip
There's nothing worse than ruminating on a situation like this. Use all your energy to tackle the issue head-on.

#170 Staff wellbeing reflections

Senior leaders: do you get the feeling that something isn't right with your team? Is morale low? It might be time to reflect on staff wellbeing.

1. Each day over a week, take a short wander about the school. Get a feel for the general vibe. Don't discuss anything with the teams, but consider the mood, atmosphere and organisation at key times.
2. At the end of each day, spend a few moments considering the wellbeing across the school. Focus on the key stages, teams or departments, thinking about the following prompts:
   • Do staff seem relaxed?
   • Do staff seem organised and ready to go?
   • Is there a strong sense of teamwork?
   • Is there any laughter or chatter among the team?
   • Are environments kept well-organised (corridors, classrooms, staffroom)?
3. Reflect on each of those questions. If staff seem rushed, tense or agitated, this indicates that things are not quite right. If lessons don't appear organised or well-prepared, is there sufficient time for planning and preparation? If teams are not working together, there could be issues between staff members or perhaps time is tight, leading to an 'every man for himself' attitude. If there is no team chat or laughter, morale could be low. If classrooms or staffrooms are messy, people have stopped taking care of these spaces. What else might they have no time to do?
4. Take action. You might try a staff meeting, an anonymous questionnaire or an email. Addressing staff wellbeing starts with finding out what is getting people down. Senior leaders have to be willing to listen and reflect on what should happen next.

Why try this?

Senior leaders have their own challenges, even if they're not teaching every day; the million and one tasks necessary to keep the school ticking over can mean it's hard to find time to consider staff wellbeing. But checking in with staff now and again can be a great way to discover what's working well across the school – and what's not.

Top tip

Book a staff wellbeing reflection period into your monitoring schedule. That way, you know you won't forget.

#171 Caring colleagues

Forming friendships at work can make a real difference to your wellbeing, but with time so tight and so much else going on, it can be hard to remember to look out for each other. Here's how to introduce the 'caring colleagues' strategy to your team.

1. Send an email pitching the strategy to your staff members. Explain that it is a light-hearted, opt-in way to champion one another.
2. Everyone who opts in will have their name placed into a hat and will in turn pick a name from the hat. Names pulled from the hat will remain a secret until the end of the school year.
3. Whoever you pick becomes your comrade. You will care for them.
4. Leave kind comments on a Post-it note, buy them a treat once in a while, talk them up and check in with them. You might even anonymously nominate them for a shout-out in the weekly email or school newsletter.
5. At the end of the year, provide tea and cakes for the caring colleagues. Everyone will try to guess their comrade and reveal who they've been secretly caring for.

Why it works
This is a fun way to give recognition to your colleagues and spread a little bit of happiness each week. It might make all the difference to someone's bad day.

Top tip
Keep the expectations low – the last thing people need is the guilt of being a bad comrade.

#172 Talk-up a teacher[19]

Recognition can be a great motivator in the workplace. Instead of granting recognition in order to improve productivity, I propose that we recognise hard work in order to improve wellbeing. Next time a colleague does something great, no matter how small, think about what made it so successful. Then choose a way to recognise it, such as:

1. Sending a congratulatory email.
2. Writing praise on a staff shout-out board (see the next idea).
3. Telling your colleague directly.
4. Leaving them a Post-it note with a kind message.
5. Talking about the impact of what they have taught you.
6. Talking-up the person to other colleagues.
7. Giving a social media shout-out on Twitter, Facebook or Instagram.

Why it works

Recognising a colleague's efforts is a great way to boost wellbeing and make people feel appreciated and valued. How often do people talk each another down at your setting? Showing recognition through talking-up spreads positive vibes.

Top tip

Responding with gratitude and praise as soon as possible will have the best impact, as the event will be fresh in everyone's minds.

---

19 Hanna Beech, 'Talk-up a teacher', *Teacher Toolkit*, 2017, teachertoolkit.co.uk/2017/11/29/one-minute-cpd-11

#173 Staff shout-outs

Gratitude is the attitude! Develop a positive and grateful environment in your school by creating a shout-outs board.

1. Pick a display board in a high-traffic area. The staffroom might be the ideal place.
2. Make a space on the display for staff to write messages to their colleagues.
3. Provide Post-its, pens and pins.
4. Email staff to tell them the purpose of the shout-outs board, encouraging them to thank a colleague.
5. Make a start by writing a message of gratitude to a team member.

Why try this?
Gratitude feels great to receive and great to give. In a busy school day, we often forget to show our gratitude, even though we really do feel it.

Top tip
To get the ball rolling, take some slips to a staff meeting, asking colleagues to fill one out before they head off.

#174 School values for wellbeing

School leaders undoubtedly have a responsibility to ensure the wellbeing of everyone at their school. This core duty requires ongoing reflection and action that puts people first. What are the values that run through everything you do at your school? The following common values can be used to support wellbeing.

1. **Resilience:** encouraging pupils to face challenges and setbacks with bounce and optimism will help to them overcome any issues they face.
2. **Respect and kindness:** encouraging pupils to respect themselves and others is key for good mental health.
3. **Diversity:** accepting and celebrating differences can aid pupils in accepting themselves and avoiding comparisons to others.
4. **Friendship:** helping pupils to foster connections with peers and staff is vital in ensuring they feel supported and valued.
5. **Appreciation:** when we have gratitude and celebrate the good things, we see the value of the lives we live.
6. **Optimism:** by teaching pupils to be positive and optimistic, we can help to reduce negative emotions, which can lead to depression.
7. **Honesty:** valuing and promoting honesty lets pupils know that they can speak openly about their feelings, without judgement.

Why values matter

Your school values should weave through every part of the school; by the time pupils leave, these values should be embedded. Make sure the values you teach are valuable!

Top tip

School values are often inherited as leaders, staff and pupils come and go. Do the school values represent your current cohort? If not, revamp your values by asking all stakeholders for their views.

Note: if a child is experiencing mental health issues or mental illness, they will require additional professional support. When someone is facing a setback, saying things like 'be more resilient' or 'be more optimistic' is simply unhelpful.

#175 **The Daily Mile**

Want to inject some energy into the school day? Many schools now use the Daily Mile initiative to encourage pupils to take up running. Here are some tips to get you started.

1. Speak to the senior leadership team and the PE coordinator to get the go-ahead.
2. Sign up at thedailymile.co.uk (it's free!) for resources and implementation ideas.
3. Find the right time for a daily run – the website suggests 15 minutes a day, which is more or less a mile, depending on the runner. Break or lunchtime are probably the best bet.
4. Complete a test run to find a mile-long route without any dangerous dips or bumps.
5. Explain the concept to teachers, pupils and parents. The website has a letter format you could use for parents.
6. Get staff on board – who might run alongside the pupils? The initiative can benefit staff wellbeing, too!
7. Decide on the details. Will pupils need trainers for the run and how will this work? How will the start and end of the run be signalled? What are the risks, if any?

Why try this?
With childhood obesity on the rise, and children spending less time outdoors and more time on devices, a liberating run each day could do the kids (and staff) a lot of good.

Top tip
If you wish to complete a daily run but feel 15 minutes is too long, try '1K a day' and reduce the run time to seven minutes. Once the routines are in place, increase the time if possible for optimal results.

#176 Mindful moments for pupils

The main aim of mindfulness is to live in the moment, clearing the mind of thoughts past and future. Research has shown that practising mindfulness has positive effects on the brain.[20] Here's how to bring it to your pupils.

1. **Try GoNoodle.** This website (gonoodle.com) offers a huge range of video clips for children, many of which help them to practise mindfulness. The site is currently free to use and primary-aged children love the clips.
2. **Use animated gifs for mindful breathing.** Search for 'breathing shapes animated gifs' online and you will find a variety of moving images to encourage a slow focus on the breath.
3. **Tell mindful stories.** Ask your class to close their eyes and focus on their breathing as you describe a relaxing experience (e.g. a walk through a beautiful meadow).
4. **Stop and listen.** Ask the children to listen to the sounds around them while focusing on their breathing. Tell them that if their thoughts wander, they can refocus by thinking only about their breathing and the sounds in the room.
5. **Try a body scan.** Ask the pupils to close their eyes and focus on their breathing. From head to toes, calmly take the children on a scan through their body, encouraging them to relax different parts as you name them. If you're not confident with this, there are plenty of body scan clips on YouTube to help you out.

Why try this?
You might think you don't have time for mindfulness, but just a few moments each day can increase pupils' focus and wellbeing.

Top tip
During their mindfulness practice, observe your class. Which children find it particularly challenging to sit and be present in the moment? Why might this be and what else can you do to help?

---

20 Antoine Lutz, Heleen A Slagter, John D Dunne and Richard J Davidson, 'Attention regulation and monitoring in meditation', *Trends in Cognitive Sciences*, 12.4, 2008, tinyurl.com/w3x432z

#177 Three good things: pupil focus[21]

In idea #166 we discussed the 'three good things' exercise by the positive psychologist Martin Seligman. Try the exercise in your classroom to see how gratitude can support pupil wellbeing.

1. Explain to pupils that by showing gratitude in our lives, we can boost our happiness.
2. Find four minutes a day to talk about gratitude with your form or class. Keep this time protected.
3. Minute 1: model your 'three golden moments' of the day. Explain that these can be tiny moments or huge successes. Write them on the board.
4. Minute 2: pupils can discuss their three golden moments. Share one or two with the whole class very briefly.
5. Minutes 3-4: ask pupils to jot down their golden moments in a journal.
6. End with a long, deep inhale and exhale.

Why it works
Research has found that this type of activity improves wellbeing and promotes optimism.[22] Eventually, with daily practice and modelling, this activity could change a pupil's way of thinking and encourage a positive mindset.

Top tip
Allow pupils to opt in or out of sharing their golden moment with the class – these moments may be very personal and some children may prefer to keep theirs private.

---

21 Hanna Beech, 'Wellbeing haven', *Teacher Toolkit*, 2018, teachertoolkit.co.uk/2018/01/24/one-minute-cpd-15
22 Martin E P Seligman, *Learned Optimism: how to change your mind and your life*, Vintage Books USA, 2006

#178 Providing special moments

How can schools provide pupils with plenty of memorable childhood experiences? Children only experience their school years once, so create some enriching moments that make pupils feel great and enhance their knowledge and understanding.

1. **Get outdoors.** Time spent in the great outdoors is so valuable but often neglected. How could you take learning outside?
2. **Allow for complete creativity.** Just like adults, children need to feel some ownership of a task in order to connect fully. Teachers have so many objectives to work through, but allowing complete autonomy once in a while will make pupils feel great. Remember that these lessons work best once pupils have sufficient subject knowledge.
3. **Get off the school grounds.** Taking part in an educational visit is a great experience that can broaden pupils' knowledge and enhance their interest in a subject. Where could you take your class this term?
4. **Don't neglect the arts.** Drama, dance, music, literature, poetry and art can be pushed out of today's curriculum. How could you use the arts to enhance wellbeing and create memorable moments for your pupils?
5. **Proms, discos and parties.** Humans are social animals. Give proper thought to end-of-year events – these are really special for your pupils.

Why try this?
Yes, we all want our pupils to remember the knowledge and skills we teach, but is that all? Some might argue that these suggestions would waste valuable learning time, but if we want to improve pupil wellbeing, enriching experiences can help.

Top tip
Ask pupils for their ideas about trips, experiences and special moments.

#179 Know the pressure points

There are certain times of the school year that we know will be tricky, so plan ahead, considering pupil wellbeing before, during and after these pressure points.

1. Reflect on the previous school year, labelling different weeks or terms as 1-mild pressure, 2-moderate pressure or 3-high pressure (in relation to pupils).
2. Look ahead at the year to come, predicting when moderate and high pressure might occur (e.g. around exams, transition or periods of significant change or expectation).
3. Ask for staff suggestions on how the pressure could be alleviated in some way. Could teachers or form tutors use mindfulness at key times? Could key staff provide wellbeing sessions for pupils? Could a free period be arranged to give kids time to reflect or revise?

Why it works

We know the pressure increases at different times of the year and wellbeing can suffer as a result. But we can make things more manageable for pupils – and for ourselves – if we are ready with a plan of action.

Top tip

Talk to the kids. Ask them when they have felt pressure throughout the term and what staff could have done to reduce this. They will probably have some valuable insights to offer.

#180 Pupil wellbeing reflection questions

Is it possible to measure pupil wellbeing? That is a matter for debate, but the first step in improving a situation is trying to understand it. These thinking prompts will help you to decide whether a pupil needs some support with their wellbeing.

1. Have you seen a dramatic change in the child's behaviour, demeanour or confidence?
2. Has this child experienced a trauma (e.g. bereavement, separation, abuse, bullying, accident)?
3. Does the child have extended episodes of low mood?
4. Does the child avoid speaking openly about their feelings?
5. Does the child often seem distracted, tired or confused?
6. Are the child's parents or carers concerned?
7. Does the child continue to lack optimism, despite support?
8. Does the child feel unsafe? Do you feel they are?
9. Does the child lack connections with others (e.g. friends, family, staff members)?
10. Are there any signs of self-harm?
11. Is the child diagnosed with or suspected to have an autistic spectrum condition?
12. Are you or other adults persistently worried about the child's wellbeing, even if you are unsure exactly why?

Why this matters

If you work with young people, spotting changes in their wellbeing and mental health is part of the job. Taking the time to think about how a child is doing will help you to see what action, if any, might be needed.

Top tip

Answer the questions with a simple yes or no initially. Take the 'yes' responses and order these from most to least concerning. Think more deeply about these before seeking the support of the pastoral team at the earliest opportunity.

#181 Put a pin in it: pupil focus

When we have a worry, it can be extremely difficult to stop thinking about it. Help pupils to focus their attention on the task in hand by using the 'put a pin in it' method that we discussed in idea #164.

1. If a child is obviously worried, ask to speak to them.
2. Tell them they seem worried and ask if they would like to talk about it.
3. If they are open to discussion, listen to them talk, but scaffold the conversation to gain a clear idea of what the worry is.
4. If the worry becomes a disclosure, follow your safeguarding procedures. You may decide to refer to the family liaison officer or SEN department. If the worry is not a safeguarding concern, empathise with the student and jot the worry down together.
5. Decide together what can be done to solve the problem – for example, 'After school, we can talk to your parents about this together' or 'At lunchtime, I will speak with the pupils about this'. Jot this down, too.
6. Explain that although the worry is still there, for now you are both going to put a pin in it. Literally place the worry, folded, on a pinboard (and make sure it is kept away from the eyes and hands of others).
7. Say that you'll come back to the worry once the lesson is over. If the child continues to be distracted from their work, ask them to recap the action you will take together and remind them to focus on the lesson right now.
8. Be sure to come back to the worry and follow through on the actions. This is the most important part of the strategy.

Why it works
Acknowledging the worry and empathising with the child show that you understand and care. Putting a pin in it means the child has a chance of focusing on the task.

Top tip
If the same child worries about different things all the time, this might indicate an underlying issue. Speak to your SEN department about your concerns.

#182 The Mental Health Media Charter, by Natasha Devon

Are you looking for some simple ways to improve discussion of mental health in your school? With help from Samaritans, Mental Health First Aid England and Beat, the mental health campaigner Natasha Devon launched the Mental Health Media Charter in 2017. The charter consists of seven simple guidelines to ensure the imagery and language used in mental health reporting is responsible. The charter, which can easily be applied to the ways in which we discuss mental health in schools, is summarised here.

1. Don't use the phrases 'commit suicide' or 'successful suicide'. Say 'died by suicide' instead.
2. Don't use images that could be triggering for people who self-harm or have eating disorders.
3. Don't label people with their illness. Say 'people experiencing anorexia/depression' instead of 'anorexics' or 'depressives'.
4. Don't give details when talking about suicide or self-harm. Think about *why* rather than how.
5. Don't use generic terms like 'mental health issues' when talking about terrorists or other violent criminals.
6. Seek to understand the distinction between mental health and mental ill health.
7. Offer good-quality sources of support if content might trigger a need for help in someone.

Why use this?
Changes in the way we talk about mental health issues and mental illness can change lives.

Top tip
Be brave in politely challenging conversations that go against these aims.

#183 Non-judgemental listening[23]

Educators tune in to the behaviours and emotions of their pupils, so they are often able to spot emerging mental health issues. Listening is vital when supporting a young person who is experiencing mental ill health or mental health issues. Try these tips to make sure they feel heard at a potentially difficult time.

1. Listen with intent to understand, as opposed to intent to respond.
2. Avoid interrupting. Allow the young person to fully express themselves.
3. Ask questions to clarify their feelings or thoughts. This shows that you are paying attention and you empathise.
4. Consider your body language, including facial expressions, eye contact, posture and seating position. Expressions or reactions that imply judgement can cause the young person to clam up.
5. Don't be tempted to offer advice or tell someone how they ought to feel. This can create feelings of guilt or inferiority.
6. Don't turn the conversation towards yourself or your own feelings or experience. This can create unhealthy comparisons and shift the focus away from the young person.
7. Don't be afraid of silent moments. These do not have to be awkward, but can instead create space for people to think and open up further. Allow the silence to spill into the space and wait for the child to speak.
8. Be careful not to minimise an issue by stating that it isn't so bad or suggesting that things could be worse. This invalidates the person's feelings.

Why try this?

As teachers, our first instinct is to support, advise and solve. But when it comes to mental ill health or mental health issues, it's vital to allow the young person to talk openly and be truly heard, without judgement.

Top tip

Be mindful of the fine line between empathy and sympathy. Remember, you want to show that you can see how difficult things are for them, rather than imply that you feel pity for them.

---

23 Hanna Beech, 'Using non-judgemental listening', *Teacher Toolkit*, 2019, teachertoolkit.co.uk/2019/09/11/one-minute-cpd-60

#184 Anxiety attacks

It can be terrifying to witness an anxiety attack, but knowing how to respond is crucial. Here's how to help a child experiencing an anxiety attack.

1. Keep calm. Don't add your stress to the situation.
2. Try to identify the trigger if you can, but don't be tempted to keep asking questions. Asking 'What's wrong?' or 'Are you OK?' is unhelpful at this time.
3. Use a calm but clear voice to ask the pupil to concentrate on their breathing. Ask them to inhale for five seconds, hold for two and exhale for another five. Repeat this exercise until the child's focus is drawn to the breath, not the trigger.
4. Praise the child but keep counting through the breaths: 'Fantastic, you are calming down, breathe again. One, two, three...'
5. When the child has calmed down completely, explain that you want to talk about the trigger together. Ask them if they are ready to talk and proceed with simple questions if they are ready to do so.
6. Questions could include: what made you feel worried? Why did this make you worried? What might happen if your fear came true? What can we do to reduce your anxiety? Who might help you with this?
7. Things *not* to say: just calm down; it's not that bad; don't overreact; stop it; this is silly/over the top/unnecessary; why are you reacting like this?; what's wrong?; you can't react like that.

Why it works
A calm and competent response to an anxiety attack can make a huge difference during the attack and afterwards, too. Making the child feel comfortable and supported, rather than embarrassed and misunderstood, can help to reduce stress.

Top tip
Normalise the experience by saying that we all worry about things. But explain that when our worries become so big that they take over, we need to find ways to take back control. One great way is to concentrate on breathing. Don't forget to log your concerns with the relevant colleagues.

#185 Self-harm: how to respond

You may have witnessed or had some experience of young people in your care self-harming, in which case you'll know first-hand how scary it can be. Educators are often left untrained in this area, which can mean they react in ways that could compound the problem. Follow these dos and don'ts if a child is self-harming.

1. **Don't** overreact emotionally with anger, fear, disgust or concern.
2. **Do** try to be neutral in your response.
3. **Don't** tell the child off. The fear of seeing someone bang their head, pull their hair or cut themselves often means we react instinctively and want to make it stop.
4. **Do** speak calmly and respectfully to the child.
5. **Don't** ask questions like 'Why did you do this?' or 'What were you thinking?'
6. **Do** assume there has been an incident or trigger, explaining that you understand they must have been feeling a negative emotion to do this.
7. **Don't** bribe, punish or make ultimatums when self-harm happens.
8. **Do** explain that self-harm is not a good way to handle difficult feelings and situations; there are different ways to reduce the stress.
9. **Don't** tell the child to be more resilient or cope better.
10. **Do** offer at least three options for reducing stress (e.g. 10 deep breaths, leaving the room, talking it over, ripping paper, etc).
11. **Don't** assume it was a one-off.
12. **Do** monitor the child's wellbeing regularly, ensuring they know that you and other key adults are available to talk to.
13. **Do** call the emergency services if there is severe harm.

Why this matters
Self-harm affects one in 12 people. Being prepared will help you know how to react.

Top tip
Always log self-harm as a concern with the welfare or SEN team, and communicate concerns with parents or carers.

Further resources

Natasha Devon, *A Beginner's Guide to Being Mental: an A-Z*, Bluebird, 2018

Adrian Bethune, *Wellbeing in the Primary Classroom: a practical guide to teaching happiness*, Bloomsbury Education, 2018

Chris Eyre, *The Elephant in the Staffroom: how to reduce stress and improve teacher wellbeing*, Routledge, 2016

James Hollinsley, *An Educator's Guide to Wellbeing and Mental Health in Schools*, John Catt Educational, 2018

Abigail Mann, *Live Well, Teach Well: a practical approach to wellbeing that works*, Bloomsbury Education, 2018

Paul Connolly, Caryl Sibbett, Jennifer Hanratty, Karen Kerr, Liam O'Hare and Karen Winter, *Pupils' Emotional Health and Wellbeing: a review of audit tools and a survey of practice in Northern Ireland post-primary schools*, Centre for Effective Education, 2011, tinyurl.com/tvgz6m4

Kirsi Pyhältö, Tiina Soini and Janne Pietarinen, 'Pupils' pedagogical wellbeing in comprehensive school: significant positive and negative school experiences of Finnish ninth graders', *European Journal of Psychology of Education*, 25.2, 2010, tinyurl.com/uw8q5l4

Teacher Wellbeing Index 2019, Education Support, tinyurl.com/yx56d88l

Chapter 9: Rapport and relationships

Teachers who have substantial subject knowledge, deliver effective instruction and assess accurately are bound to have successful outcomes with their pupils. But there's another important factor: building genuine relationships. Not only can this have a positive impact on learning potential, but it's also fun. One major benefit of working in the education sector is that you get to hang about with kids, and kids are great – they are funny, honest, energetic, real and open-minded.

There are some strong views out there about the importance of building relationships versus the importance of effective teaching instruction. But, in my view, it's not about whether a rapport with pupils improves learning or doesn't improve learning. Comparing the importance of rapport and instruction is like comparing the importance of air and water; attempts to crown one over the other are a bit reductive. The point is, having a rapport with pupils is good for us and good for them.

Interestingly, scientists and neuroscientists have considered the idea that the need for human connection is comparable to other basic needs, such as water and food. Research has shown that maintaining social connections has positive effects on wellbeing, both emotional and physical[1] (if you want to find out more about this, the scientist Matthew Lieberman[2] has explored how severed or poorly connected social bonds can negatively affect education and

---

1   Bert N Uchino, 'Social support and health: a review of physiological processes potentially underlying links to disease outcomes', *Journal of Behavioral Medicine*, 29, 2006, tinyurl.com/u7dr7vb

2   Matthew D Lieberman, *Social: why our brains are wired to connect*, Oxford University Press, 2013

health). And the idea that relationships are significant in managing behaviour is echoed in the Education Endowment Foundation's *Improving Behaviour in Schools* guidance report,[3] which discusses the benefits of pupils feeling valued and supported.

For us, as educators and human beings who continue to exist outside the school gates, it's important to consider the finding that positive social connections contribute to emotional and physical wellbeing. Bearing this in mind, we can aim to build the strongest rapport possible with our pupils. We can give them time to share their thoughts, build trust through supportive and calming approaches, show empathy, and allow them to learn more about us as real people. Rapport will help to forge better relationships between 'them' and 'us'.

In my experience, when a strong rapport exists, pupils are more likely to ask questions, offer ideas and talk openly about their learning. The better the rapport I have with a pupil, the more likely they are to listen intently to me, complete the work I present, rise to challenges and be honest when they need my help. There is trust and respect.

I've also enjoyed the benefits of having a rapport with my pupils – the connections I make help them to show empathy towards me. One example that springs to mind is when I'd had one of *those* mornings at home and a nine-year-old pupil approached me after class, asking 'Miss, are you all right? You don't seem yourself today.' He was looking out for me, just as I had for him.

None of this is to suggest that good teaching can't occur without rapport, but simply that having a rapport isn't going to harm learning and might even benefit it, allowing adults and children to connect in meaningful ways and thus optimising learning potential. Another advantage of understanding the benefits of rapport is that it provides an opportunity for self-reflection. Sure, we love our jobs, but we also need to truly connect with the people in our lives outside school. We owe it to ourselves to ensure that our own basic needs are met: food, water *and* social connections with those whom we hold most dear.

Take a moment to consider how connected you are with family, friends, colleagues or even pets. Note down the names of six people (or animals!) who are very important to you.

---

3   Igraine Rhodes and Michelle Long, *Improving Behaviour in Schools: guidance report*, Education Endowment Foundation, 2019, tinyurl.com/y2pqq7zt

1	
2	
3	
4	
5	
6	

Now give each a score between 0 (totally disconnected at present) and 5 (fully connected at present). Take a few moments to reflect on any scores between 0 and 3, asking yourself what is stopping you from being more connected with this person – after all, you've identified them as very important to you.

The psychologist Daniel Goleman has written about the three ingredients of rapport: full mutual attention, in which we put down whatever might distract us and focus fully on the other person; physical synchrony, where we subconsciously move in harmony with each other; and positive emotions that indicate an optimal brain state.[4] In the classroom, the first is the best starting point for building a rapport. After all, it seems only fair that pupils have the full attention of their teacher.

---

4   Daniel Goleman, 'The chemistry of connection', 2014, danielgoleman.info/daniel-goleman-the-chemistry-of-connection-2

#186 Invisible children

With so many pupils to teach, some children can fly under your radar. Try this method with your team to identify your 'invisible' children.

1. During a staff meeting, ask your colleagues to make a list of the children in their class or form. Give them up to two minutes to do so.
2. When the time is up, give them a class list to check against. Ask them to identify the children they forgot.
3. Discuss the fact that the children at the forefront of our minds are often the most confident or concerning, leaving the quieter or more compliant children to become invisible. Explain that we tend to recall the students we have a better rapport with.
4. For the rest of the week, ask staff to focus on their invisible children, fostering a relationship with them in as many ways as they can.
5. At the next meeting, discuss the outcomes together.

Why it works
When we identify those pupils with whom we are yet to forge strong relationships, we can begin to address the situation one child at a time.

Top tip
Ask support staff to identify their invisible children, too, increasing the number of pupils who feel connected to an adult in school.

#187 Remembering pupils' names[5]

Forgetting a child's name or getting it wrong isn't ideal. The following methods will help you to learn your pupils' names in a flash.

1. Give out name cards to the pupils randomly. Ask a pupil to stand up and read the name on their card. Take the card from them and give it to the correct person. The card holder can direct you with 'hot' or 'cold' clues.
2. Ask the pupils to state their name to the group, as well as an animal or food that starts with the same letter. For example, 'I'm Isabelle, iguana and ice cream.' This might help you to make associations.
3. Consider asking pupils for their preferred pronoun. Giving young people the chance to express this shows respect and openness.
4. Put name cards in a pile and pick one, calling out the name. In round 1, the child has to stand up and shout 'I am…'. In round 2, the table with that child cheers and you have to pick out the child. In round 3, the pupils stay silent and you have to place the card with the correct child.

Why try this?
Building a relationship with pupils begins with knowing their names. These methods are fun and will also help to build class rapport.

Top tip
Refer to pupils by their names as often as possible. Once you know first names, move on to surnames. Promise to reward them each time you get their name wrong – that certainly improved my memory!

---

5   Hanna Beech, 'Remembering pupils' names', *Teacher Toolkit, 2018,* teachertoolkit.co.uk/2018/09/17/one-minute-cpd-32

#188 'Getting to know you' games

Play these simple games to get to know your pupils.

1. **Three lies and one truth.** Tell the children four pieces of information about yourself, only one of which is true. The pupils have to guess which one. Then choose a child to tell their three lies and one truth.
2. **Smart questions** (see opposite). Write a set of questions to help with getting to know someone. Colour-code each question red, purple, blue, yellow, orange, brown, green or pink. Buy some Smarties and place them in a bowl. Close your eyes and take one Smartie; answer the question according to the colour key. Choose pupils to select a Smartie, too.
3. **Question of the day.** Pick a question of day to answer in a class discussion. This question should enable you all to learn something about each other – for example, 'What is your favourite meal?'
4. **Guess who?** Choose one child and keep their identity secret. Pupils can ask yes or no questions to try to guess the chosen child – for example, 'Do they have brown hair?' and 'Do they enjoy football?'
5. **Class Grammys.** Ask pupils to vote for their classmates under titles such as 'most improved attitude', 'most helpful classmate' and 'outstanding achievement in art'. Reward the chosen pupil, offering congratulations and applause.

Why it works

Rapport might not naturally spring from a class that's constantly all business. A light-hearted game every so often can make a real difference.

Top tip

Don't spend more than 15 minutes on a game. Beyond that it might lose its appeal or consume too much curriculum time.

'GETTING TO KNOW YOU' QUESTIONS

Colour	Questions
Red	What is your full name? When is your birthday? Who is in your family?
Purple	What is your favourite food? What is your favourite subject? What is your favourite animal?
Blue	Who inspires you? Who makes you laugh? Who would you like to meet?
Yellow	Do you play any sports? Which sport would you like to try? Can you swim?
Orange	Have you got any pets? What is your dream pet? Which animal would you be?
Brown	What is the best thing to do? Do you prefer outdoors to indoors? What is your special talent?
Green	Which country would you visit? How do you travel to school? Where have you visited?
Pink	What is your favourite film? What is your favourite book? Who is your favourite author?

#189 People watching

Think you know your pupils? Observe them interacting socially and you might need to think again! Try this five-minute method to gain a deeper understanding of your class.

1. Think about a child or group of pupils you believe you know really well. Predict how they might respond in different social situations.
2. During a group task or breaktime, casually get on with something near to the children. Appear busy.
3. Listen intently to their interactions and observe how they work or play alongside one another.
4. Ask yourself: are they active or passive? Do they fall into a role within the group (e.g. leader, follower, disengaged, domineering, extroverted, introverted, class clown)?
5. Reflect: did they act as you expected? Were they more or less confident than you predicted?

Why try this?

Subtly observing pupils can be eye-opening, offering you a new perspective on a familiar person.

Top tip

Don't take this too seriously – it isn't about judging or spying on pupils, more about growing your understanding of the young people you teach. Avoid discussing your observations with the children.

#190 Early investments (for leaders)

How well do you know the youngest children in your school? Try these methods to get to know them better.

1. Make an effort to learn the names of your new pupils. Watch them respond with a smile and a puzzled 'How do you know my name?' when you address them.
2. Speak to form tutors or class teachers about their pupils – they are the experts. They will be able to identify the children you should get to know early on.
3. Be present at the gate, during breaktimes and in between lessons. Visit classes. The more you see of the pupils, the more you'll learn about them.
4. Meet their parents. Investing in the parents of new pupils is so important. If you can engage them now, you'll save yourself the challenge of forming relationships unnaturally later on.

Why it works
Invest early on and you'll save time and effort later – it's much harder to form a relationship when the pupils and their families have become part of the school without connecting to the senior leadership team.

Top tip
Don't be tempted to only become familiar with potentially problematic pupils. Knowing all the children well will mean you can celebrate, understand and enhance everyone's time at your school.

#191 Casual questions

Finding it difficult to form a relationship with a pupil? Ask some casual questions to start building a bond.

1. Find time to chat to pupils during breaktimes, transition times and free lessons.
2. If you haven't yet developed a solid rapport with a child, avoid personal questions about family or emotions; these might cause more friction than connection.
3. Try a 'Would you rather…' question. These are fun and irresistible.
4. Ask 'If you could choose any pet/job/holiday destination, which would it be?' These questions can open up lots of conversations. Younger audiences might like the book *You Choose* by Nick Sharratt and Pippa Goodhart.[6]
5. Try questions like 'If you could have one wish, what would it be?' or 'What do you wish would change about the school/community/world?' These allow pupils to use their imagination while expressing their views.
6. Ask 'Do you prefer … or …?' questions. It could be film, food, sports, music, lessons, actors – anything! These can start a discussion that allows you to express your view, too.
7. Ask 'What would you do if…?' questions, which encourage pupils to think on their feet.

Why it works
It's easy for teachers to always ask personal or academic questions of pupils, but more casual questioning allows for exploration and imagination. Casual questions allow educators to get to know the children on a totally different level.

Top tip
Pose the question to the child sitting next to the one you want to get to know. You can then casually ask, 'What do you think?' to encourage them to share their thoughts.

---

6   Nick Sharratt and Pippa Goodhart, *You Choose*, Random House, 2004

#192 The importance of trust

Trust is essential to building genuine relationships, but for some pupils, trusting adults might not come easily. Here are five important points to consider.

1. According to the psychologist Dan Ariely,[7] we tend to become more trusting when we believe that our interactions will extend for a longer period of time. This can easily translate to schools, where pupils spend so much time with the same adults. Long-term relationships allow people to prove over and over that they can be trusted.
2. Ariely also discusses the value of transparency. In an education context, that might include ensuring that pupils understand what is happening, and making expectations and sanctions clear and predictable. It could also involve opportunities for open two-way feedback.
3. Give pupils responsibilities and trust them to fulfil them. This will strengthen your relationships.
4. The management professor James Davis has discussed three drivers of trust in the context of a customer and a company,[8] which can be easily translated to education:
   - Ability: can the business do what they say they can do?
   - Benevolence: do they care about me?
   - Integrity: do I agree with their values?
5. Do what you say you will do. This will allow you to be seen as trustworthy.

Why this matters
Fostering trust could help pupils to let their barriers down and feel safe in your presence.

Top tip
Trust can decline quickly. If trust is broken, take time to consider the steps you must take to reestablish it.

---

7   Dan Ariely, 'The trust factory', *Dialogue*, 2016, tinyurl.com/wl3x85p
8   James Davis, 'Building trust' (talk), TEDxUSU, 2014, tinyurl.com/m94ddf3

#193 Can I get you anything else?

What do teachers and waiting staff have in common? Perhaps more than you might think. Here's how you can use the skills of waiting staff to serve learning to your pupils.

1. **Greet and seat.** Welcome the pupils and make sure they are comfortable in the environment. Give them something to help them make good use of their time as others find their seats.
2. **Offer something worthwhile.** Make sure your lesson content is interesting, challenging and thought-provoking.
3. **Courtesy check.** Check in with the pupils while they work, asking 'Is everything OK with your task?' and 'Can I get you something else?' Up-level or scaffold if they haven't quite got what they need.
4. **Circulate and be available.** Stay visible as pupils work.
5. **Thank them for coming.** Show the class you appreciate their efforts.

Why it works
Being truly available to the class will let them know that they can rely on you. People like people who help them out.

Top tip
Being there to help doesn't mean children can disrespect you; be careful that they don't take advantage.

#194 Classgram display

Want to create a learning environment that really belongs to your class or form? Try a Classgram display, inspired by Instagram.

1. Find a prominent classroom display space.
2. Make lettering for the title 'Classgram' and prepare 12 square pieces of card (20 x 20cm is a good size). Position them in four rows of three (how images are organised on an Instagram profile).
3. Tell the class that you have created a Classgram display where special school moments can be shared.
4. Take photos of those special moments: a class presentation, a school trip or that eureka moment in maths.
5. Print and place the special moments on the Classgram display, with a short caption (and maybe some hashtags for fun).
6. Update the board as regularly as possible, to keep it relevant and ensure all pupils can be featured.

Why it works
This builds celebration into the classroom, gives pupils ownership over the learning space and really helps to establish rapport.

Top tip
Ask pupils to contribute images of their personal achievements. Don't forget to add some snaps of yourself and the teaching assistants, too!

#195 Amazing anecdotes

Help your pupils to get to know you a little better through anecdotes.

1. Talk about when you were younger. Children love to hear about an adult's childhood – aside from helping them to connect to you as an actual human being, it baffles them a little!
2. When something amusing happens to you outside school, remember to tell the class about it. Start with 'You'll never guess what happened to me on Sunday' to grab their attention.
3. When reading, say 'This character reminds me of...' and tell a short anecdote about an interaction with that person.
4. Tell the children about your interactions and friendships with the other staff – for example, 'The other day in the staffroom, Mr Jones and I were talking about that film. We thought...'. This helps them to imagine you interacting socially within school.
5. When talking about safety issues (fire, water, roads, etc), tell the pupils about your experiences. It's important to keep the anecdote appropriate for young audiences, but discussing safety in a real context can help pupils to see the gravity of the issue.
6. Tell the class about your struggles and how you overcome them. This enables them to see you as a real person and shows them that problems can be surmounted.

Why try this?
Watch the pupils' faces as you tell them a real story about you. If you want to build rapport, it just works.

Top tip
Keep anecdotes short; teaching time is tight enough as it is.

#196 Accepting gifts

Do you really want that little bundle of twigs or scrunched-up list of times tables? Probably not, but change your perspective from trash to treasure when a child gives you an offering and it could boost your rapport.

1. When a child gives you a 'gift', look pleasantly surprised.
2. Offer immediate acknowledgment, thanking them for the kind thought.
3. Show the gift to someone else in front of the child – not the whole class (they might not like that), but perhaps their close friend or the teaching assistant.
4. Place the gift at the front of your desk or on a visible shelf, leaving it there for at least a few days.

Why this matters

This isn't groundbreaking, but it is easy to forget. When there's a parent at the door, the phone is ringing, Billy is under the table and you've put the photocopying somewhere, Frank's drawing of a volcano can elicit a curt 'Thanks Frank. Go and sit down now please.' Ouch.

Top tip

You could write a short thank-you note to the child, sending this home with them.

#197 The Benjamin Franklin effect: do me a favour

Want to get a child onside? Get them to do you a favour! According to David McRaney, the author of *You Are Not So Smart*,[9] this effective approach was used by Benjamin Franklin to win over people who didn't like him.

1. Plan a favour the child can easily manage; you don't want it to be too challenging or boring.
2. Pull the child to one side.
3. Present the problem and pose their support as the solution.
4. Explain why their special skill set or support is needed.
5. Ask if they are happy to help you. This is a bit risky, but nine times out of 10, they'll agree.
6. After the favour has taken place, say thank you and extend the favour over a period of time if possible.

Why it works
It's hard to stay disconnected from someone who values you and needs your help.

Top tip
Get other staff involved, too, asking them to think of a favour for the child. Giving the child a feeling of purpose will better connect them to the school.

9   David McRaney, *You Are Not So Smart*, Oneworld Publications, 2012

#198 Pay a compliment

Sometimes you need fast and simple ways to establish rapport. It never hurts to make pupils feel good about themselves, so why not try paying compliments.

1. **Be observant.** Notice when a pupil does something positive.
2. **Plan a compliment.** Think about how best to compliment the child and whether they prefer public or more private praise.
3. **Pay the compliment.** Be genuine and remember to compliment the act as opposed to the child.

Why it works

Everyone likes to be complimented!

Top tip

A simple 'Nice haircut' or 'Love the coat' can be a great way to make a child feel noticed, but don't become reliant on superficial compliments. Try to offer compliments that relate to ethos, character, outcomes or effort.

#199 Noticing the little things

If you spot something different about a child, show them that you're paying attention. Here are some things to look out for.

1. **Changes in appearance:** haircuts, new shoes or growing taller. These are easy to spot and easy to point out.
2. **Changes in attitude or effort.** When a child makes a marked improvement in attitude or effort and it goes unnoticed, this could reduce the momentum of the positive change. See it, say it!
3. **Changes in ability or outcome.** When a child's outcomes have improved, let them know that you've noticed and you're proud.
4. **Changes in circumstances.** Whether it's a new sibling, moving house or joining the netball team, show the child that you're aware of the change and allow them the chance to celebrate it with you.

Why it works
Recognition of a positive change makes a child feel seen and valued.

Top tip
Let the child overhear you telling a colleague about their change.

#200 Celebrating successes

When we focus solely on the goals and forget the people, motivation can dwindle. Remember to celebrate class achievements to build rapport, especially when it's been a period of 'all business'. Here are some ideas to get you started.

1. If your class achieves a great success, find a slot for free time. This is a chance for you to play, chat and connect with individuals. Every second of the teaching day counts, but even 10 minutes of free time for pupils can really pay off.
2. Put on a surprise for your pupils. A bit of spontaneity can revitalise a class – try a tea party or host some karaoke. Again, time is tight, but I guarantee they will appreciate your efforts.
3. Celebrate big accomplishments. When the class has finished a project, don't just close the books and rush on to the next thing. Share the work and bring in some treats that relate to it – for example, if pupils have completed a project on Africa, bring in some cultural food and music and display the projects on the tables for peer exploration.
4. Share home-grown successes. Many pupils attend clubs, enter contests or have hobbies outside school. When a pupil achieves something amazing, be sure to share it with the class, allowing them to ask questions about the journey towards success.

Why try this?
You're playing the long game. Part of maintaining great relationships is acknowledging when something special has happened. Show that you care by responding to success.

Top tip
If you are deviating from routine, don't forget those pupils who might not appreciate a sudden change to the timetable. Give them a heads-up beforehand – you could even ask them to help you set things up.

#201 Stop and listen

How can you boost rapport with staff, parents and pupils with immediate effect? In 1999, *Harvard Business Review* published an article by the psychiatrist Edward Hallowell[10] in which he discussed his idea of 'the human moment: an authentic psychological encounter that can happen only when two people share the same physical space'. According to Hallowell, the human moment has the following prerequisites:

1. **Physical presence:** when someone seeks your attention, stop what you're doing. Put things down, turn your focus away from your task and turn towards the person who has come to talk to you.
2. **Emotional attention:** actually listen. You might be distracted, but really listening to the person's needs and thinking about what they are saying will enable you to understand why they have chosen to communicate with you.
3. **Intellectual attention:** respond and acknowledge with a potential action if appropriate; make a quick note if needed.

Why it works

Rapport is about connecting. Without disconnecting from a task and turning your attention towards the person, rapport is not able to grow – or, even worse, can be destroyed.

Top tip

Emails are great for many reasons, but using technology to connect restricts the development of rapport. Where possible, go and see people for genuine face-to-face connection.

---

10 Edward Hallowell, *'The human moment at work'*, *Harvard Business Review*, 1999, tinyurl.com/y9zssypk

#202 Knowing your purpose

With so much going on, it's easy to forget our true purpose in education. In his TEDx talk 'How to know your life purpose in 5 minutes',[11] the film producer Adam Leipzig suggests that knowing your life purpose might be the secret to happiness. Give his five-minute method a try when you're feeling swamped and rapport with your pupils (or colleagues) has dropped off the priority list. Provide a one-sentence answer to each of the following prompts.

1. Who are you?
2. What do you do?
3. Who do you do it for?
4. What do those people want and need?
5. How do they change as a result?

I've included my answers below, to model the method for you.

1. *My name is Hanna Beech.*
2. *I am a deputy headteacher.*
3. *I do this for the pupils and staff of my school.*
4. *These people need leadership, guidance, encouragement and challenge.*
5. *As a result, they will feel fulfilled and make progress towards their goals.*

Why it works
According to Leipzig, this works because only two of the prompts are about you. This encourages you to be outward-facing.

Top tip
Watch the talk if you have 10 spare minutes; it will give you a deeper understanding of Leipzig's thinking.

---

11 Adam Leipzig, *'How to know your life purpose in 5 minutes'* (talk), TEDxMalibu, 2013, tinyurl.com/v9mrjzw

#203 Giving pupils purpose

If purpose is the key to happiness (see the previous idea), how can we make sure our pupils have purpose in school? Making sure they feel connected positively is a great way to enhance their respect for education. Try these strategies to give children purpose in your setting.

1. **Assign jobs.** Book monitor, librarian, line leader, even paperclip manager – it doesn't matter what the role is. The point is that giving pupils responsibility for their space and the running of the class helps them to connect with school life.
2. **Link learning to real life.** Giving every lesson a purpose is really important – why learn something that appears to be pointless? If pupils know you are teaching them purposeful lessons, they'll respect you for that.
3. **Do me a favour.** Ask pupils to do you favours. Nothing extravagant – just passing on a message or helping a classmate with their work will do.
4. **Common goals.** Remind the pupils that you're all on the same side – you have common purpose. This will make for better teamwork towards those goals.

Why try this?
All children, especially those with attendance issues, will benefit from feeling better connected to school and to you through a sense of purpose.

Top tip
To avoid a decline in efforts, rotate jobs and responsibilities after a few weeks or each term.

#204 **Honesty is the best policy**

There is always one pupil that you feel you might 'lose' if you're honest with them, but one of two things will happen if you sugarcoat the truth in an attempt to keep them onside:

1. They will never receive the feedback they need and, as a result, will not make significant changes.
2. They will see right through you, feel they can manipulate you and take advantage of this.

Respect and rapport can be destroyed in this way, so be totally honest with them. If they are failing due to truancy, tell them. If they are coasting and could do better, tell them. If they are trying their best but not progressing, tell them.

Why it works
Once you've been honest with the pupil, together you can find ways to make improvements.

Top tip
Value honesty in class. If you want to create a situation where you can be honest, expect the same from the children in your care.

Further resources

Daniel Goleman, *Social Intelligence: the new science of human relationships*, Arrow, 2007

Robin Dreeke, *It's Not All About 'Me': the top ten techniques for building quick rapport with anyone*, People Formula, 2013

James Allen Sturtevant, *You've Gotta Connect: building relationships that lead to engaged students, productive classrooms, and higher achievement*, Incentive Publications, 2014

CS Lim, Keow Ngang Tang and SF Tan, 'Building rapport with pupils to enhance teaching: implications from observing three primary excellent teachers', *Pertanika Journal of Social Science and Humanities*, 21.3, 2013, tinyurl.com/ru5ekbj

Jason J Barr, *Developing a Positive Classroom Climate: IDEA Paper #61*, IDEA Center, 2016, tinyurl.com/wa5gdpp

Katrien Vangrieken, Filip Dochy, Elisabeth Raes and Eva Kyndt, 'Teacher collaboration: a systematic review', *Educational Research Review*, 15, 2015, tinyurl.com/rfs4xyj

Chapter 10: Teaching and learning

The words 'teaching' and 'learning' are often treated as one, but they're really not the same thing. Of course, teaching and learning are deeply connected because of their reliance upon one another: teaching without learning isn't worth much at all, and learning without teaching is likely limited and prolonged. For the sake of reflection, let's first explore teaching in its most basic terms. The dictionary definition of the word 'teach' is: 'Impart knowledge to or instruct (someone) as to how to do something.'[1] That's it. That's what it all boils down to: imparting knowledge and delivering instruction.

It can really help to think about teaching in such fundamental terms. The educators Shaun Allison and Andy Tharby take a fuss-free approach in their book *Making Every Lesson Count*,[2] which identifies 'six principles to support great teaching and learning'. These are: challenge, explanation, modelling, practice, feedback and questioning (see idea #206). Their book provides a common-sense framework for everyday classroom practice; it unpicks each of the six suggested principles and offers ideas for effective teaching approaches. Another educator who has distilled the art of teaching into its most essential elements is the late Barak Rosenshine (see idea #205). His Principles of Instruction[3] have influenced the practice of many teachers, myself included.

---

1   en.oxforddictionaries.com/definition/teach
2   Shaun Allison and Andy Tharby, *Making Every Lesson Count: six principles to support great teaching and learning,* Crown House Publishing, 2015
3   Barak Rosenshine, 'Principles of instruction: research-based strategies that all teachers should know', *American Educator,* 36.1, 2012, tinyurl.com/gltfvv4

With teaching being the crux of the job, it's no wonder that we seek strategies to master our craft. Teachers love the teaching aspects of their role. In fact, I believe that teaching is one of the most mindful activities a person can engage in. We can enter a 'flow state' of optimal consciousness, where the mind is sharply focused and performance is heightened. In the flow state, brain activity moves from the beta waves of our normal waking moments to the borderline between the alpha waves (where daydreaming occurs) and theta waves (associated with REM sleep).[4] In my view, there are reasonable grounds for the hypothesis that this all-consuming flow state is why teachers are at risk of exhaustion. As wonderful as flow is, could being in this state deplete our energy and lead to fatigue? Later in my career, I would love to conduct research into flow states in teachers and how they contribute to our wellbeing (positively and negatively), but for now, I'm throwing the idea out there as food for thought.

So, it turns out that teaching is just about imparting knowledge and delivering instruction. Job done, then? Well, maybe not. So many struggles and confusions have stemmed from such a simple concept. The contexts and narratives that surround teaching are many and varied, leading it to become far more complex than any definition might suggest. In my experience, anything that involves lots of people quickly becomes complicated, and teaching certainly involves a lot of people. To add to this, these people happen to be young, developing humans who might well be hormonal, emotionally charged and socially immature. Not so simple after all.

Even with the best will in the world, imparting knowledge or delivering instruction won't automatically lead to rich learning. You may have observed that, sometimes, it seems as though the children get in the way of the teaching. You have the best lessons, resources and instruction, yet the teaching becomes ineffectual. This common problem (where learning and teaching become detached from one another; where teaching is offered but learning doesn't result) leads me to the work of one of the most renowned education authors of recent times. The cognitive psychologist Daniel Willingham (see idea #237) has considered why students don't enjoy school, suggesting that the human brain isn't naturally good at thinking and will avoid this effortful task where possible.[5] If Willingham's body of work could be neatly summarised in a single quote, for me it would be this: 'Memory is the residue of thought.'[6]

---

4   Steven Kotler, 'Flow states and creativity: can you train people to be more creative?', *Psychology Today*, 2014, tinyurl.com/s558oqu

5   Daniel T Willingham, *Why Don't Students Like School?*, Jossey-Bass, 2010

6   Ibid.

The reason this quote is so profound is because the concept is so straightforward. The idea that the things we think about are the things we will learn can bring clarity to our role as educators. Get the kids to think about the important bits. Teaching and learning are again intertwined.

The complexities of human brain function remain relatively unknown, but some interesting insights into learning have emerged from neuroscience. In my view, developing an understanding of what learning is and *what it isn't* will benefit teachers' classroom practice. Yet others argue that neuroscientific discoveries, which are in their infancy, are irrelevant to education and that 'neuro-nonsense' is being fed to educators.[7] Whatever your views, my advice would be to keep a close eye on developments in the field of cognitive neuroscience; use the findings as you wish, but bear in mind that neuroscience can be misapplied or overused in the classroom. Remember to step back from the theory and reflect on your day-to-day practice. To find out more about links between cognitive neuroscience and education, explore the work of Dr Paul Howard-Jones.

The acts of teaching and learning are exciting and exhausting in equal measure. Teaching and learning are the bread and butter of working in education and they thread through every element of school life, so if there is anything you ought to spend time developing a better understanding of – whether you are a classroom teacher, teaching assistant or executive head – this is it. To gather your thoughts about teaching and learning at your setting, consider the following thinking prompts and the adjectives (three for each) that you would use to complete them.

In an ideal lesson, teaching is…
In an ideal lesson, learning is…

Now think about how close to reality those adjectives are in your setting. Whatever your reality is, just thinking about how you want teaching and learning to unfold will help you to plan for improvement.

In this chapter, you will find a variety of approaches to either immediately apply to your classroom practice or to reflect upon further. Teaching and learning are both such broad spheres, so the ideas have been selected with the intention of providing information, sparking thought and encouraging reflection, allowing you to get to grips with what really is the heart of the job.

---

7   Eleanor Busby, 'Schools should be wary about using "neuroscience nonsense" in classroom, academic says', *Tes*, 2017, tinyurl.com/t8nw9j6

#205 Rosenshine's Principles of Instruction

Teaching and learning can easily become overcomplicated. There are thousands of ideas and approaches out there, but what do the most popular usually have in common? They are simple. In a renowned article,[8] Barak Rosenshine offers 10 research-based principles of instruction. Here's a quick summary.

1. Provide a daily review of the previous learning.
2. Offer small chunks of information to avoid overload.
3. Ask plenty of questions to check the understanding of as many pupils as possible and further embed learning.
4. Give students worked examples and models to show them 'how'.
5. Guide pupils through their practice, as opposed to allowing them to explore or embed errors when learning new concepts.
6. Reduce errors by checking pupils' understanding at each stage of the lesson.
7. Secure a high success rate during your input, practice and independent work by closely monitoring pupils' responses and performance in a lesson.
8. Offer pupils a scaffold for tricky tasks.
9. Ensure plenty of independent practice is offered and monitored.
10. Provide weekly or monthly review opportunities to recap and rehearse previous learning.

Why try this?

Autonomy and individual flair are important in teaching, but it's sensible to build your practice on a set of principles rooted in research.

Top tip

Read the full article to develop a better understanding of Rosenshine's ideas. Leaders of teaching and learning can ensure staff are at the very least aware of his principles by sharing the article in a staff meeting or placing it on a noticeboard.

---

8 Barak Rosenshine, 'Principles of instruction: research-based strategies that all teachers should know', *American Educator*, 36.1, 2012, tinyurl.com/gltfvv4

#206 Making Every Lesson Count

In their book *Making Every Lesson Count*,[9] Shaun Allison and Andy Tharby suggest 'six principles to support great teaching and learning'.

1. **Challenge:** to ensure pupils hold high expectations for achievement.
2. **Explanation:** to ensure pupils gain knowledge and skills necessary to achieve.
3. **Modelling:** to ensure pupils have a clear understanding of how to apply their knowledge or skills.
4. **Practice:** to allow pupils to embed the learning.
5. **Feedback:** ensuring pupils think about and further develop their knowledge and skills.
6. **Questioning:** to enable pupils to think hard.

Why it works
Allison and Tharby used these principles to form a teaching and learning policy at their school. Their structured approach still allows for that all-important teacher autonomy.

Top tip
To implement these principles at your setting, ask staff to consider how each aspect is reflected in their teaching practice. Generate interest through genuine discussions about everyday practice.

---

9   Shaun Allison and Andy Tharby, *Making Every Lesson Count: six principles to support great teaching and learning*, Crown House Publishing, 2015

#207 A teaching policy and a learning policy

A teaching and learning policy isn't a necessity, but if you're going to have one, make sure it's simple, effective, and built by and for your team. Better still, try creating two separate documents, one for teaching and one for learning.

1. Before a staff meeting, ask teachers to reflect individually on what is important to them in teaching and in learning. This should only involve a few moments of thought – no extra workload!
2. Begin the meeting with table discussions of the question 'What is great teaching?' Make a list of all the identified priorities, which might include clear instruction, appropriate challenge or effective questioning.
3. Ask each table to distil the list into the five most significant ingredients of great teaching.
4. Share these around the room. As a group, decide on the top five across the school. These five will form the teaching policy.
5. Repeat this process with great learning in mind. Features of great learning might include focused pupils, pupils asking questions, pupils learning from errors, etc.
6. Create the teaching and learning policies as one-page documents that are accessible and user-friendly (think simple statements).
7. Share these with the team and place posters in classrooms.
8. Try calling the documents 'guidance' as opposed to policies.

Why it works

Creating bespoke policies for teaching and learning will make them more relevant to your setting and more relatable for staff. When staff have invested in something, they're more likely to value and use it.

Top tip

Share the learning policy with pupils, ensuring their understanding of each element.

#208 Pointless v purposeful planning

How much time do you or your team spend on planning? Planning is arguably the most time-consuming activity for teachers, so follow these dos and don'ts to make sure planning at your school is purposeful, not pointless.

Senior leaders

1. **Don't** expect submitted weekly plans.
2. **Do** have some simple guidelines about how to plan effectively.
3. **Don't** demand a given planning format.
4. **Do** be aware of what type of planning happens across your school.
5. **Don't** formally monitor daily plans.
6. **Do** discuss planning as a team to share good practice.
7. **Don't** expect teachers to plan excessively.
8. **Do** provide quality resources (examples include knowledge organisers and schematic maps) and ample time for teachers to plan effectively.

Teachers

1. **Don't** spend too long focusing on daily plans in isolation.
2. **Do** consider progressive, longer-term plans, as well as plans for retrieval practice.
3. **Don't** try to do everything on your own.
4. **Do** collaborate with colleagues or online professionals to share ideas and resources.
5. **Don't** spend too long recreating resources that already exist.
6. **Do** use textbooks and other resources *if* they align with your intentions.
7. **Don't** create plans for monitoring purposes.
8. **Do** create plans that enhance and guide your delivery and the pupils' learning.

Why try this?
Planning is a huge contributor to effective teaching and learning. When lessons are planned well, the result will be better performance from your pupils, fewer behaviour incidents and better outcomes.

Top tip
Remember that everyone is in this together. Help teachers by ensuring there are no huge planning demands and help the senior leadership team by ensuring there is no mystery around what is being planned.

#209 Daily planning: simple and smart

Could your planning slides be unintentionally limiting learning? The tips below, intended to optimise learning rather than minimise it, summarise some key findings from the instructional design experts Ruth Colvin Clark and Chopeta Lyons.[10]

1. Gifs and clip art may liven up your slides, but unnecessary images draw pupils' attention towards the irrelevant. Instead, use visuals that are context-relevant.
2. Photographs and videos draw attention away from the objectives when they are overly detailed. Simple line drawings are more effective.
3. Images of processes reignite thought about content, connecting pupils' thinking to prior learning.
4. Placing words alongside (relevant) images is more effective than words alone.

Why try this?
Many teachers rely on presentations, so it's important for them to promote good learning outcomes.

Top tip
Keep explanations simple by avoiding the use of large bodies of text on slides and presentations.

10 Ruth Colvin Clark and Chopeta Lyons, Graphics for Learning: proven guidelines for planning, designing, and evaluating visuals in training materials, John Wiley & Sons, 2010

#210 Teaching inputs

Teaching inputs don't just come at the start of a lesson. An input is any contribution from the teacher that is consumed by the children in order to embed or expand their knowledge or skills. Inputs might need to be reiterated or built upon halfway through the lesson. Here are some simple tips to make sure your teaching inputs are effective, whether they come at the start of the lesson or are used to take the narrative of your lesson forward.

1. **Tell pupils the purpose of the lesson.** This can be a real motivator for learning. Sometimes the purpose is really obvious – learning about money, for example. Sometimes the purpose is trickier to explain, but you can always find a way to justify why the lesson is relevant to the pupils' education or lives.
2. **Drive home the key messages.** Know exactly what it is that you need the pupils to take away for successful learning in this lesson. Repeat the key elements and ask pupils to demonstrate what they understand.
3. **Listen.** Listening to pupils' responses is a great way to help you decide where to take the learning. If you assess what has been retained with questioning, you can gain a good understanding of what needs to be taught next.
4. **Teach the vocabulary.** With new learning often comes new vocabulary. This can become a real barrier unless you make very clear the pronunciation and meaning of new words.

Why try this?
The introduction or consolidation of learning through effective teacher inputs is arguably the whole point of teaching.

Top tip
When pupils don't seem to be connecting to the input, slow things down. Break down each step or go back to explore the building blocks of the new learning.

#211 Midway-point teaching

As pupils move towards the midway point of a lesson, they should be somewhat secure with the learning that they are tackling. In an ideal world, I would expect to see progress towards an end goal, some struggle and a high level of concentration. If you come to the midway point and notice that pupils are floundering, this could mean they haven't grasped the concept well enough, or they find it unmotivating – perhaps the work is too easy or just not that interesting. Here are a few tips for improving the lesson through midway-point teaching.

1. Scan the classroom. Are pupils displaying on-task learning behaviours? These might include focused conversations, self-talk, good outcomes emerging, and pupils looking at their work and completing it.
2. Identify any children or groups displaying off-task learning behaviours: off-task conversations, slouching, huffing, messing around or a lack of progress towards the intended outcomes.
3. Tackle the off-task behaviours by providing some midway-point teaching. You might need to re-teach or take the learning back a few steps, or offer more challenging work. Or it could be that a motivational pep talk is required.
4. If off-task learning behaviours outweigh on-task learning behaviours, it's worth stopping the entire class for some midway-point teaching.

Why it works
Sometimes a lesson begins really well but slowly goes downhill. Taking the time to look for signs of learning can enable you to move the lesson forward.

Top tip
A second opinion is useful. If you are fortunate enough to have an additional adult in class, ask them to scan the room throughout the lesson to see whether some midway-point teaching is required.

#212 Modelling

Modelling is one of Rosenshine's Principles of Instruction (see idea #205) and it's a natural, go-to strategy for teaching. Here are seven suggestions to maximise your modelling.

1. **Plan your modelling.** Spending a short time thinking about 'how' you will model a concept or outcome can really boost your confidence. Sometimes the simplest concepts are the hardest to model.
2. **Model live.** Providing a live model shows pupils the process, rather than the outcome.
3. **Go with the flow.** Modelling too quickly or too slowly will affect how well your pupils proceed with the learning. Scan the room to decide if you ought to speed up or slow down. Regularly check the learning!
4. **Exploit modelling throughout the lesson.** Use the input to model to the whole class; adapt the learning time to model to those who need further instruction; and before the end of the lesson, provide pupils with the chance to model their learning to each other.
5. **Narrate your modelling.** Talking as you model allows pupils to hear your thinking. Sometimes you're actually modelling how to think about a process, rather than the process itself.
6. **Simplify.** Break down longer processes by modelling one part at a time.
7. **Use worked examples.** Provide a worked example to help key pupils.

Why try this?
Modelling takes up a large proportion of a teacher's day, so make the most of your modelling to optimise outcomes.

Top tip
Reduce modelling over time to allow pupils to think for themselves.

#213 Ending a lesson slowly[11]

The end of a lesson can sometimes feel like a rush as we plough towards new learning. To give a lesson the ending it deserves, provide pupils with the opportunity to summarise aspects of their learning. Allocate around one minute for partner discussion and two minutes for sharing ideas with the rest of the class. Pick one of the following as a focus.

1. **Three final words:** ask pupils to choose three words that summarise the learning.
2. **Three final feelings:** ask them to select three words that describe how the lesson made them feel. This works best for PSHE, RE, philosophy and RSE lessons.
3. **Three final facts:** ask pupils to recap three key facts from the lesson.
4. **Three final questions:** allow pupils to pose three questions based on the day's learning.
5. **Three final strategies:** discuss three key strategies or skills used during the lesson.

Why it works

This method allows pupils to reflect upon the lesson, drawing key aspects of learning together. And ending a lesson slowly helps teachers to understand what the pupils have gained.

Top tip

Model your 'three final facts' or 'three final thoughts' to the class. Ask pupils to retrieve and show this information on a mini whiteboard – this will ensure they have thought about the lesson.

11 Hanna Beech, 'Ending a lesson slowly', *Teacher Toolkit*, 2017, teachertoolkit.co.uk/2017/11/01/one-minute-cpd-7

#214 Differentiated teaching inputs

There have been some terrible responses to differentiation over the years that have added to workload and, in some cases, decreased learning outcomes. Thankfully, thinking around differentiation is changing. To make the best use of differentiation in your classroom, try these suggestions to support a range of learners in one teaching input.

1. Teach to the top, but go slowly if necessary and be clear. Challenging pupils by delivering content that gets them thinking and extends their knowledge, skills or understanding will keep them engaged and optimise progress.
2. Be flexible. If you notice that the input is too easy or too challenging, be responsive to the learners by adapting the content you offer. You will notice if the pitch is too high or too low as pupils will probably become disengaged. Using frequent questioning to check for understanding will help you to establish where to take the teaching next.
3. Use the team. If you are lucky enough to have additional adults in class, make sure they work with key pupils during the input to prompt, paraphrase and question.
4. Vary your questioning and target your questions appropriately.
5. Provide resources that might help pupils, such as multiplication grids or word banks.
6. Scaffold any partner-practice questions so the questions become progressively harder. In this way, all pupils can work through the questions with their partner, but those who are confident will work through them more quickly.
7. Try mixing partners by ability to enable them to learn from one another.

Why this matters

Reflecting on how to ensure that the teaching input suits pupils' needs can help you to get the lesson off to the right start.

Top tip

Let those pupils who have 'got it' before the end of the input go ahead and start their task. If they finish early, great – the additional time at the end of the lesson can be used for further variation and mastery.

#215 Differentiation for mastery[12]

How can your most confident learners help other students? This strategy allows pupils to act the experts and help others in their class. It aims to maximise pupil understanding through the articulation of what they know to help their peers.

1. Set up a table at the back of the room. There should be two chairs on one side of the desk and two on the other side. Prepare a set of questions on a clipboard relating to the topic or method being taught.
2. When your most able pupils have completed their recorded task (or perhaps you've already identified two pupils who are ready for mastery) ask them to sit at the expert table.
3. They can explore the prepared questions together, ready to be interviewed.
4. Send two pupils across to the expert table. Ask them to quiz the 'experts' on the topic.
5. Provide the interviewers with an opportunity to ask their own questions, too.
6. If you feel they are ready, ask the interviewers to become the new 'experts' to pass on the knowledge they've gained from the interview process.

Why it works
Pupils gain ownership over their own learning and become the facilitators of others' learning. Power to the people! Giving pupils a chance to teach helps them to consolidate what they know. This method provides meaningful and valuable ways for children to deepen their own understanding.

Top tip
Be certain that your pupils are totally confident with a concept before you ask them to act as experts.

---

12 Hanna Beech, 'Differentiation for mastery', *Teacher Toolkit*, 2017, teachertoolkit.co.uk/2017/11/08/one-minute-cpd-8

#216 Differentiating explanations[13]

Do your pupils pick things up at different rates? I suspect so. There are many strategies to differentiate across the classroom, but here is one that is simple, achievable and effective.

1. Explain to the class that they will receive three layers of explanation from you: the first is the most basic, the second will build upon that and the third will broaden the explanation further. For example:
   - **Basic:** In Ancient Egypt, when people died, their bodies would be mummified to be preserved for the afterlife.
   - **Building:** This process would involve…
   - **Broad:** We know this because…
2. After the basic explanation, ask pupils to review their understanding of the concept. If most of the class have grasped the basics, you can start to build upon this.
3. Continue until you get to the point where you can offer a broader explanation.
4. For those who pick things up very quickly, add a fourth layer: beyond. This can be an opportunity for highly confident pupils to explore the concept beyond what has been directly taught, by conducting their own enquiry or solving a range of challenge tasks.

Why try this?
Beginning with the basics puts all pupils on an equal footing, drawing learners together. No one is left behind and you have an idea of how much each pupil has understood.

Top tip
If there are individuals stuck at the basics after all three layers of explanation, go back to basics once more. This will stop them feeling overwhelmed.

---

13 Hanna Beech, 'Differentiating explanations', *Teacher Toolkit*, 2017, teachertoolkit.co.uk/2017/11/23/one-minute-cpd-10

#217 Explanation station[14]

Do you find yourself repeating the same instruction or explanation over and over again? Set up an explanation station to demonstrate your strategy without having to actually monitor or manage the area.

1. In your classroom, set up a table called the 'explanation station'. This will be a zone for pupils to visit during the lesson if they are unsure about the strategy, even after you've explained it.
2. Set a timer and see how many variations of explanation you can prepare in five or 10 minutes. You could try: an instructional poster; a visual prompt or diagram with steps; a QR code with a link to a website; worked examples; or a pre-recorded step-by-step breakdown of the strategy using the Explain Everything app (provide headphones!). You might even ask support staff to sit at the table to deliver live explanations.
3. When pupils arrive for the lesson, inform them that the station will be available for use to help them embed the strategy.

Why it works
This method allows you to spend time supporting or challenging core groups of pupils without being interrupted by others who want to clarify the method. Pupils take ownership over their learning and solve their own misconceptions.

Top tip
Your most confident learners could help to create strategy posters as an extension task; these can be placed at the explanation station for tomorrow's lesson.

---

14 Hanna Beech, 'Giving instructions', *Teacher Toolkit*, 2018, teachertoolkit.co.uk/2018/02/07/one-minute-cpd-17

#218 **10 quick questioning techniques**[15]

Questioning is undoubtedly a key tool for teachers. Through questioning, we gain an insight into what pupils know; this gives us vital clues for where to take the teaching next. Although questioning comes naturally to teachers, we may find ourselves falling into traps that inhibit learning. So how can you make the most of questioning in class? Try these 10 no-fuss approaches.

1. Make a statement and ask pupils to agree or disagree with you, justifying their response.
2. Ask a table to respond collectively to the rest of the class.
3. Scan the room for the 'right child' for the question.
4. Pose a question for groups to discuss. Listen in and paraphrase back to the class on their behalf.
5. Avoid questions that begin with 'who' (e.g. 'Who can tell me…?', 'Who wants to explain…?'). These can provide an opt-in, opt-out vibe.
6. Add 'why?' or 'how?' once a response has been given, even if the response is not what you would expect.
7. Create multiple-choice questions (but be careful with the options you provide!).
8. Make an incorrect statement, asking pupils to prove why you are wrong.
9. Vary questioning with lower-order (recall) questions and higher-order (thinking) questions.
10. Don't over-question. Questions are a tool for assessment and to generate thinking. Choose your questions carefully and remember, if the pupils still don't know after you've probed their thinking, just tell them.

Why try this?
Teachers spend much of their day posing questions. Mixing up questioning approaches and ensuring a balance of open and closed questions will keep responses interesting and useful.

Top tip
Notice who you are drawn to for responses and instead scan for pupils who you've not yet questioned in the lesson.

---

15 Hanna Beech, '10 quick questioning tips', *Teacher Toolkit*, 2018, teachertoolkit.co.uk/2018/12/05/one-minute-cpd-42

#219 More inclusive questioning[16]

Do you find that only a few pupils opt into discussions, put their hands up or are vocal in class? When we begin questions with 'Who knows...?', 'Who can tell me...?' or 'Who wants to...?', we are allowing pupils to either opt in or opt out. Here are some alternatives.

1. Instead of asking 'Who knows what happens when we mix sugar and water?', try 'I've been wondering what happens when we mix sugar and water. Ben, what do you know about this?'
2. Instead of 'Who can tell me what an adverb is?', try 'I know that adverbs have a function. Ella, share something you know about adverbs.'
3. Instead of 'Can you tell me the name of Henry VIII's reign?', try 'I'd like to discover what you know or don't yet know about Henry VIII's reign. Nisa, tell everyone what you already know or something you want to discover about this.'

Why it works
Rephrasing our questions can completely change the way our pupils respond. Asking 'Can you...?' risks the obvious answer of 'No, I can't', but by rephrasing, we encourage pupils to fully participate.

Top tip
Remember to give pupils a fair time to think and then respond – don't be afraid to wait for 10 seconds for a child to gather their thoughts. If they still don't respond, tell them you'll find time to come back to them and be sure to do so.

---

16 Hanna Beech, 'More inclusive questioning', *Teacher Toolkit*, 2018, teachertoolkit.co.uk/2018/01/31/one-minute-cpd-16

#220 Extending pupil responses

How can questioning be used to drive the learning forward, rather than just drive the lesson forward? Too often we are tempted to ask a question, grab the correct answer and charge on to the next part of our plan. Instead, slow down by using these simple and adaptable prompts to extend pupils' responses.

1. What else do you think/know about this?
2. Why didn't you say...?
3. Tell me another point that relates.
4. Prove why you are right.
5. What helped you to decide this?
6. What if I argued that...?
7. Could you be wrong?
8. Would this also apply to...?
9. Explain this again, this time using...

Why try this?

Extending pupils' responses is a great way for you to assess how much your pupils truly understand and what they don't yet know. It also helps learners to articulate and strengthen their own understanding, while offering their peers the chance to learn from them.

Top tip

Write prompts on flash cards and dish these out during partner discussions. Pupils should get into the habit of extending each other's responses, too.

#221 Teacher talk: quality over quantity

Many experienced teachers have been told that they ought to talk less. One consultant told me after an observation that my teacher talk should be no longer than 10 minutes. Looking back, it seems a strange piece of advice to give to an NQT; it implies that all concepts can be explained, modelled and grasped within 10 minutes. In the past, teacher talk has been considered a waste of pupil-led learning time, but more recent research has shed light on its power. Here are five simple ways to make sure your teacher talk is engaging and on point.

1. **Plan what you need to say.** This may sound obvious, but taking the time to really consider what you need to get across will help you to make the key messages clear to the learner.
2. **Streamline.** Teacher talk can easily become waffle, with long or back-and-forth explanations taking over. If you find yourself losing direction, just stop for a moment to gather your thoughts and refocus on the learning priority.
3. **Show an interest in what you are saying.** If you demonstrate a genuine interest in the topic through animated talk, pupils are more likely to follow with interest.
4. **Be flexible.** Although planning what you will say is key, you need to include some flexibility in your explanations or discussions. Be direct, clear and interested when talk moves in a direction you didn't expect.

Why this matters

Much of a teacher's day is spent talking and explaining, so take the time to make your teacher talk impactful.

Top tip

Beware of tangents. Pupils can be really artful, redirecting the teaching towards their own areas of interest. A small tangent can be useful at times, but don't allow yourself to be steered away from the learning outcomes.

#222 Using your 'teacher voice'

All teachers develop a 'teacher voice' and usually this happens without much conscious thought. If you've ever filmed yourself teaching and watched it back, it's likely that your first response was, 'Do I really sound like that?' Maximise the attention that pupils pay to your teaching by trying different ways of using your voice in the classroom.

1. **Volume.** Varying the volume can make pupils listen keenly to what you say and maintain their attention.
2. **Pitch.** I once knew a teacher who was told that her voice was too high-pitched and shrill. This feedback took it a little far, but there is something to be said for varying the pitch you use, so your teacher talk is not delivered in a monotone.
3. **Pauses.** Taking a pause at the right time can be a powerful way of grabbing pupils' attention.
4. **Speed.** I have observed teachers who spoke so quickly that I had no idea what was being said. Then there were those who spoke so slowly that my mind began to wander. Changes in speed keep things interesting. Try to make purposeful variations in speed while you talk.
5. **Moving and gesturing.** Hand and arm gestures and using the space around the room can make for more interesting delivery of information.

Why try this?
Putting a little thought into your teacher voice could make your teacher talk far more appealing. Using an effective teacher voice also models excellent public speaking.

Top tip
Record yourself and see what you notice about your voice.

#223 Homework for memory, not the activity, by Ross

Does setting homework make a difference? Is homework a meaningful contribution to learning? Does it promote higher achievement and teach study skills and responsibility? Very little research has considered the quality of the tasks set, pupils' responsiveness and the amount of work proportional to spare time. Without evaluation of such conditions, the evidence linking homework to achievement will remain insufficient.

The psychologist Mihaly Csikszentmihalyi coined the term 'flow'[17] to describe a state of feeling content and immersed in a task. We can use this theory to inform how we set homework. The challenge is gauging whether pupils can complete the work set without the expertise of the teacher. And if we reset work in line with the theories of retrieval practice to support memory retention, how can we avoid pupils and parents saying, 'We've done this homework before'?

1. Try setting no regular homework at primary level and instead provide a termly overview of ideas that families 'may' want to try – for example, projects or outings. The Department for Education has an excellent activity passport, available online.[18]
2. Use simple quizzes or online tests for maths, reading and spelling. There is no marking and it removes much of the stress of collection and checking. This also supports retrieval practice, puts the onus on the pupil, not the teacher, and offers the pupil an easy way to self-assess their performance and growth.

Why try this?
If we set meaningful tasks that learners have self-selected and have a clear objective, they are more likely to find a happy medium between being over-challenged and under-challenged; they can move from apathy to flow.

Top tip
Seek out Csikszentmihalyi's book *Flow* to learn more about the concept.

---

17 Mihaly Csikszentmihalyi, *Flow,* Rider, 2002
18 gov.uk/government/publications/my-activity-passport

#224 Comparative judgement, by Ross

Teaching and learning is a complicated business. And increasing levels of accountability and the need for teachers to 'show progress' mean it is becoming a more pressurised business, too. Add to this the developments in the field of cognitive science, particularly cognitive load theory, plus the demands for teachers to teach critical thinking skills, and it's clear that teaching and learning are becoming even more complex and nuanced. Sadly, our accountability regimes choose to analyse the complexity of teaching, postcode demographics, funding and accountability by assessing the individual teacher. But one way to reshape this is by tackling one of the biggest topics in education: assessment.

Given the current popularity of research- and evidence-informed methods, this is an exciting time to be in the profession. Despite Thurstone's law of comparative judgement dating back to 1927, few teachers have heard of the psychologist Louis Thurstone. His method asks the judge (or teacher) only to make a valid decision about quality and therefore, according to research, 'offers a radical alternative to the pursuit of reliability through detailed marking schemes'.[19]

I'm a huge fan of comparative assessment and the comparative judgement model being used for exams. There are ways to achieve this in lessons, too, and across a team of teachers, with some exam boards already offering this tool to assess a pupil's performance over the course of the year, rather than in a one-off exam. This debate has come to the fore after the Covid-19 crisis, with Ofqual asking teachers to judge the grades that students were likely to have achieved had they taken their exams in summer 2020. Ofqual also asked teachers to rank each student relative to others that they judge would have gained the same grade.

Fingers crossed, we may have a reformed examination model post-Covid-19, and given the experience of teachers and pupils working remotely during lockdown, we may see a new assessment model evolving towards 2030.

Why try comparative judgement?
All good teams and departments should moderate on a routine basis. If your team is just you, put systems in place to moderate your bias and predictions.

Top tip
The low-tech approach to comparative judgement is to spread pieces of work over a table and move them around like a sliding puzzle until you have them in a rank order you are happy with.

---

19 Alastair Pollitt, 'The method of adaptive comparative judgement', *Assessment in Education: Principles, Policy and Practice*, 19:3, 2012, tinyurl.com/yar27ua7

#225 Teach Like a Champion

Doug Lemov's wildly popular book *Teach Like a Champion*[20] is packed with teaching ideas. Here are four of his suggested strategies.

1. **Stretch it.** Lemov suggests that we often breeze through questions, accepting basic answers. We ought to instead stretch the thinking by offering a pupil an additional, more challenging question to answer. Simple, yet effective.
2. **Work the clock.** Using the clock to set task times and countdown activities keeps teachers and learners working at the right pace. Lemov says that setting times for a task sets the expectations.
3. **Call and response.** Asking a question of a class and expecting them to respond in unison is highly engaging for pupils and a useful assessment tool for teachers.
4. **Do now.** The teacher sets up a short, manageable and relevant task for pupils to complete as soon as they enter the classroom, leading to less wasted time and less off-task behaviour.

Why read Teach Like a Champion?
Lemov offers lots of tried-and-tested ideas to implement.

Top tip
The updated version of Lemov's book, *Teach Like a Champion 2.0*, offers additional suggestions for teaching and learning.

---

20 Doug Lemov, *Teach Like a Champion: 49 techniques that put students on the path to college*, Jossey-Bass, 2010

#226 **Selfie-squares**[21]

How can you maximise your team's teaching? This method, an adaptation of the 'teaching squares' development tool,[22] will help your colleagues to help each other.

1. Divide staff into groups of four.
2. Group members each film themselves teaching.
3. They privately reflect on what they see, choosing a point to focus on and improve.
4. Each person gives a one-minute presentation to the others in their square, explaining what they will aim to develop in their own practice and why.
5. Every colleague in the square adopts a role: teacher, note-taker, pupil-questioner, feeding back. Three-quarters of the square visit the 'teacher' for 10 minutes, focusing on the development point.
6. The trio discuss what they saw, agreeing on the feedback that will be shared.
7. Informal yet direct feedback is given to the teacher.
8. The teacher reflects meaningfully on the feedback, seeking further support, resources or research if necessary.
9. The members of the square switch roles, with each person taking on each role as the process continues.

Why try this?
A study published by the Harvard Graduate School of Education found that 'work environments that promote positive collegial interaction are likely to support student learning'.[23]

Top tip
Ensure individuals offer feedback on their experiences to the senior leadership team. This will encourage further reflection through a coaching model.

---

21 Hanna Beech, 'In it together', *Teacher Toolkit*, 2019, teachertoolkit.co.uk/2019/01/24/one-minute-cpd-45
22 Neil Haave, 'Teaching squares bring cross-disciplinary perspectives', *Faculty Focus*, 2018, tinyurl.com/vj953z9
23 Susan Moore Johnson, Matthew A Kraft and John P Papay, *How Context Matters in High-Need Schools: the effects of teachers' working conditions on their professional satisfaction and their students' achievement*, Harvard Graduate School of Education, 2011, tinyurl.com/y2woc65g

SELFIE-SQUARES

Foci	
Teacher	Focus

Timetable					
Cycle number	Date/Time	Teacher	Pupil-questioner	Note-taker	Feeding back
1					
2					
3					
4					

Outcomes				
Cycle number	1	2	3	4
Trio meeting date/time				
Trio feedback date/time				

#227 Overcoming observation nerves[24]

Lesson observation can make you feel as if you're under scrutiny – and I am yet to meet anyone who enjoys that feeling! How can we feel more in control when being observed?

1. Don't make big changes to your classroom environment, teaching methods or content to suit an observation.
2. Remind yourself that observations can help you to improve your practice. There is no bad feedback. There is only feedback.
3. What's your worst fear? Ask yourself if that would ever really happen. And even if the worst *did* happen, what would follow? Often the outcome of your worst fear will only be that you get feedback that suggests something should change.
4. Don't give yourself time to overthink the observation. Look after your wellbeing by enjoying mindfulness, exercise or socialising with friends.
5. Enjoy the observation. That may sound impossible, but use your adrenaline to show off what you do every day.

Why it works
Lesson observations might be necessary at your setting, so prepare yourself by addressing negative feelings. This will help you to feel open and ready on the day.

Top tip
Talk to someone about feeling nervous. Colleagues will be able to relate and provide support.

---

24 Hanna Beech, 'Beat those observation nerves', *Teacher Toolkit,* 2018, teachertoolkit. co.uk/2018/06/20/one-minute-cpd-28

#228 Teaching with memory in mind[25]

If pupils can remember what we teach, then our work has been successful. As research uncovers more and more about memory and retention in education, here are a few suggestions to help you make the most of memory in your classroom.

1. Avoid blocking learning. Weaving learning to practise a variety of skills is believed to have a better impact on long-term retention than simply teaching the same learning skills in a block.
2. Once you've taught something, ask yourself, 'When might they forget this by?' and re-teach the learning just before it is fully 'forgotten'. The act of remembering and retrieving the previous learning will strengthen the pupils' long-term learning.
3. Use testing before you begin a topic – this gives pupils a chance to retrieve their knowledge and you a chance to see what has or hasn't been retained.
4. Use testing after a longer break. We often teach something and then test a pupil's ability immediately afterwards, but to see what has really been learned, we ought to test pupils after a longer period of time.
5. Be careful not to 'over-model' a skill once you've taught it. Be sure to allow pupils to use their own memory to recall and remember the steps for success. Make the learning 'desirably difficult' (read more about this in the work of Robert Bjork[26]).

Why try this?
Applying research approaches could enhance the children's learning.

Top tip
Tell pupils exactly what it is you want them to remember, emphasising its importance.

25 Hanna Beech, 'Teaching with memory in mind', *Teacher Toolkit*, 2018, teachertoolkit.co.uk/2018/07/04/one-minute-cpd-30
26 Robert A Bjork, 'Creating desirable difficulties to enhance learning', in Isabella Wallace and Leah Kirkman (eds), *Best of the Best: progress*, Crown House Publishing, 2017

#229 Memory and maths[27]

Do your pupils forget core maths strategies? Try these seven ways to embed mathematical strategies once and for all!

1. Repeat the strategy verbally, working through examples step by step.
2. Model the strategy silently, asking a child to narrate as you model.
3. Ask pupils to talk their partners through the strategy, missing out one key step. Partners have to identify the missing step.
4. Ask pupils to create an instructional poster for the strategy or make a vlog to explain it.
5. Provide the strategy steps on strips of paper. Ask pupils to order the steps as quickly as they can. As a challenge, throw in a random step to see if they can identify it as unnecessary.
6. Share the strategy with parents and carers to ensure consistency between home and school approaches.
7. Buy some menu holders for each table and place strategy posters inside them.

Why try this?
Many mathematical strategies can contain multiple steps, making them easy to forget. Once a strategy is fully understood and embedded, it can become automatic, making the work easier.

Top tip
Once a strategy is embedded, remove the support and scaffolding to allow pupils to retrieve the steps from their memory instead.

---

27 Hanna Beech, 'How to embed math strategies', *Teacher Toolkit*, 2019, teachertoolkit.co.uk/ 2019/02/06/one-minute-cpd-47

#230 Steady sentences[28]

How can we help emerging writers? Here's a 'count, repeat, write' strategy to try with children who are yet to master retaining and forming a sentence they wish to write.

1. Ask the pupil to orally plan their sentence. They may need some assistance if they are struggling with ideas or lacking vocabulary.
2. Model saying the sentence aloud, asking the pupil to repeat the sentence after you. Repeat this step until they can say the sentence without prompts.
3. Next, repeat the sentence once more, this time counting each word on fingers as you say it.
4. In the pupil's book, use a pencil and ruler to draw a horizontal line for each word. Space them out.
5. Repeat the sentence orally, pointing to a horizontal line as you say each word.
6. Ask the pupil to write each word on the drawn lines to form their sentence.
7. Either observe silently or leave the pupil to complete the sentence. Once it is written, check the sentence with the pupil, making any adjustments to omitted or misplaced words.
8. Repeat for each sentence, focusing on quality not quantity, and remembering that each idea may feel like Everest for the pupil.

Why it works
This method has worked incredibly well with emerging writers in my classes (aged 6-11). It slows down the thinking process and allows for just the right amount of autonomy/support. Over time, pupils begin to develop independence in writing basic sentences.

Top tip
Although spelling is very important, try to consider pupil self-esteem when checking their sentences. Focus on sentence formation and structure first.

28 Hanna Beech, 'Steady sentences', *Teacher Toolkit*, 2018, teachertoolkit.co.uk/2018/03/28/one-minute-cpd-23

#231 Triple-sided flash cards[29]

Flash cards are a brilliant way of practising key skills. This triple-sided flash card technique aids basic knowledge and application of skills; you could make the cards yourself or ask your pupils to make a bank of cards to share around the room for revision sessions.

1. Create a flash card by folding an A5 piece of card in half.
2. On one side, add a silver dot or border. On the reverse, add a gold dot or border.
3. On the silver side of the flash card, provide a basic question, such as $36 \div 5$. You may wish to provide more than one question (all relating to the same skill).
4. On the gold side of the flash card, write a contextual problem relating to the skill – for example, 'Egg boxes hold six eggs. How many egg boxes can I fill with 54 eggs?'
5. Now open the folded card up and jot down some simple steps for the method and a worked example.

Why it works
This resource allows for three levels of differentiation during your revision sessions. Pupils can peek at the method if they are stuck, practise the silver steps and then move to gold.

Top tip
If pupils make the flash cards, be sure to provide opportunities for the questions to be checked by peers or adults before they are shared around the room.

29 Hanna Beech, 'Revision', *Teacher Toolkit*, 2018, teachertoolkit.co.uk/2018/03/21/one-minute-cpd-22

#232 **Know your flow**

As Ross discussed in idea #223, Mihaly Csikszentmihalyi coined the phrase 'flow state'.[30] According to Csikszentmihalyi, flow states allow for optimal performance and are incredibly enjoyable. But how do you know if you are experiencing a flow state? Here's a brief summary of the eight characteristics of flow.

1. Total concentration.
2. Clarity of goals.
3. Transformation of time (speeds up or slows down).
4. Feels intrinsically rewarding.
5. Feels effortless.
6. There is a balance between challenge and skill.
7. There is an absence of self-consciousness.
8. There is a feeling of control over the task.

Why this matters
Firstly, flow states could have benefits for your wellbeing and performance. Secondly, helping your pupils to experience flow could benefit their wellbeing and performance, too.

Top tip
Consider this: if you look around the room and see a distinct lack of the eight characteristics of flow, what is your next move? Read more about flow in idea #233.

---

30 Mihaly Csikszentmihalyi, *Flow*, Rider, 2002

#233 Getting into the flow

According to Csikszentmihalyi, 'flow' enhances creativity, optimises performance and boosts happiness.[31] Yes please. So, how can educators make the most of flow states in the classroom?

1. **Spread the word to staff.** Sharing an article or hosting a staff meeting about Csikszentmihalyi's work and the benefits of flow could spark interest in your team.
2. **Reflect.** Ask staff to consider what gets them into flow states. If you can identify this in yourself, you can do more of it!
3. **Loop the kids in.** Explain Csikszentmihalyi's work to your pupils. Even key stage 1 kids can grasp simple explanations of flow states.
4. **Reflect.** Ask pupils to consider what gets them into flow states. Help them to see how good flow can feel and how they can benefit from this.
5. **Plan for flow.** What types of learning experiences enhance flow in your pupils? Full-on flow for every lesson might not be realistic, but try to provide opportunities for flow-inducing learning where you can.
6. **Look for flow.** During lessons, scan the room to see how immersed pupils are. You could use the eight characteristics of flow (see the previous idea) to guide you.

Why try this?
High performance, creativity, deep concentration and enjoyment – that sounds like a fabulous classroom environment to me.

Top tip
If a child lacks often lacks flow and focus across all subjects, perhaps it's time to intervene with discussion and support.

---

31 Mihaly Csikszentmihalyi, *Flow*, Rider, 2002

#234 Conversation is key

Talking is such a key skill for young learners: research backs up the idea that developing language and communication skills in children supports and enhances their academic achievements. Conversation isn't just polite, it's a necessary life skill that children can greatly benefit from. Here are four ways to generate effective conversations within and beyond school.

1. **Teach it.** Explicitly teaching pupils how to hold a conversation ensures they know the ins and outs of two-way talk.
2. **Host it.** Spark one-on-one conversations with pupils, modelling excellent listening and contributing.
3. **Promote it.** Encourage conversations in class by facilitating talking points for your pupils and praising those who hold successful conversations.
4. **Prompt it.** Support conversations at home by providing 'ask me about' prompts. For example, if pupils have been learning about rivers in class, the prompt might be 'Ask me about the famous rivers I've been studying'. These prompts will avoid the common answer of 'nothing' when parents ask pupils what they have been learning about that day.

Why try this?
A group of scientists from Harvard University and the Massachusetts Institute of Technology found that talking with children via back-and-forth conversation led to meaningful brain and language development.[32]

Top tip
Read more about my views on the art of conversation in an article I wrote for *Tes*.[33]

---

32 Rachel R Romeo, Julia A Leonard, Sydney T Robinson, Martin R West, Allyson P Mackey, Meredith L Rowe and John DE Gabrieli, 'Beyond the 30-million-word gap: children's conversational exposure is associated with language-related brain function', *Psychological Science*, 29.5, 2018, tinyurl.com/rxyxb9e
33 Hanna Beech, 'If we don't teach the art of conversation, who will?', *Tes*, 2019, tes.com/magazine/article/if-we-dont-teach-art-conversation-who-will

#235 Prioritising talk in Reception

Research conducted by Durham University[34] found evidence that 'the boost in attainment from an effective first year of school remained with students right through to the end of secondary school'. This highlights the importance of making sure the first year of school is successful for all children – and one vital skill that pupils must develop during their first year is 'talk'. Ensure talk is encouraged throughout Reception year with these 10 tips.

1. **Teach new words every day.** Planning relevant vocabulary to be taught will keep talk high on the agenda.
2. **Create a 'correct back' culture.** When children mispronounce or misuse a word, repeat the correct pronunciation or use back to the child. You might ask them to repeat it back to you, too.
3. **Talk the talk.** All adults in the classroom should speak correctly to give children the best possible models to follow.
4. **Use questions.** Effective questioning that encourages children to elaborate, justify and reconsider will promote good conversational skills.
5. **Don't forget listening.** An important part of learning effective talk is learning to listen.
6. **Use synonyms.** For example, when a child says, 'It's cold', repeat their phrase back to them with an additional synonym: 'It's cold and chilly.' This extends their vocabulary.
7. **Praise great talk.** When a child uses a new word or speaks with confidence, let them know this is recognised and valued by praising them: 'That was a brilliant use of the word "flickered" – what a great word!'

---

34 Peter Tymms, Christine Merrell and Katherine Bailey, 'The long-term impact of effective teaching', *School Effectiveness and School Improvement*, 29.2, 2018, tinyurl.com/scpywo4

8. **Extend ideas for the child.** For example, if the child talks about their favourite fruit being an apple, extend this by saying, 'My favourite fruit is an orange because it is really juicy and sweet.'

9. **Make use of songs, stories and rhymes.** These can be a great way to extend vocabulary, model sentence structure and help children to understand sounds.

10. **Use intonation when speaking.** Modelling how to vary the tone, volume and pitch of your voice in different situations can help children to explore using their own voice in a variety of ways.

Why try this?
So much of our lives relies on effective communication and use of language. The sooner children can develop confidence with talking, the better.

Top tip
If your Reception team plan the vocabulary, stories, rhymes and songs they will be exploring with their classes, these can be collated and shared with families, who will then likely support the learning at home.

#236 The EEF's Preparing for Literacy guidance

It is commonly agreed that developing literacy in learners has multiple benefits. The Education Endowment Foundation's *Preparing for Literacy* guidance report[35] presents seven practical, evidence-based recommendations for developing early literacy, language and communication. Here's a summary of the suggestions.

1. **Prioritise the development of communication and language.** Engaging in rich conversations with children allows good modelling of communication.
2. **Develop children's early reading using a balanced approach.** Employing approaches such as storytelling, singing songs and reciting rhymes alongside the development of systematic phonics is noted to be more effective than using one single approach.
3. **Develop children's capability and motivation to write.** Provide a range of opportunities to communicate through writing, prioritise expressive language and ensure that pupils develop fast, accurate and effective handwriting.
4. **Embed opportunities to develop self-regulation.** Make sure activities are suitably challenging and pupils have the chance to self-regulate through activities such as 'plan-do-review'.
5. **Support parents to help their children to learn.** This can be achieved through encouraging parents to read to and with their children, and through school-led workshops on how to read and talk effectively with children.
6. **Use high-quality assessments.** The right assessments will help to make sure pupils receive the support they need to make good progress.
7. **Use high-quality targeted support to help struggling children.** Adults must be well-prepared and trained to support groups of children who are falling behind.

Why try this?
This guidance report is based on a solid foundation of evidence, so is worth exploring.

Top tip
Read the full report to gain a deeper understanding of the recommendations.

---

35 *Preparing for Literacy: improving communication, language and literacy in the early years – guidance report*, Education Endowment Foundation, 2018, tinyurl.com/r7pnuom

#237 Willingham's Principles of the Mind

How can we use what we know about brain function and capacity to maximise learning? If you haven't read Daniel Willingham's book *Why Don't Students Like School?*,[36] put it top of your 'to read' list. This is a summary of Willingham's nine Principles of the Mind.

1. **Curiosity.** Humans are naturally curious but not naturally drawn to thinking. Ensure that pupils are presented with relevant problems to spark their curiosity. Keep the instruction varied and consider pace.
2. **Knowledge.** Factual knowledge comes before skills. Ensure pupils have sufficient knowledge before you aim for critical thinking.
3. **Memory.** According to Willingham, memory is the residue of thought. People will remember what they think about, so consider what you want the pupils to remember and how you will get them to think about it.
4. **Understanding.** We understand new things in relation to what we already know. Find ways to connect what kids already know and what you want them to learn next, making comparisons to support understanding.
5. **Proficiency.** Extended practice leads to proficiency. Find ways to provide rich and meaningful practice.
6. **Cognition.** Novices and experts think differently. Help pupils to develop a deep understanding; don't expect them to create new knowledge themselves.
7. **Differences.** Pupils are more alike than different in how they learn. Forget the dated and debunked theory of teaching to individual 'learning styles', and instead focus on the content of your lessons.
8. **Intelligence.** Although people do differ in intelligence, intelligence is malleable and can be maximised with effort and practice. Always praise effort rather than ability.
9. **Teaching.** Teaching is a cognitive skill that develops with practice. Being an educator isn't easy, but effort and feedback can lead to improvement.

Why try this
Willingham's findings have influenced many teachers and the direction of their teaching greatly.

Top tip
Read the book! It will give you an in-depth understanding of Willingham's ideas.

---

36 Daniel T Willingham, *Why Don't Students Like School?*, Jossey-Bass, 2010

#238 Considering cognitive load

Cognitive load theory, developed by John Sweller in the 1980s, suggests that our working memory has limited capacity. So, how can you take cognitive load theory into account when preparing and teaching your lessons?

1. Planning is key. Be sure to plan your lessons into relevant, manageable parts.
2. Direct pupils to the most important parts of the learning.
3. Know when to slow the lesson to allow for learning to be digested.
4. Take time to repeat core content.
5. Check for understanding throughout the lesson.
6. Provide visual prompts alongside your teaching.
7. Avoid overcomplicating lessons with too many resources or activities that divert from the learning.
8. Ensure pupils have enough support to begin the lesson and remove this at the right pace, allowing them to embed learning with independence.

Why try this?
Considering cognitive load theory as you plan and deliver your lessons will make sure pupils aren't overwhelmed with information.

Top tip
Read the document *Cognitive Load Theory in Practice: examples for the classroom*.[37]

---

37 *Cognitive Load Theory in Practice: examples for the classroom*, Centre for Education Statistics and Evaluation, New South Wales Department of Education, 2018, tinyurl.com/ybc22n3c

#239 Dual coding for effective teaching outcomes

How often do you use visuals alongside your verbal explanations? This process is known in the world of cognitive science as dual coding. Dual-coding theory, initiated by Allan Paivio in 1971, suggests that using verbal and visual cues when teaching enhances the learning outcomes. Here are some ways to use dual coding in the classroom.

1. When planning, consider which parts of the teaching are vital for the pupils to remember.
2. For these key parts of the teaching, find or create simple visuals that enhance your verbal explanations.
3. Place these images strategically on your slides or print them for your working wall. Drawing a concept as you teach is a great way to use dual coding.
4. When teaching, direct attention to the visual so that pupils can link together the verbal and visual aspects of the learning.

Why try this?
Pupils can refer back to the visuals you created or presented to help them recap key parts of the learning.

Top tip
Keep images and drawings simple.

Further resources

David Eagleman, *The Brain: the story of you*, Pantheon Books, 2015

Mary Aiken, *The Cyber Effect*, Spiegel & Grau, 2016

Jon Tibke, *Why the Brain Matters: a teacher explores neuroscience*, Sage Publications, 2019

Tricia Taylor with Nina Dibner, *Connect the Dots: the collective power of relationships, memory and mindset in the classroom*, John Catt Educational, 2019

Paul A Kirschner and Carl Hendrick, *How Learning Happens*, Routledge, 2020

Pooja K Agarwal and Patrice M Bain, *Powerful Teaching*, Jossey Bass, 2019

Tina M Owen-Moore, *The Alliance Way: the making of a bully-free school*, Harvard Education Press, 2019

Lee Elliot Major and Steve Higgins, *What Works? Research and evidence for successful teaching*, Bloomsbury, 2019

Fiona Millar, *The Best For My Child: did the schools market deliver?*, John Catt Educational, 2018

Evidence Based Education: evidencebased.education

Visible Learning Meta^x: www.visiblelearningmetax.com (John Hattie's new database of what works best in education)

Google Scholar: scholar.google.co.uk (a teacher's first port of call for searching research)

Mendeley: mendeley.com/library (for academic referencing/writing)

Families of Schools Database: educationendowmentfoundation.org.uk/tools/families-of-schools-database (for school comparison)

FFT Education Datalab: schoolslikeyours.ffteducationdatalab.org.uk (for school comparison)

Schools financial benchmarking service: schools-financial-benchmarking.service.gov.uk (for evaluating how well a school performs with a budget)

Conclusion

Education consumes. It consumes our time, our energy, our thoughts. But the thing about education is that its rewards are huge. When you work with young people, there's a distinct feeling that is hard to describe – it's kind of like pride mixed with urgency and hope.

When you meet others who work in education, your conversations almost instantly turn to teaching and learning, to pupils and their behaviours and their lives, because working with these young people is so important and so fascinating. We seek connections with those who also dedicate their lives to education, forming friendships in the real and the online world. Co-workers in schools often connect on a deep level, relying upon one another for professional dialogue and for camaraderie.

One of the reasons we spend so much time thinking about our pupils is the fact that there are just so many details to consider: their learning, progress, welfare, social interactions, communication skills, attendance, aspirations, limitations, home lives – the list could go on (and on). Each child is unique in their learning and personality, both of which adjust and evolve as they move through the academic year. Due to the complexities of working within schools, there is a need for continuing reflection on the education we provide and how we provide it.

Teachers must also be learners. There isn't one person in education who knows it all or has 'finished' learning about the profession. For that reason, CPD is indispensable. It's a crucial way of making sure that your time and efforts are not wasted. If we must spend time thinking about our work (and let's face it, we do this constantly), then we should ensure that what we think about makes a positive difference to the children in our care, as well as to ourselves.

When we look back on our best teaching moments, we often recall those proud 'eureka' instances when a child suddenly grasps the knowledge or skill we have been trying to instil. And that's what CPD is for educators: it gives us our own eureka moments. It's a means by which we can think, learn and truly improve. In reading this book, you will have been exposed to a wide range of ideas, theories and research, allowing you to reflect, plan and create simple ways to not only help your students, but also to improve your practice, your team and your setting. This book is as much about *you* as it is education. Time spent considering your wellbeing and your development is always time well spent.

In chapter 10, I included a quote from *Why Students Don't Like School?* by Daniel Willingham. It bears repeating, this time within the context of our own professional development:

'Memory is the residue of thought.'

What has inspired deep thought for you while reading this book? What will you take with you and how will you use it? Like any good CPD, it's what you do with it that counts. So, what are you going to do now?

CPSIA information can be obtained
at www.ICGtesting.com
Printed in the USA
JSHW020142310720
6912JS00002B/5

9 781913 622107